Rambling
Down the
Suir

By the same author:

WALKS GUIDES
The Wicklow Way
Ireland's Long Distance Walks
Ireland's Waymarked Trails
Irish Waterside Walks
Ordnance Survey guide to the Wicklow Way
Ordnance Survey guide to the Western Way
Ordnance Survey guide to the Beara Way
Waterford Walks

GUIDES
Day Tours from Dublin

TRAVELOGUES
By Cliff and Shore
By Swerve of Shore
Walking Across Ireland

ANTHOLOGY
A Walk in Ireland

ARCHITECTURAL HISTORY
The New Neighbourhood of Dublin (with Dr Maurice Craig and Joseph Hone)
Doorways of Ireland

HISTORY
The Wicklow Military Road: History and Topography

Rambling Down the Suir

The past and present of a great Irish river

MICHAEL FEWER

ashfield PRESS

Published in 2009 by

ASHFIELD PRESS • DUBLIN • IRELAND

ISBN: 978-1-901658-74-3

CERTIFIED
CARBON
NEUTRAL°
publication

CarbonNeutral.com
CO₂ emissions reduced to
net zero in accordance with
The CarbonNeutral Protocol

This book is typeset by Ashfield Press
in 11 on 13.5 point Quadraat and Zapfino

Designed by SUSAN WAINE
Printed in Ireland by GPS COLOUR GRAPHICS LIMITED, BELFAST

Contents

Preface
7

CHAPTER ONE
From the Source of the Suir to Templemore
10

CHAPTER TWO
Templemore to Thurles
40

CHAPTER THREE
Thurles to Cahir
62

CHAPTER FOUR
Cahir to Clonmel
94

CHAPTER FIVE
Clonmel to Carrick on Suir
136

CHAPTER SIX
Carrick on Suir to Waterford
176

CHAPTER SEVEN
The Suir at Waterford City
206

CHAPTER EIGHT
Waterford to the Sea
238

Select Bibliography
278

Index
280

Preface

I WAS BORN WITHIN a hundred metres of the river Suir, where its waters, swelled by many tributaries, are broad and majestic as it passes by Waterford's long Quay. I spent hours as a child observing the river from the first-floor front windows of my maternal grandfather's apartment near Reginald's Tower, marvelling at the ships manoeuvring in the strong tidal flow, with smoke belching and klaxons booming, and wondering at the endless herds of cattle being driven on board ships moored at the Quay. These memories, and a recently discovered grainy photograph of my mother and grandmother waving from the deck of the SS *Great Western*, as it pulled away from the Quay in the nineteen thirties bound for Fishguard, inspired me to consider writing about the Suir. When I discovered that little has been written about this great river, I decided to embark on this book.

During my field research, I walked the course of the river where I could: where good fishing is to be had, rough anglers' paths can be found leading out from most settlements, and a few stretches are popular walking routes. For long reaches, however, the river is bounded by a wonderful but often impenetrable natural wilderness, where flora and fauna forced out of the intensively farmed hinterland has found a home. I explored some of these secluded and remote stretches of the river for hours without meeting another soul, and it was clear that I was following an ancient, disused route through an all but forgotten landscape. Upstanding remains of Gaelic lordships in the form of earthen-mounded sites and the vestiges of monasteries are common along the Suir, as are the more robust stone-built castles and priories of the Normans. Evidence of a one-time populous peasantry is to be found only in the crumbling stones of their remarkably numerous, tiny places of worship. As I passed along this riverine corridor, I sensed I was in the company of the shades not only of those peasants, but of Gaelic chieftains, Viking explorers, Norman warrior-colonisers, and Gaelic and European monks. In many Suirside villages and towns I met their descendants.

My exploration of the Suir was a rich and uplifting experience, not only because of the glorious landscapes through which the river led me, but through the people it introduced me to, many of whom gave invaluable assistance to me in my work. I finished my research with one strong conviction: the river and its banks, whether in the countryside or in its towns and villages, represent a valuable but vulnerable trove of heritage that local authorities need to take more account of. In particular, it was clear to me that a great number of the medieval buildings that I came across, which roofless, have weathered the winters of so many centuries, will succumb to this particular century and be subsumed back into nature unless radical measures to save them are taken. We have sadly come to the end of a time of plenty, during which we possessed more than enough resources to protect and preserve for the future these important reminders of our past, but didn't. It may be decades before it becomes possible again to take the necessary measures, by which time, for many sites, I believe it will be too late.

I have relied on the assistance of many to bring this project to a conclusion. Jonathan Williams, as always, was inspiring and encouraging beyond the call of duty. My wife Teresa keeps me going through all, and makes it possible for me to write. Dick Cronin has once again been a stalwart travelling companion of inestimable knowledge, insight and humour. It is a pleasure to work with Ashfield Press, John Davey, Susan Waine and Judith Elmes, who make the transition from manuscript to completed book seem easy. My son Donal gave sensible advice about the text and prepared the initial maps. Mike O'Neill helped with the du Noyer images, for which my thanks is due to the Royal Society of Antiquaries of Ireland. Liz and Peter Burke introduced me to the landscape and people of the Devil's Bit, Jerry Dwyer gave me insights into Thurles, Shay Hurley showed me the two sides of Clonmel, Michael Coady provided a lyrical window onto Carrick, Jim Power took me on a Suir voyage, and Anthony Brophy shared his thoughts about the Suir at Waterford. Leslie and Cora Dowley, Jane Twomey, Ned and the late Kitty Burke, Paddy Drohan, Andy O'Meara, Jim and M.B. Kennedy, Marie Tynan Devanney all helped me on my way, and to them all, I dedicate this book.

MICHAEL FEWER
26 March 2009

Chapter One

Map of the River Suir

From the Source of the Suir to Templemore

RIVERS ARE AMONG the most beautiful and, when of superior size, the grandest features of our natural scenery. Mountains have an impressive gravitas, even from afar. Lakes have a passive, reflective beauty. Rivers, however, while they have a close association with mountains and lakes, glaciers, cataracts, forests, meadowlands and even ocean shores, have an animation, a geographic spread, and a usefulness to humankind that sets them apart as one of the most pervasive elements of our natural world. They have been closely associated with the societal and economic development of man since earliest times, and have always held a central place in primitive religions, as well as being at the core of present-day Gaiaesque philosophies.

In Ireland, man has interacted with rivers since he first arrived on these shores nearly 10,000 years ago. Mesolithic peoples carried out their hunting and gathering from temporary settlements close to coasts and rivers, and Neolithic peoples learned early of the value of rivers not only for the fish and shellfish they offered, but to irrigate and drain land used for food crops. Since farming began, man has been involved in attempts to control rivers, to contain them, to reclaim them, to draw off the power of flowing water to grind grain or crush rock, or to use the river's own physics to allow river craft to travel up or down its route.

The Suir is one of Ireland's greatest rivers, flowing 183 kilometres from where it rises in County Tipperary to where it enters the Celtic Sea in the company of the Barrow and the Nore, the other two of the 'Three

Sisters', with whom it drains most of the south-eastern part of the island.

I learned many years ago from my Christian Brothers geography textbook that the river Suir rises on the Devil's Bit Mountain in County Tipperary. I first spotted this strange-shaped eminence as I drove along the Dublin to Limerick road years later, and over time it became familiar from afar with the unmistakable round-shaped 'bite'. More a range of hills than a mountain, the Devil's Bit is one of a series of upfolds in a field of hard Old Red Sandstone. This rock is made up of eroded fragments of older, long gone mountains, reduced to sands and gravel by primordial weather and washed down and deposited in ancient estuaries and lakes around 360 million years ago. These layers of sands and gravel in time became mountains themselves, and in the south of Ireland what remains of those mountains today stretches from Kerry through the Devil's Bit, the Knockmealdowns and the Comeraghs before becoming exposed again along the picturesquely pink, cliff-girded coast of Waterford Harbour.

The Devil's Bit range is made up of a ridge of low summits: Devil's Bit Mountain (480m) in the south, and Kilduff Mountain (445m), Borrisnoe Mountain (442m) and Benduff (450m) at the northern end. Part of the range was composed of softer rock which eroded away eventually over millennia to leave the characteristic gap, the devil's 'bite', relating to the legend that the devil, on one of his aerial passages over Ireland, took a bite out of the hill, and then, farther east, spat it out, creating the eminence we now know as the Rock of Cashel. This legend may have had origins in one of the old names for the hill, *Slieve Aildiuin*, 'the mountain of the cliff fort', but sounds similar to *Slieve Aill Deamhan*, 'the mountain of the cliff of the demon'.

In my venture to follow the Suir from source to sea, my first task was to identify and locate the source, the place from where water began to flow, it is said in the annals, 'on the night that King Conn of the hundred battles was born'.

At least three streams rise on the eastern slopes of Borrisnoe Mountain, north of Devil's Bit Mountain, to come together to form the Suir on the plain below; when I was there in the wet summer of 2007, there seemed to be many more. Although I found that local people had vague ideas about which of them was in fact the true Suir, no one I met initially seemed to be certain. The only official indication I had was the Ordnance Survey map, which has a note in fine blue print stating 'The Source of the River Suir' on one of the three main streams rising on Borrisnoe.

My wife, Teresa, and I were invited by friends, Peter and Liz Burke, who live at Killawardy just below Devil's Bit Mountain, to stay with them while we explored the area and sought the source of the Suir, and we were delighted to accept. There is nothing better than local knowledge, and over the course of a number of visits to the area Peter and Liz

Andy O'Meara of
Boharnarooda

introduced us to their home place and the people who live on the flanks
of Devil's Bit Mountain. They also took us wandering the network of
boreens of Borrisnoe in search of the true Suir, and in the course of one
of these pleasant rambles we met Andy O'Meara of Boharnarooda out
walking his dogs. A short stocky man in his eighties, he soon had Peter
and his part of the Burke family placed, and they swapped family news
as only people who live in a country area can. It became clear that Andy
O'Meara was very knowledgeable about the area and he had a quiet
confidence behind his twinkling eyes. I told him I was looking for the
source of the Suir.

'Then I'm your man', he said. 'I'll take you there, if you like.'

He took us along the road and into a dense forestry plantation that
cloaked the hillside. We followed the forestry road as it gently climbed
and zig-zagged uphill, and although I am sure the landscape has been
transformed by forestry over the past few decades, Andy brought us,
without hesitation, straight to the spot. From a point on the forestry

road near a sharp bend, he pointed out a rivulet that flowed down through an open area bordering a section of forest. I clambered down off the forestry road and followed the rivulet gingerly through thick, tussocky grass interspersed with patches of spongy sphagnum moss until, about twenty yards from the road, it disappeared. Higher up than this I found no evidence of flowing water. When I made my way back to Andy, he told me that when he was young an ancient whitethorn tree had marked the spring where the Suir rose. As a child he had taken water from it to make tea when he and his family were cutting turf on the bog. The area has been covered with trees since 1958 and the whitethorn tree had been smothered by the conifers: they had soaked up the water from the land, so the stream was a lot smaller than it used to be. When Andy was young, there were small trout in it as far up as this, and he remembered catching them by hand. This kind of confident and detailed first-hand evidence is seductive, and on the basis of what Andy said, I would have been convinced that I had found the source, except for the fact that his location did not agree with that shown on the Ordnance Survey Map.

During the course of another ramble, however, we struck gold. We met a local woman, Marie Tynan Devanney, who claimed that her late father and mother's cottage was the nearest house to the place where the river Suir rose.

'We call it the last house that God built,' she said, and she insisted that we all come and see it there and then. At the end of a steep boreen we found a neat whitewashed cottage with a gay red tin roof tucked into the eastern flank of the mountain, looking out at a spectacular panorama of horizon that stretched from the Slieve Blooms, by Lugnaquilla, Mount Leinster and Slieve na Mban to the Comeraghs. It had been Marie's childhood family home, and after her parents died, she preserved and cared for it, using it occasionally for guests and family parties. A wooden plaque on the wall has the name Annfield, and the array of potted plants along the front was clearly regularly cared for. The out offices, which had not been used for farming purposes for some years, were whitewashed and spotlessly clean and, inside, the well-worn tools and paraphernalia of a small farm were carefully hung on the walls or stacked in corners.

The cottage had the simple traditional layout of a typical nineteenth-

'The last house that God built'

century small farmer's cottage: a kitchen with an inglenook fireplace, a parlour for entertaining and two tiny bedrooms.

Cooking and baking had been done in the traditional way over the kitchen fire, and a blackened kettle and pots still hung on the crane. Next to the fireplace was a white-lidded enamel bucket from which Marie offered me a drink of pure, cool Suir water.

'We have a well here on the farm,' she said, 'but this water comes from below the first bridge across the Suir, not far from the source. I get a bucket of it every day or so – we like it particularly because it has no lime in it.' Indeed, it tasted fresh, cold and sweet.

Marie told us that her parents had gone on holiday only once in their life, and that was for the week of their honeymoon. Then they returned to this cottage for the rest of their lives and worked the marginal

Ruined cottage at Borrisnoe

mountain land, joined in the labour by their children as the years passed. She told us of childhood memories of early morning starts for school and long days spent during the holidays working up in the fields on the flanks of Borrisnoe. Leaving home with a handful of porridge oats in their pockets, she and her siblings produced a morning meal by milking their cow and making a cold porridge, sweetened in autumn with juicy blackberries. Lunch was often nettle soup, boiled in a can on an open fire, with mushrooms in season.

'We worked hard but we always seemed to be happy. We didn't know of any other life,' she said. The last house that God built is a shrine to Marie's parents and the hard but happy life they and their children lived on the mountainside.

As we said goodbye and left this peaceful place, she directed us downhill to the first bridge over the Suir, which we had passed before without noticing. A tinkling stream descended from the coniferous wood that covers this part of the hill and passed under the road. On the downstream side of the road a few tiny steps led down to a sparklingly clear pool, where Marie was accustomed to draw her Suir water. We had not time on that occasion to follow the stream uphill to its source, but I returned at a later date on my own to attempt to do so.

Climbing the bank on the upstream side of the road, I found myself in a dark and neglected wood. I carefully made my way across undulating pine-needle-covered ground, scattered with a treacherous minefield of fallen branches, towards the stream, tinkling its way merrily downhill, glinting with silver as it cascaded over rocks. I followed it uphill, and soon reached the edge of the forest, where it was joined by another smaller stream from the south. I continued along the bank of the bigger watercourse, with more difficulty now because it flowed through a cordon of overhanging gorse and stunted trees. Upstream of another little tributary the amount of water decreased and the flow became sluggish as the stream, more of a rivulet now, disappeared under a small but dense copse of bushes. Rounding the bushes, I found nothing on the other side but sedgy grass. As I walked on, however, I suddenly discovered that the Suir had only dipped beneath the surface: the sedgy grass was but a thin skin over a concoction of black mud and cold water, into which I sank up to my shins. If the source of a river is the point where it emerges from the earth, I had certainly found it. I had planned when I reached the source of the Suir that I would sit and ruminate poetically about my journey with the river down to the sea 183 kilometres away. The river thought differently, and instead I trudged and squelched uncomfortably back to the road and my car.

After a steep fall from its source and crossing under the road, the Suir swings to follow the road briskly through a green, scrubby landscape, hugging the bedrock and frequently tumbling down tilted shelves of sandstone. A local man told me that there is not as much water in the Suir as there used to be. He could remember as a young lad hearing from his doorway the roar of the water plunging off the mountain, but that is

no longer the case. Here the river passes by the sites of a couple of long-abandoned cottages, probably dating from the same period as the Tynan cottage above. Such places are common in many parts of rural Ireland, particularly in counties such as Leitrim, Cavan and Mayo, and I have come across many on cross-country walking explorations. They have a strange stillness and a tangible sadness that you will not find in many other places. As an old friend commented when we came across a similar ruined cottage in County Wicklow, if you stand still and listen intently, you may hear the sound of happy children at play. Sometimes in springtime bunches of brilliant yellow daffodils burst forth from the rank grass surrounding such sites, evidence perhaps of little gardens of long ago.

The Burnt House

Nearly two kilometres from its source, the river is swelled by two tributaries from the south, one of them Andy O'Meara's Suir. Not far downstream are the remains of the first of the many watermills on the Suir. Called by locals the Burnt House, it is a roofless, steep-gabled, substantial stone building with tall chimneys, and looks to me to be of the late seventeenth century. Ivy cloaks much of the structure, and semi-mature trees grow out of its fireplaces. Local lore has it that it was a flax mill, and in the nineteenth century it was owned by the Sligo flax company Brookes Hanley. The brilliant powder-blue flowers of flax in bloom are rarely seen in Ireland today. Introduced to Ireland from Roman Britain, flax was once grown widely both for its fibre, used in cloth-making, and for the oil extracted from its seeds, linseed oil, once used for cooking and lighting.

A local story tells how a band of flax workers who had lost their jobs in Northern Ireland in the nineteenth century came south, in desperation, to seek work. They had been turned away at this mill, and went on to Templemore, where they were also unsuccessful in obtaining work. Outside the town they stopped in despair at a sheebeen where they were sold poteen. They got roaring drunk and returned to burn down the mill, and that is said to be the way the ruin got the name the Burnt House.

A couple of kilometres below, the river passes Garret's Mill, a robust stone-built structure standing on the brink of a deep ravine through which the Suir cascades. I was told that the great steel millwheel was sold for scrap during World War II, and it looks as if the building has been used until recently as a dwelling. Just downstream from the old mill, the river passes under its first named bridge, Garret's Mill Bridge, where the rush of the watercourse off the mountain slows down as the gradient of the terrain levels out. Here, a few kilometres from its source, the Suir, having risen at an altitude of about 350 metres, has already lost 200 metres, leaving only 150 metres of fall to the sea almost 180 kilometres away. From here it meanders through open country as neat and slow-moving as a narrow canal, and passes under Skehanagh Bridge. At Killough it passes under its first main road, the N62, and, swelled by more tributaries, takes an abrupt turn to the right, flowing under Knockanroe Bridge and decidedly southwards for the first time.

Directly west now is the Devil's Bit, where a modern tradition has developed of gathering for the rosary and mass on what is locally called Rock Sunday, the Sunday nearest 25 July, St James's Day, and I arranged

to begin my journey down the Suir by visiting the Devil's Bit and attending the Rock Sunday celebrations. After a rainy, blustery week, Rock Sunday dawned bright and sunny, with a scattering of fluffy white clouds crossing a blue sky. Hurling enthusiasts had been enjoying an exciting season, and the Tipperary team was doing well in the run up to the All Ireland Hurling Championship. At very short notice, however, that Sunday was fixed for an important match against neighbouring County Clare, long-time hurling rivals. When it comes to traditions, inter-county hurling is on a much higher plane than the celebration of Rock Sunday, and with the very reasonable expectation that those who were not going to make their enthusiastic way to Croke Park for the match would be watching it on television, the celebrations at the Rock were cancelled. I was disappointed to miss the festivities,

The Suir at Skehanagh Bridge

(*Above*) Garret's Mill

The view from Devil's Bit towards Lough Derg

(*Right*) Rock Tower, a nineteenth-century folly below Devil's Bit

but we made our way to the Bit anyway, and joined a few family groups wandering up towards the cross on the summit.

A dramatic and tall round tower called the Rock Tower on the OS map stands just below the 'bite'. Local tradition has it that it was built by the Cardens, the local landlords, as a folly in the nineteenth century. Just above the tower we came a grotto overlooked by a statue of the Virgin Mary erected by the Presentation Brothers in 1946. Beyond

we found a well-beaten track to the summit worn in the soil over the years by thousands of pilgrims' feet. It meandered upwards through shoulder-high heather interspersed with fraughans, and we paused to sample and enjoy the astringent flavour of their tiny purple berries. Rising out of the heather were great blocks of sandstone, around which the path threaded its way. The rock here was in the form of what the Victorians called pudding stone, made up of a mix of water-rounded pebbles cemented together and indeed looking like a geological pudding. As we climbed, the rich emerald landscape of Tipperary was revealed behind us, allowing us an excuse to take a breather and admire the view. A little scrambling was needed to get to the summit plateau, topped by a great white cross, but it was a rewarding arrival.

Only the view to the north was blocked by the long ridge to Borrisnoe, but in all other directions we could see to the horizon. Identifying familiar landscape features, we reckoned we were overlooking nine counties. Laois stretched to the north, and beyond the Wicklow hills were unmistakable, low on the north-eastern horizon. Mount Leinster and the Blackstairs marked Carlow, while the whaleback of Brandon Hill in Kilkenny was visible. The Comeraghs and Knockmealdowns led the eye through County Waterford, and continuing clockwise past the Galtys, the next eminence was Keeper Hill in Limerick. To the west the long sliver of silver could only be Lough Derg on the Shannon, beyond which the dark landscape of Clare and Galway lined the horizon, and of course all round us the rich chequered pattern of the fields of Tipperary stretched into the distance. Although I knew it was close by, I was a little disappointed that there was no sign of the river Suir.

Another ancient name for the Devil's Bit is the Rock of Bearnan, or the rock of the little gap, and the fact that it is an easily identified feature for many miles around may have contributed to it becoming an important site in pre-Christian times for harvest celebrations and assemblies, particularly at the festival of Lughnasa. Pieces of gold regalia of historic date, a five ounce ceremonial hat and a decorated gorget or collar have been found nearby on two separate occasions', perhaps evidence that there was considerable activity here in the Bronze Age. What is interesting about the pagan tradition of assembly at the Rock of Bearnan is that it was continued without any Christian involvement by local people

until well into the twentieth century. The first time it received an official Christian imprimator was in 1946 when the Presentation Brothers choose it as a site for their grotto of a statue of Holy Mother Mary, Queen of Ireland. Late in 1954 a great cross was erected on the summit to celebrate the Marian Year.

A drawing of the gold hat found near the Devil's Bit

The original pagan celebrations may have lost their old meanings over time, or were disguised or reinterpreted as Christianity spread through the land. Those surviving folk memories of the festive activities, although clearly involved with celebrating the harvest, are fragmentary and confused. They tell of the local people refusing to pay their tithes, and instead gathering ceremonially at the base of the 'bite' to symbolically bury the tithes, and with them the notices received from the authorities demanding payment. These stories sound like a later version of the more traditional Lugnasa gatherings, during which the first sheaves of the crop being harvested are buried as a symbolic thanksgiving offering to the gods.

In recent centuries the assemblies at the Rock of Barnane took place on the Sunday nearest St James's Day, 25 July, which is within six days of the pagan feast of Lughnasa on 1 August. After masses in the many little churches in the vicinity, the people converged on the Devil's Bit , where picnic feasts were enjoyed. The plentiful fraughans are in season at this time and they, and probably a spiritous liquor derived from them, formed part of the picnic menu. The picnicking took place in the shelter of the 'bite' between the two tors, and after lunch those who were able would climb the rest of the way to the summit, and festive music and singing would begin. Fiddles and melodeons were the instruments most represented, but in one year, 1941, the Local Defence Force marched out from Templemore, accompanied by their brass band, to take part in the gathering.[1]

The afternoon was filled with ball games, races and athletics, and opportunities were presented for boys and girls of different parishes to freely meet and court, something that was not in former times as easy as it is today. As always in these circumstances, local entrepreneurs also turned up to sell cakes, fruit, sweets, lemonade and strong liquor. Occasionally there were faction fights between two local family groups, the Cummins and the Darrigs, known as the Blackfeet and the White-feet. No representatives of these families seem to be in the area today.

I found that the people of this part of Tipperary have qualities of civility and hospitality that recall an older, more convivial Ireland. Such attributes seem now, alas, to have disappeared from many parts of our countryside, much of which has become culturally urbanised owing to the low density, ribbon-development expansion of Irish towns and cities. The industrial and commercial nature of present-day agriculture is far removed from the qualities of land and animal husbandry and of neighbourliness, which was still strong in Ireland less than thirty years ago. I found that arriving in this part of rural Tipperary was like leaping back those thirty years to a kind of place that I had begun to think was becoming extinct in Ireland, where the genuine friendliness of the people, the old-style hospitality, the sheer comfortableness and relaxed nature of the locality pours over you. Visiting one another is clearly an important activity. Callers at a house, great or small, are warmly invited in, and, no matter what time of the day or night, the woman of the house seems to want nothing more than to feed her visitors. I found that more than once when visiting, if there was a television on, it was promptly turned off, even if a favourite show was being watched, its importance immediately taking second place to the old tradition of hospitality to, and interest in, visitors.

The Templemore/Devil's Bit area is not on any main national artery

---

1   *Tipperary Star,* 19 and 26 July 1941.

road, there is no vibrant populous urban centre, no significant industries, no beaches, no lakes, no outstanding or dramatic scenic beauty
that would attract tourists in large enough numbers to unbalance the
traditional ways. There is a strong kinship between the people of the
different parishes, where everyone knows everyone else, and from my
conversations it was clear that the old values are cherished even by the
young. I was told that the rate of marital break-up in the area is a mere
fraction of the national figure.

After our descent from the Devil's Bit we visited the nearby ruined
church and graveyard in the parish of Killea, where the Suir rises. I was
particularly attracted to this ruin since I knew that at the end of my
journey along the Suir, overlooking Waterford Harbour, there is another
ruined church called Killea. Other than a couple of ivy-covered outcrops
of masonry, there is little left of the Tipperary Killea, and it has probably been in ruins since the sixteenth century. Recent archaeological
examination of the site revealed pieces of dressed stone of medieval
origin built into the boundary walls, a quern stone and parts of a
fifteenth-century ogee-type window. A bullaun stone, something
commonly found in old churchyards, was also dug up. A bullaun is a
stone with a scooped out, font-like basin, originally thought to be a
pestle for the grinding of the altar bread grain, but more recently considered to be of pagan origin, suggesting a very ancient date for the site.

The forest of lichen-dappled tombstones and Celtic crosses in the
churchyard include a stone commemorating the Rev. Paul Higgins
(c.1628-1724), a legend in the area. He studied for the Catholic priesthood on the Continent and was ordained in Rome in 1669, but after he
returned to Ireland, in the face of the severe penal laws, he was
persuaded to change sides and he joined the established church. He took
up a post in Trinity College, Dublin, teaching Gaelic reading and writing
and while there he helped prepare the first Gaelic translation of the
Bible. Higgins also preached a sermon in Gaelic once a month, which
became a popular event, attracting outsiders as well as students. Eventually, he received a lucrative appointment as Rector of Drom and Templemore, and spent the rest of his life in Devil's Bit country. He became
much loved by the local people, Catholic and Protestant, but there were
always doubts about his real allegiance: it is said that preaching once in

[27]

Jim Kennedy of
Clonakenny with his
working model of a
Ransome threshing
machine which he built
to one-quarter scale

Templemore an awful thunder and lightning storm burst from the heavens, and Higgins roared above the noise to his congregation 'Get on your knees and make the sign of the cross, ye devils, or you'll burn in hell!' It is said that just before he died, aged 96, the local Catholic priest visited the Rev. Higgins, who asked him if there was any chance of receiving absolution for his sins. The priest is supposed to have said there was a better chance that the Suir would run uphill, and as he left he saw that Higgins's tears at this news were running up his forehead.

Knowing I had a lot of questions about the area that they might not be able to answer, Liz and Peter Burke took us to meet Jim Kennedy and his wife, 'MB', at Clonakenny, a couple of miles east of where the Suir rises. Here also, as friends of Liz and Peter, we were made welcome, and before long sandwiches, cake and tea were conjured up from the kitchen. Jim and his wife are popular musicians, and play at local parties and weddings, but Jim is also known as an inventor of all kinds of gadgets, a lover and repairer of clocks, and he can make almost any part of any machine in the workshop attached to the house. I found him fascinating, a possessor of an amazingly wide range of largely self-taught skills. He showed me around his workshop, an artificer's treasurehouse, a place of workbenches and tools, the walls hung with strange equipment – clocks, tilly lamps, oil cans, wheels of all kinds, and even a laminated wooden propeller from an old aeroplane. Jim collects old tools, particularly tools that are no longer made, and light engineering machines, ancient and modern, drills and lathes, both normal size and miniature. With great ceremony and not a little drama, he used a tweezers to take from a tiny cylindrical box a drill bit that was almost invisible to the naked eye. In that tiny shed with little space to manoeuvre, Jim enjoys refurbishing antique furniture, and has recently finished building an astonishing one-quarter scale working model of a Ransome threshing machine, for which he made all the parts.

We eventually got down to matters relating to the Suir, and Jim proved to have an encyclopaedic knowledge of the river, with answers for all my often unusual questions. Before I knew it, hours had passed; not wanting to overstay our warm welcome, we made our farewells and made our way back to Killawardy.

———

After about five kilometres flowing south through open grasslands which look as if they flood in wintertime, the Suir is joined by a broad tributary before it passes under a substantial bridge of three arches at Knock-nageragh, which carries the R433 westwards across the river to Temple-more. From the parapet of the bridge, the Devil's Bit can still be seen clearly. Until a century ago many thousands of acres to the east of the river and around Templemore were owned by the Cardens, who arrived in Ireland about 1665 and settled into the medieval Templemore Castle. When it was destroyed by fire in 1740, they built Templemore Priory. Either because of their great wealth or poor judgement, or perhaps a bit of both, they had this house pulled down in the early nineteenth century and built a new house called Templemore Abbey on another site. Some years later the Abbey was transformed into a huge Tudor-Gothic pile, with finials, battlements and crockets to the designs of Ireland's premier house architect of the time, William Vitruvius Morrison.

Perhaps the best remembered and most infamous of the Cardens was John Rutter Carden (1811-66), who owned land between the Devil's Bit and the Suir. He was a deeply unpopular landlord, widely known locally as 'Woodcock' Carden, after the number of times he was shot at by certain of his tenants. His tenants were many and the marginal mountain land was poor, yet Carden was not prepared to put up with those whom he felt were non-industrious. To make more room on his land for grazing cattle, he carried out many evictions, driving up to fifty families from their homes, and by 1852 the 150 children on the roll of Barnane school had dwindled to just ten.[2] His actions made him and his agents a target for ambushes by disgruntled and evicted tenants, but he seemed to have a charmed life and fought back fearlessly. On one occasion he chased on horseback two men who had shot at him, knocking one insensible and capturing the other. Binding them both and leading them from his horse, he delivered them to Nenagh Jail, where they were eventually hanged. He was besieged in his home at Barnane Castle a few times by angry tenants who ploughed up his lawns until he fortified his home and installed a cannon on top of the building.

Carden was infamous for another incident: the attempted abduction of a young girl when he was forty-one. He fell in love with a beautiful eighteen-year-old English girl, Eleanor Arbuthnot, who was living at Rathronan House in Clonmel. When she rejected his advances, he became obsessed with her and decided to kidnap her. The plan was to take the girl to his yacht which was moored off the Galway coast, and then sail to the Isle of Skye and the house of a friend. The attempt at abduction went disastrously wrong, however. Carden and a few of his men ambushed a coach carrying Eleanor and her two sisters as it came to the gateway of Rathronan House. The young women resisted vigorously, and, assisted by staff of the house, managed to beat off their attackers. Carden fled, but the police captured him near Holy Cross. After a trial in Clonmel which attracted a great concourse of people of all classes, he was sentenced to serve two years with hard labour, a verdict which, the Times reported, 'was received with loud cheers and many ladies in the gallery enthusiastically waved their handkerchiefs'. Only

---

2   Máirtín Ó Corrbui, *Tipperary*, Brandon, 1991.

the cellars of Barnane Castle remain today, but its walled gardens and a number of mock towerhouse follies in the area, including that just under the Devil's Bit, are reminders of the one-time wealth of the Carden family.

The Templemore Abbey Cardens had, to the west of the town of Templemore, an enormous walled demesne that was well treed and rich in wildlife. It attracted much trespassing and poaching, and a wonderful local song, penned by a local man from Curraduff, Killea, called 'Carden's Wild Demesne', describes the plenitude of grouse, pheasant, partridge and hare on the lands, and the fine walks and woods. It goes on to decry the ownership of so much by so few, and finishes with these lines:

> So rise up me bold Tipperary boys and hasten to the fray,
> And join your gallant comrades from Drum and brave Killea,
> We'll free the land St Patrick blessed, and break the tyrant's chain,
> We'll hunt and shoot and reap the fruit, on Carden's Wild Demesne.

Sir John Carden, the last of the family to live in Templemore Abbey, left it in 1909. In 1920 it became the local base for British Army Auxiliaries, which probably led to it being burned and demolished in 1922. The Cistercians at Roscrea are said to have bought all the cut stone for £500, leaving only the gatelodges as evidence of the one-time existence of a great house.

The town of Templemore lies a kilometre west of the Suir in the townsland of Kiltilane, which means the church of St Silean. It seems reasonable to surmise that the ancient church lies in Templemore town park, beneath the ruined thirteenth-century Teampull Mór, which gives the town its name. Teampull Mór graveyard, situated between the park and a pitch and putt course, is densely filled with gravestones and broken funerary monuments of the better-off locals, including the Cardens, whom I suspect are eternally turning in their graves at the idea of ending up surrounded by vulgar multitudes playing mini-golf. A nineteenth-century directory states that one side of the graveyard, 'tastefully enclosed, is sacred to the Carden and Willington families' and that the

Cardens unsuccessfully tried to prevent the public from gaining access to it. Whatever about the mini-golf, by the looks of the empty beer cans and crisp bags filling the spaces between the tombs, the occupants of the cemetery must also often have unsavoury night-time company.

The park, a beautiful wilderness within minutes of the town centre is also the site of a ruined castle built by the Butlers, where the Cardens lived for nearly a hundred years until it was destroyed by fire. The town that grew to the south of the castle in the park was granted a market in medieval times which must eventually have become an important one, judging from the great market square that characterises the town.

The remains of the old Butler castle in the town park

The barracks at Templemore was originally intended for Thurles, but the Presentation Sisters there felt it would be inappropriate to have an army barracks close to a convent school. Named Richmond Barracks, the buildings were originally designed to accommodate 1,500 men and 54 officers, and included a hospital, a chapel, a prison, and a stables. This development had a major effect on the prosperity of the town and became an important social and cultural influence on its inhabitants, who at the time numbered about 3,000. The game of cricket was introduced by the military and a cricket ground was laid out in the barracks recreation grounds as early as 1840. While initially the game was played by the army and local gentry, such as the Cardens

and Trants, by the 1860s it had gained in popularity throughout Tipperary, and a team made up of the ordinary folk of Templemore was competing throughout the county by the mid-1860s. At the time of the establishment of the GAA in 1884, cricket was the most popular field sport in County Tipperary.

Inevitably, the constant and highly visible presence in the town of the soldiers in their uniforms, marching with bands, would have induced countless local young men to join up, and soon a tradition Templemore military families became established. The Church of Ireland church in Templemore is rich in memorial plaques commemorating members of local families who joined up and helped build the British Empire. The few words inscribed on these plaques paint a picture of great endeavour: from one we learn that the bodies of Major Richard Willington and Lieutenant Colonel James Ring lie in far-off graves in the Punjab 'in the East Indies', mourned by local families in 1868 and 1898 respectively, and from another we learn that Robert Ring died in Mandalay in Burma

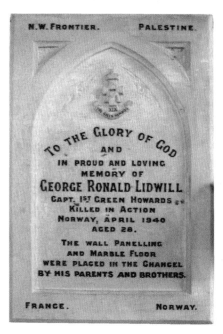

N.W. FRONTIER.   PALESTINE.

TO THE GLORY OF GOD
AND
IN PROUD AND LOVING
MEMORY OF
GEORGE RONALD LIDWILL
CAPT. 1ST GREEN HOWARDS &
KILLED IN ACTION
NORWAY, APRIL 1940
AGED 28.
THE WALL PANELLING
AND MARBLE FLOOR
WERE PLACED IN THE CHANCEL
BY HIS PARENTS AND BROTHERS.

FRANCE.   NORWAY.

in 1890. More recently, many local families lost sons in World War II: George Lidwell died aged twenty eight in the brief Norwegian campaign in April 1940 and his brother Arthur was twenty four when he died of wounds received in the battle for Normandy in July 1944. A third brother, Robert, fought in Crete, North Africa, Sicily, and France and survived the war with a rank of Lieutentant Colonel to die in 1994 in his eightieth year. Even the desperate battle for Monte Cassino in Italy is remembered here, through local man Richard McKinley, who died in the fighting there in March 1944.

Church of Ireland church houses several memorial plaques commemorating local men who died fighting for the British Empire

(*Above*) Memorial to George Lidwill who was killed in the Norway campaign in 1940

For every local officer, there must have been many local working class Catholics whose military service, even in the war against Hitler, is shamefully unrecognized and certainly not memorialized in the Catholic Church of the Sacred Heart on Church Avenue.

The surrounding high walls of Richmond Barracks were not only ideal for defence, but when it was decided to turn the barracks into a prisoner-of-war camp in 1914, they helped to confine prisoners. The First Battle of the Marne took place in early September of that year, less than a month after hostilities broke out. Over three days an inexperienced British expeditionary force joined with French allies in a desperate attempt to check the advance of the German army and drive them back to the Aisne river. They succeeded, the Germans dug in on the east bank and prolonged trench warfare began. A large number of German and Austrian prisoners were taken during the retreat to the Aisne, and some 2,000 of them found themselves in a prison-of-war camp hastily erected in the great square in Richmond Barracks. Before long, the exotic newcomers had become well known and much liked by the townspeople: Protestant prisoners paraded under guard to St Mary's Church of Ireland each Sunday for Service, and Catholics paraded to the Church of the Sacred Heart, singing popular German songs as they marched. The local newspapers claimed that the prisoner of war camp put Templemore on the map, and that 'tourists from all parts come to see the town's cosmopolitan inhabitants'. It was felt that 'so many foreigners within its gates is calculated to greatly re-enliven the town'. The barracks had been unoccupied for three years before the Germans arrived, and one can easily imagine the boost to general business which more than 2,000 souls and their guards would have meant.

Within a few months of the opening of the camp, however, the government became aware of the danger of having such a large number of trained enemy soldiers on Irish soil. The Irish Volunteers had been founded in Dublin in November 1913 to protect nationalist aspirations and counter the Ulster Volunteer Force, founded in January of the same year. Nationalists of all persuasions were attracted to the Volunteers, and by September 1914 their numbers had risen to a phenomenal 180,000. The government was justifiably nervous, concerned that if an uprising was to take place, the 'springing' of a couple of thousand battle-trained Germans and Austrians would make the suppression of the rebellion all the more difficult. Arrangements were hastily made, and in February 1915 the 'town's cosmopolitan inhabitants' were shipped to a camp in England. Naturally there was general disappointment and not a little dismay in the town when the Germans and Austrians were taken away, but a few weeks later the Munster Fusiliers arrived to a great welcome at the railway station, to set up a training camp at the barracks. The area to the west of the barracks, today the Garda College Golf Links, was turned into a mock battlefield, with trenches, dugouts and barbed wire, recreating the battlefields in France, and over the following years thousands of Irishmen who volunteered for the British Army were trained there for the war in France. Many of those who left Templemore railway station for the Western Front never returned: of the estimated 300,000 men who volunteered for the British forces during World War I, over 40,000 died.

Richmond Barracks was essential for the economic survival of Templemore. Conscious of the need to retain the British presence in the town, particularly after the end of the war, a group of interested citizens made efforts to ensure that regiments stationed at the barracks would regard it as an ideal station. Funds were collected to provide appropriate off-duty activities for the soldiers, and a recreation and games room was established in the town hall in the middle of the market square where tea was served to off-duty soldiers.

Within five years, however, the political climate had changed dramatically, and the same town hall was burned in August 1920 by troops from the barracks as a reprisal for the shooting of an RIC inspector in the town. On another occasion when three English soldiers were killed in an IRA ambush, a mob of soldiers emerged from the barracks to burn and wreck houses in Patrick Street and Main Street. Towards the end of the War of Independence, in addition to the Northamptonshire Regiment in the barracks and the Auxiliaries in Templemore Abbey, Black and Tans were billeted in the RIC station in Main Street, now the Centenary Co-Op.

When the British Army marched out of Richmond Barracks in February 1922 after 112 years of occupation, their place was taken by a small force from the 2nd Tipperary Brigade of the IRA. The Barracks was under the command of Commandant Leahy, who seemingly at the time hadn't made up his mind whether he should align his force with those who had voted for the Anglo-Irish Treaty or those who had rejected it. In the tense time before the outbreak of the Civil War, he managed to 'confiscate' a precious armoured car which had been given to the Provisional Government by the British, complete with its Black and Tan drivers. When in July 1922 a force of the newly uniformed National Army

The Garda Training College at Templemore

arrived in Templemore with the intention of occupying the barracks and getting hold of the armoured car, Leahy would not allow them in. This was before a shooting war had broken out in earnest, and what transpired reads like the script of a Keystone Cops movie. It was difficult for Leahy to effectively garrison such a large establishment with a small force of men, and a party of National Army soldiers managed to steal in. Their aim was to take the armoured car and race out through the gates in a derring-do escape, but they found that a mountain of sandbags had been piled against the gate, making it impossible to drive a vehicle through. Instead they disabled the car by removing its essential parts, and escaped back to Liberty Square, where the National Army had set up its headquarters.

While the officers of the National Army were discussing what to do next, one of them, who had decided that he was on the wrong side, left the meeting, gathered the parts and brought them back to Leahy in the barracks where they were refitted in the engine. Leahy, believing that the armoured car would be more useful to the cause in the capital, sent it to Dublin. In the midst of these confusing events, the commander of the National Army, having been well reinforced from Kilkenny, decided to lay siege to the barracks, and deployed his men around the complex. At the last minute Archbishop Harty of Cashel and Emly interceded and succeeded in preventing any bloodshed by persuading Leahy quietly to withdraw with his forces.

The barracks was occupied by the National Army until 1929, after which, except for the period of World War II, it was left vacant for thirty-five years. By the early 1960s the National Garda Training Depot was straining at the seams, and a delegation from Templemore approached the then Minister for Justice, Charles Haughey, to see if Richmond Barracks could be opened again as a Garda Training College. Haughey visited Templemore a short time after. He was impressed at the potential of the barracks, and renovation work was put in hand in mid-1963. In February 1964 the new National Garda Training Centre was opened, ensuring the future of Templemore and its people.

Chapter Two

Templemore to Thurles

A COUPLE OF KILOMETRES east of Templemore the Suir continues its journey southwards, passing under Knocknageeragh Bridge where it broadens to about five metres wide. The next bridge is a simple steel girder railway bridge, and a short distance farther downstream is Aughall Bridge, which takes the R502 to Templemore. When I passed here, the heavy rains of the night before had swelled the waters of the Suir, roiling them to a thick, muddy brown colour. The river was sweeping at breakneck speed under the bridge. A pair of cormorants flew over, about forty feet up, heading west. They were a reminder to me that, although I felt that I was far inland and the open sea of the Shannon Estuary was fifty miles off, the extensive waters of Lough Derg and the Shannon were less than twenty-five miles away. As I watched the birds a new silver and green Iarnród Éireann train crossed the nearby railway bridge and swished past almost soundlessly.

To the south-east is the village of Castleleiny, where a tributary of the Suir passes under the quaintly named Washpin Bridge. It must have had some importance in the past, for it is noted on a map dated 1811 prepared by John Killaly, one of the only four places named in the area, the others being The Devil's Bit, Clonakenny and Templemore. Killaly's map shows an ambitious scheme to link the rivers Barrow and Shannon and the Grand Canal with the Suir by way of an extensive canal system. The Suir section of the canal had its summit east of here and descended to Cashel and then Cahir, finally running closely parallel to the river from Clonmel to Carrick on Suir, where, after 41 locks, navigation shifted to the river. The project never came about, and today Castleleiny is a sleepy little hamlet with just a chapel, a post office, a pub and a tiny bridge over a tributary of the Suir. A scholar named Liam Meagher ran a school of classical education here in the late eighteenth century, where Latin and Greek were taught through the medium of the history, culture and literature of Greece and Rome. It must have been an important school, for students attended from all over the country, sometimes up to one hundred at a time. They were boarded out in the village and the surrounding area, in return for which they did labouring work in their spare time. The school fees were eight shillings and a penny halfpenny per quarter, a substantial amount of money at the time.[1]

Hedge schools were widespread in the late eighteenth and early nineteenth centuries and a product of the Penal Laws, anti-Catholic measures enacted between 1695 and 1709, one of which banned Catholic schools. The historian W. E. H. Lecky described this particular law as a 'universal, unqualified and unlimited proscription': not only were Catholics forbidden to attend school, but Catholic teachers were not permitted to teach under pain of being regarded as a Popish clergyman, and were prosecuted as such. The hoped-for result of these restrictions was to persuade Catholics to avail themselves of Protestant schools, which would result in them becoming loyal Protestant subjects: those Catholics who did not take that option would be marginalised in a state of ignorance.

To avoid imprisonment, Catholic teachers taught their pupils in secret, in any available rural shed or cabin or sometimes in rude shelters under trees or hedges; thus the name 'hedge school'. While many of the schools provided an education of the highest quality and were run by scholars and poets such as Eoghan Rua Ó Suilleabháin and Brian Merriman, by the early nineteenth century standards were very mixed. The most popular books used in some schools were what were called 'Burton books'; my grandmother would have referred to them as 'penny dreadfuls'. They were cheaply put together with crude woodcut illustrations, 'uncouth sculpture' as one commentator says, and their content was 'loose and immoral'. The most popular texts were *Laugh and be Fat* and *The Irish Rogues and Raparees*, which John Edward Walsh describes as 'the first a collection

---

1   Mairtín Ó Corrbui, *Tipperary*, Brandon 1991.

of the most indecent stories, told in the coarsest language; the second celebrated the deeds of highwaymen'.[2] I cannot imagine that texts of this sort would have been central to Liam Meagher's school in Castleleiny: many of his graduates went on to continue their studies for the priesthood in the Irish Colleges on the Continent.

Downstream of Aughall Bridge and Penane Bridge, 18 kilometres from its source, the Suir meanders through a flat and almost treeless countryside, but as it approaches the village of Loughmoe the natural course of the river has been altered by an embankment which guides the waters eastwards to serve a large mill. The great five-storey stone building, with its intact slated roof and twenty-five gaping windows, does not look as if it has been disused for long, and what must have been the millers house beside it has been recently renovated as a fine residence.

Remains of mill on the banks of the Suir at Loughmoe

2   John Edward Walsh, *Sketches of Ireland Sixty Years Ago*, McGlashan, 1857

At the gateway is a disused cottage that might have been the home of Mary Grant, one of the last women to be hanged for murder in Ireland. Hers is a story that reiterates the great divide in Irish society which characterises the helplessness of the poorer classes at the hands of the unprincipled members of the landed classes. At the beginning of the nineteenth century Mary was alone one day in the cottage when the son of the local landlord, Gilbert Maher, called, and tried to have his way with her. In defence, she struck him with a hatchet and killed him. Panicking, she hid his body in a ditch, but the word got out and she was arrested for his murder. Because she was poor, she had little chance of justice, and she paid for her act of self-defence by being found guilty and hanged in Clonmel. Probably as a result of this injustice, Mary Grant's brother, 'Captain' Jer Grant, became a notorious highwayman and terrorised Tipperary for some years until he was caught, and in August 1816 he also departed this life at the end of a rope.

There was a motte and bailey at Loughmoe in medieval times, part of a defensive perimeter for the Norman colonisation of the Suir valley against the incursions of dispossessed Gaelic lords who had resettled farther west or in the upland wilderness of the Slieve Bloom Mountains to the north. In the fifteenth century the manor came into the ownership of the Purcell family, who built a towerhouse, one of about 130 such medieval fortifications to be found along the Suir valley. It is an impressive construction as towerhouses go: its large rooms and rounded corners suggest that it was of a higher quality than usual. By the unsettled years of the early sixteenth century, this Anglo-Irish family was living much as their Gaelic neighbours were, keeping a hospitable house with resident poets and harpers, raising cattle and augmenting their grazing stock from time to time by carrying out raids on neighbouring Gaelic and Anglo-Irish lands alike. By the mid-sixteenth century the county of Tipperary was described in contemporary papers as in a state of 'utter desolation and waste, saving for a few castells', and the castles were 'standing like islands in a sea of looting'.[3]

A little more than a hundred years later, when the political situation was more settled, it became fashionable for the gentry to build more

---

3   Peter Somerville-Large, *The Irish Country House*, Sinclair-Stevenson 1995

spacious houses that, while defensible against poorly armed rabbles and a disgruntled peasantry, had larger windows on the upper floors, providing a brightness in the rooms that was always absent in the old towerhouses. The Purcells extended their towerhouse at Loughmoe with a generously fenestrated central section and a tower-like wing at the far end balancing the old tower. In addition to the delicately mullioned Elizabethan windows, the new section sported decorative string courses at every floor, tall chimneys and rounded parapet gables, and would have been a spectacular sight to behold in its time.

It still is an impressive sight, standing on the banks of the Suir well away from the road, and the landowner, a young and friendly shaven-headed farmer, gave me permission to go across his fields to explore the ruins. Today, the 'new', Jacobean part of the building is open to the sky, since the floors and roof were of timber, while the

The ruins of Loughmoe Castle: the Jacobean section is on the right

The richly carved fireplace at Loughmoe Castle

old towerhouse, with its stone-vaulted roof, is still comparatively intact. In the upper room there is a massive stone fireplace richly carved with armorial crests, the letters 'FP', and a Star of David, all decorated with sinuous vines and leaves. In the newer block the dressed stones have been taken from all the lower windows, and have probably found their way over the years into the houses in the village, and only the danger of attempting to harvest the upper windows has left most of them in place.

Standing in the upper room of the old towerhouse, I tried to transport myself back to the time of the Purcell lordship of this area. One could imagine the crackling, flaming fire in the great fireplace casting flickering golden light on the faces of a gathering as they listened attentively to the family bard singing a praise song of the Purcells, showering poetic insults on their enemies. The view out of the the castle windows has not changed greatly over the past few hundred years. What was probably a

richly stocked, walled kitchen garden to the north-east today is a grassy paddock, while to the east the meadow that gently slopes, uninterrupted, down to the Suir cannot be much different from what it was in the Purcell's time. In the farther distance it is likely that one would have seen forest where there is now a patchwork of hedged fields, but the prospect of the grey-blue undulating Galty Mountains lining the southern horizon is the same as seen by the Purcells, as is the unmistakable profile of the Devil's Bit ten kilometres away to the north. My sixteenth-century reverie was broken by the whistling rush of a Cork-bound train on a line just west of the castle which definitely was not there in the seventeenth century. Today the Purcells have long gone, leaving behind this magnificent ruin, home now only to many hundreds of jackdaws, whose raucous cacophony of calls echo off the windowless walls.

Roof level of Jacobean section

South-westerly view from Loughmoe Castle towards the Galty mountains

(*Above right*) Loughmoe graveyard with castle in the distance

In the old churchyard of Loughmoe is the tomb of the two McCormack brothers, from nearby Killahara, hanged in 1858 for the murder of a local land agent named Ellis. The McCormacks were innocent of the crime: the man said to have carried out the shooting went to the local bishop and admitted it after the brothers had been sentenced. The authorities, however, refused to reverse the decision, and the brothers were executed and buried in the yard of Nenagh Gaol. The sense of injustice that the general populace felt on the execution of these two innocent young men festered for many years after, until in 1910 it manifested itself when the brothers were disinterred and reburied in Loughmoe after the largest funeral Tipperary had ever seen. The ten-mile route of the cortege between Nenagh and Loughmoe was lined with mourners who had come from far and near, all businesses were closed down for the morning, and the windows of houses were shuttered.

Daniel Cormack
HANGED INNOCENTLY
~ AT NENAGH ~
11TH May 1858
Aged 18 Years
~ R · I · P ~
HIS REMAINS TRANSLATED
· HERE 11TH MAY 1910 ·

The McCormacks' tomb is a semi-subterranean structure covered with a confection of rich decorative stuccowork, depicting framed panels of flowers and grapevines, and the coffins of the two brothers can be seen through richly ornamented wrought iron gates. On one of my visits I found a man painting the tomb and carefully touching up the stucco details. I asked him if I could take a few photographs, and he said 'No bother!' and stood back to let me have a clear view of the tomb. He told me he was working there because there was going to be a reburial of the brothers the following month.

Tomb of the brothers Cormack wrongfully accused of murder and hanged in 1858

(Above) The brass plate on one of the coffins

'They'll be using two "dead coaches", you know, horsedrawn hearses, to transport the two coffins on a little procession around the village and then to the church for mass before the lads would be returned to their tomb', he said.

He told me that even the coffins had been rebottomed and revarnished, but when I suggested that there must not have been much left of the two unfortunate brothers at this stage, he just smiled.

'The whole parish will be out,' he said, 'and there'll be lots of people coming from all round, particularly to see the hearses: sure, a lot of the young generation have never seen such things except in a book, but to see it in real life beside you – jet black horses with jet black feather plumes – that's a sight. If you are around then with your camera, if only to get a shot of the horses, you'd be made up. I'd say there will be quite a few photographers.'

I asked who was organising this unusual ceremony, and he told me that the parish priest and the tidy towns committee had arranged it.

The nineteenth-century Catholic chapel that stood nearby was a plain structure, but in the last years of that century an imaginative parish priest had the building embellished with elaborate octagonal turrets, a reredos that the architectural historian Maurice Craig has called 'especially fine', and an exotic entrance gateway. All this was regrettably demolished about 1980, and the only echo of the opulence of those later additions is to be found in the McCormack tomb, which is likely to have been the work of the same stuccadores.

Nineteenth-century chapel at Loughmoe, demolished about 1980

South of Loughmoe the Suir swings east at Clonamuckoge and flows through a hedgeless meadowland to pass under Rossestown Bridge, a fine three-arched structure and the river's thirteenth bridge. To the east is the densely wooded Brittas estate. The Langleys, who came to Ireland in the mid-seventeenth century, about the same time as the Cardens, lived in Brittas Castle, a short distance from the Suir, and when it burned down about 1820, Major Henry Langley embarked on the construction of a massive replacement home. He had William Vitruvius Morrison, architect of Templemore Abbey for the Cardens, design for him a great moated castle based on Warwick Castle in England from where the Langley family originated. Work began in the early 1830s with the erection of a great limestone gate tower, a tall triple-arched structure spanning two turrets. As the construction proceeded, however, Major Langley was struck on the head and killed by a piece of falling masonry, and the project was abandoned. The great gate remains, however, incongruously but dramatically rising from the partial moat, beside the comfortably modest single-storey house that is home

Limestone gate tower of Brittas Castle

to the present owners of Brittas. South of Brittas, the Suir runs parallel to Bohernamona, a pleasant name for what was once a bog road, and enters the town of Thurles.

In times past Thurles was an important Norman establishment, with a large motte and bailey which contemporary accounts suggest was 100 feet high. It was demolished about 1800, but the remains of nine tower-houses survived in the town into the early nineteenth century, in addition to the castles at the east and west gates. The only easily accessible survivor today is Bridge Castle on the banks of the Suir, where the east gate was formerly. It is still largely intact, and provides storage for a ladies boutique next door. The manageress of the boutique kindly allowed me to climb to the roof, provided I did not stand on the nests of the jackdaws and pigeons that littered the stairs. Bridge Castle was origi-nally one of two castles at that point: an eighteenth-century gunsmith named Blackwell, who lived in the other one, stamped the motif of a gate on the guns he manufactured.

With the road from Dublin to Limerick a long way to the north and the road from Dublin to Cork 9 kilometres to the south, Thurles is somewhat remote. However, the main railway line from Dublin to the south-west passes through the town, and has been a major influence in the survival of Thurles as an important educational, industrial and commercial centre for rural Tipperary, evidence of which is the high quality of much of its traditional architecture and craftsmanship. Fine stuccowork, in particu-lar, can be seen throughout the town, but the finest examples, perhaps, are the façades of Kickham House on the south-west corner of Liberty Square, and Haye's Liberty Market opposite.

Kickham House is where the body of the writer and Fenian Charles Joseph Kickham lay for the night of 27 August 1882 before his burial on the following day. Kickham was born in 1826 near Cashel, but was brought up at Mullinahone, near the Anner river and in sight of Slieve-namon mountain, both of which feature often in his writings. In his youth he was greatly influenced by *The Nation* newspaper, and his early writing included articles he wrote for it while still in his teens. Although partly blinded and deafened in a childhood accident with gunpowder, he

took an active part in local politics, founding the Mullinahone Confederate Club and joining the Young Ireland movement. After the failure of the ill-timed and poorly planned rising at Ballingarry in July 1848, for which he organised a supply of pikes, he joined the Tenants Rights League and the Fenians.

Kickham House, Thurles, named after the writer and Fenian Charles Kickham

In 1865, at the age of thirty-nine, Kickham was sentenced to fourteen years in Pentonville Prison in London for his membership of the Fenians. He was never a particularly healthy man, and he was released after four years because of ill-health. He wrote his novel *Sally Cavanagh* while in prison. *Knocknagow*, a novel of rural Tipperary and his best-known work, was published in 1873. His fame in Ireland had increased to such an extent that when he died at Blackrock, County Dublin in 1882 eleven marching bands and ten thousand mourners followed his funeral cortege to Kingsbridge Station. When the remains arrived at Thurles and were met by similar crowds, however, the local priest had the doors of the cathedral closed, to make sure that Kickham, who had been excommunicated owing to his Fenian membership, would not lie in

[53]

state there overnight. He told the mourners that he could not allow the corpse into the cathedral without the permission of the Archbishop, Dr Thomas William Croke, who was away. It may not have been convenient for the Archbishop, who trod a narrow line between upholding law and order and supporting the Fenian cause, to be present in Thurles at the time. So, instead of lying in state in the cathedral, Kickham was 'waked' in the home of a kind Quaker family named Larkin. The following day the funeral took place to Kickham's home place, the village of Mullinahone. It is said that no priest was allowed at the graveside.

The exotic neo-Romanesque Cathedral Church of the Assumption of the Blessed Virgin Mary is a surprising building to find in a town like Thurles, and all the more surprising when one learns that it is the work of J.J. McCarthy, often called 'the Irish Pugin', who is not known for work in the Romanesque style. He designed seven cathedrals and over forty churches in Ireland during his career, which began at a time when the Catholic Church was beginning to flex its muscles and show its wealth. His departure here from the Gothic style was strongly influenced by the client, Archbishop Leahy, a well-travelled prelate with a good knowledge of architecture. The façade is thought to be based on that of the cathedral of Pisa, built between 1063 and 1350, although the building at Thurles is of dramatically more human scale and considerably less ornamented. As at Pisa, the baptistry forms a significant structure detached from the main building. Unfortunately, I found the baptistry closed, and had to admire the remarkable baptismal font through a glazed door. Made from a single block of marble, it portrays a great metre-wide stylised clam shell with four snakes sinuously slithering up from the base and around the rim.

The ambience of good church interiors are added to greatly by sacred music, and I was fortunate to hear a school choir sing accompanied by the organ, filling the space with rich and melodious harmonies. The interior is elegant and colourful: the colonnades of columns in red Cork marble have capitals and bases of Caen stone, and all the capitals, which were carved in situ, are of different designs. Much of this carving work was carried out by a young Cork stone mason named Michael O'Riordan, who died before the work was finished.

The original marble tabernacle, now located at the rere of the

chancel, is thought to have been made by Giacomo della Porta (1537-1602) a pupil of Michelangelo and one of the architect/sculptors of St Peter's Basilica. It had stood in the Jesuit church in Rome for over 300 years until, discarded during nineteenth-century renovations, it was spotted by Archbishop Leahy while he was attending the First Vatican Council in 1869. He managed to buy it for a small amount and bring back to Thurles to grace his new cathedral.[4]

Cathedral Church of the Assumption of the Blessed Virgin Mary, Thurles

St Mary's Church of Ireland church and graveyard is up a narrow

---

4   Peter Galloway, *The Cathedrals of Ireland*, Institute of Irish Studies 1992

St Mary's Church of
Ireland church, Thurles

street. On the gate piers of the graveyard are two plaques that indicate how the history of Ireland and England are so closely intertwined. One proclaims that Elizabeth, Viscountess of Thurles and mother of James Butler, 1st Duke of Ormond (1587-1673) is buried here. She was the progenitor in her second marriage of not only Nano Nagle, founder of the Presentation Order of nuns, and Rev. Theobald Mathew, Apostle of Temperance, but of both Prince Charles and Diana, Princess of Wales. The plaque on the opposite pier states: 'William Loughnane, 1898-1921, killed by British Forces March 1921, aged 23, is buried in this churchyard'. A third plaque suggests that the concept of the global economy is not a recent phenomenon: the earliest church on this site was erected in the early Norman period, and in 1292 it was mortgaged to Italian merchants.

I was taken aback when I entered the graveyard to find two large gleaming pieces of artillery, one a field gun dating from the Great War and the other an anti-tank gun from World War II, but I quickly learned that St Mary's has been dedicated as a military garden of remembrance, commemorating Irish soldiers in war and peace. Men who fought and died in the British forces in the two world wars are listed on wall plaques, including local man John Cunningham, who as a corporal in the East Yorkshire Regiment won a Victoria Cross at the Battle of the Somme in 1916. Another Thurles man, William Bradshaw, who served as a surgeon in the British Army and who won the Victoria Cross for exceptional gallantry during the Sepoy Rebellion in 1857, is also buried here. There is a memorial to those who were killed during UN peace-keeping missions, including the ten soldiers who died in the horrific Niemba ambush in the Congo in 1960, which introduced the name of an obscure African tribe, 'Baluba', to Ireland's vocabulary. I was present at the ceremonies in 1960 when the 33rd Battalion, the second Irish Army peace-keeping force to be sent to the Congo departed from Baldonnel Aerodrome. After a blessing by Archbishop McQuaid, they boarded US Airforce Globemasters that were to take them the 6,000 miles to a very disturbed country in tropical Africa. The men were wearing the standard bulls-wool uniform and forage caps, and climbed the ramps into the huge aircraft carrying their WWI rifles and their gear on their backs. They also carried a plastic bag containing sandwiches and couple of oranges for the journey. In contrast, the US Airforce personnel were well-turned out in stylish, modern uniforms, and they looked on somewhat bemused at the Irish Army's finest. The contribution of Ireland's soldiers to peace in the Lebanon is little heard about, but clearly is well appreciated by the Lebanese: a ceder tree is planted in St Mary's which is one of 47 presented by the Lebanese people to honour the 47 Irish soldiers who died in their land on peacekeeping duties between 1978 and 1986.

As the 1880s dawned, Ireland was in poor shape. Within living memory there had been three disastrous rebellions and a horrendous famine, and in the early 1870s a worldwide industrial slump resulted in Ireland being flooded with cheap surplus stock from Britain, undermining once again unprotected Irish industry. Three very bad harvests from 1877 to 1879, and particularly the failure of potato and oat harvests in the west, brought many rural communities close once more to famine. Such was the national climate when, as the winter of 1884 set in, a group of men met in Thurles, and started a movement that has been as influential in Ireland as any church or political party. The main athletic sports played in Ireland were English in origin, and it was felt that the sports and pastimes of the Gaelic race were being ignored. The hard-working Irish needed an element of healthy recreation in their lives, and to revive traditional Irish sporting activities in the best possible way, the Gaelic Athletic Association was founded. If Thurles is the Bethlehem of the Gaelic Athletic Association, the manger was Hayes's Hotel in Liberty Square, called Main Street in the 1880s. Run by Miss Lizzie Hayes and advertised as a commercial and family hotel, it was already a century old, and boasted, in the same way that hotels today boast of gyms and swimming pools, a large commercial room, a ladies drawing room and first-rate billiard and smoking rooms. In one of those billiard rooms the GAA was born.

Among the seven people present on that night were Michael Cusack, a 37-year-old teacher from Carron in County Clare and 43-year-old Maurice Davin from Carrick on Suir. Maurice was a member of a family celebrated for their athletic prowess, and an accomplished athlete in his own right. Although circulars had been widely issued with notice of the meeting, it was a small attendance, but those present were encouraged by over sixty letters and telegrams from prominent people expressing warm support for the initiative. The outcome of the meeting was the foundation of the Association 'to preserve and to popularise native Irish pastimes and thereby to reawaken national pride and self-reliance', with Maurice Davin elected the first president. The agreed objectives of the association were sent to Dr Croke, Archbishop of Cashel, Charles Stewart Parnell and Michael Davitt, requesting them to become patrons.

The Archbishop accepted in a letter that regretted the gradual demise of such Irish sports as 'ball-playing, hurling, football-kicking according to Irish rules, casting, leaping in various ways, wrestling, hand-grips, top-pecking, leap-frog, rounders, tip-in-the-hat...' and while he felt he thought lawn tennis, polo, croquet and cricket were excellent in their own way, the archbishop described them as alien sports. He also decried the falling off of popularity of snap-apple night, pancake-night, and bonfire night: '... they are all things of the past, too vulgar to be spoken of, except in ridicule by the degenerate dandies of the day'. He saw the foundation of the GAA as a peaceful, cultural revolution and stated that if the Irish continue to condemn 'the sports that were practised by our forefathers, effacing our national features as though we were ashamed of them, and putting on, with England's stuffs and broadcloths, her masher habits and such other effeminate follies as she may recommend, we had better, at once and publicly abjure our nationality, clap hands for joy at the sight of the Union Jack, and place "England's bloody red" exultantly above the green.' A fine statue of Archbishop Croke stands on a plinth at the west end of Liberty Square, and he is also remembered at GAA headquarters in Dublin, where Ireland's largest and finest stadium is named Croke Park. I was surprised, however, to find no monument in Thurles to the principal founders of the GAA.

When Parnell and Davitt later also agreed to become patrons, the new association received the political support it needed. Over the following few years its popularity spread throughout the country and it became one of the most successful mass-movements of its day. Appropriately, Thurles Sarsfields Club, representing Tipperary, won the first All-Ireland Senior Hurling Championship in 1887, beating Galway.

Over the years the GAA has given the nation, or at least its nationalist citizens, considerable spirit and pride, and it has gone on to become the largest amateur sporting organisation in the world. The depth of its culture of anti-Britishness, born out of those dark days of the nineteenth century and the massacre of twelve spectators and one player by the Black and Tans at Croke Park in November 1920 was such that it is only in recent years that the association's ban on its players playing 'foreign games', in other words English games, and its ban on members of British forces or Royal Ulster Constabulary becoming members, was abolished.

The nationalist spirit raised its head in these parts again in 1920,

Example of stuccowork in Thurles

when another cleric assisted in further rejecting the influence of the colonial power in Thurles by the non-democratic and arbitrary changing of street names in the town. Rev. Dr. Michael O'Dwyer, dean of St Patrick's seminary in the town, formed a committee to review the existing names, and to come up with alternatives appropriate to the new sense of pride and identity brought about in the Irish people by the War of Independence. There was little opposition; it would not have been politically correct at the time to oppose the moves and, indeed, it might have been dangerous to raise objections, and twenty-two other names of places in the town devised by O'Dwyer's committee were put before the Urban District Council and were unanimously adopted. It did not matter that many of the existing names had historic significance; places like Pudding Lane, Pike Street and Carney's Lane were wiped from memory and were replaced by Smith O'Brien Street, Wolfe Tone Place and Kickham Street.

The Suir flows under the bridge at the east end of Liberty Square, passing between old and new Thurles. On the east bank opposite Bridge Castle is an example of twenty-first century Thurles, the spanking new and architecturally dramatic Source Arts Centre, which houses a bright

The old and the new. Source Arts Centre and Bridge Castle in the background

colourful library, a restaurant and a theatre with seating for 250. I hope this complex will encourage the people of Thurles in what must be worrying times: the demise of the sugar beet factory in 1988 and the looming closure of the Erin Foods factory have left a serious shortfall in local employment prospects. A local woman emphatically told me that the biggest asset in the town was the railway station, because it allowed most of the working population to commute to work as far afield as Dublin and Cork. The rest, she said, lived off servicing the wealthy farming communities in the agricultural hinterland.

The website for the Source Arts Centre informed me that the management host film, theatre, opera, dance, ballet, music and visual arts events in a gallery space. I hope that the facility will provide inspiration to the citizens of Thurles on a widely inclusive basis, but I am not sure: when I took a walk around the facility, the advertised play was a black comedy with the title 'Wiping My Mother's Arse'.

Flowing south and out of the town, the Suir takes in a tributary from the east, called the Drish, before it crosses under the Cashel road and meanders into an open, hedgeless landscape.

Chapter Three

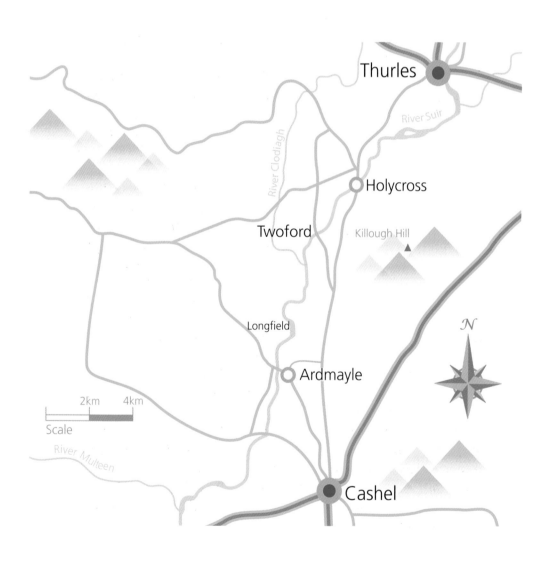

Thurles

River Suir

River Clodiagh

Holycross

Twoford

Killough Hill

Longfield

Ardmayle

2km   4km

Scale

River Multeen

N

Cashel

Thurles to Cahir

ELOW THURLES the Suir flows through a landscape like a great watermeadow to reach Cabragh a few kilometres south-west of the town. The establishment of a mill here may well have been the reason why the river divides into two watercourses, creating an island nearly a kilometre long. Only an ivy-shrouded stone structure and a few fragments of sluice gates remain of the mill, and the Suir flows unimpeded westwards under two stone bridges to become one again. The river now swings south and, willow-fringed, reaches the great weir at Holy Cross Abbey.

The Abbey of Mary, St Benedict and the Holy Cross was founded in about 1169 by Domhnal Mor O'Brien, whose name, as we will see, crops up frequently in matters to do with the medieval Suir. Not long after the abbey's foundation, it was recolonised by Cistercian monks, who not only brought modern ecclesiastical practices to Ireland, but also pioneered the development of agriculture and fishing. In every new territory where they established a monastery, the Cistercians cleared and drained the land, erected elaborate fish weirs in the rivers and set up well-ordered farms, over time changing the face of what was up until then a relatively untamed and wild landscape.

The wealth of Holy Cross in later years was attributable to the relics of the True Cross that were held by the monks there and which attracted a great number of pilgrims. Most relics of the true cross extant in Western Europe at this time seem to have come from a single large piece of timber, said to be part of Christ's cross, which was purchased by Richard Coeur-de-Lion in the Holy Land. The relics at Holy Cross had vague provenances. One of them was said to have been given by Pope Pascal II to Muirchertacht O'Brien, grandson of Brian Boru, which inspired him to establish a monastery to house it. However, it was not until after his death that his grandson, Domhnal Mór, managed to establish the monastery. The other relic mentioned in the stories was said to have been a gift of an English Queen, possibly Isabella, widow of King John.

During Henry VIII's Reformation, laws were enacted suppressing religious foundations, during the course of which ownership of monasteries, friaries and their lands were acquired by supporters of the king. At time of the dissolution of Irish monasteries the abbey seems to have escaped, possibly because the abbot of the time, one Philip Purcell, a married layman, had previously converted to Protestantism. In 1563, however, Elizabeth I granted the abbey, lands and possessions to Thomas Butler, tenth Earl of Ormond, whom we will meet again at Carrick on Suir. It seems he neglected the place and let the buildings fall into decay, but he did not interfere with the workings of the abbey, which continued quietly to have abbots appointed and to receive pilgrims for another two hundred years. It is recorded that Hugh O'Neill, 2nd Earl of Tyrone, made a detour to Holy

Holy Cross Abbey as painted by George du Noyer c.1860, and (right) modern-day view from the banks of the Suir

R.S.A.I.

Transept of ceiling, Holy Cross Abbey

Cross on his march into Munster in 1600 with his army, 'when the Holy Cross was brought out to induce protection'.[1] The following year Hugh O'Donnell similarly stopped at Holy Cross to receive the blessing of the monks. In 1603, however, a great gathering was held on 30 August, the feast of St Bernard, that attracted the attention of George Carew, President of Munster, who sent a large force to disperse the crowds, and the abbot of the time narrowly escaped capture by fleeing to France.

---

1   The Four Masters, *The Annals of the Kingdom of Ireland* 3rd ed., Castlebourke, 1998

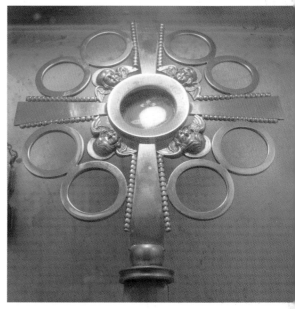

There was a major scandal in 1623 when one of the relics of the Holy Cross was stolen. Even the pope, Gregory XV, got involved, writing a letter confirming that 'a certain person named O'Kearney' had taken away the relic, 'so that he might divert into his own house the offerings of the Catholics', and urging the hierarchy to be firm with such 'usurpers', but to forgive them. The relic was apparently returned after a few months.

By the late eighteenth century there was no more than a parish chapel at Holy Cross and the great collection of relics had been reduced to part of a brass crozier, a tattered brown mitre, and what remained of the true

Stonemason's mark on column in Holy Cross Abbey

(*Above*) Gold reliquary at the Abbey

cross after many slices off it had been sold over time.

In 1896 the Commissioners of the Church of Ireland handed what remained of the abbey into the care of the State as a national monument, which probably saved it from further deterioration. In 1969 because of the relatively good condition of the buildings, it was agreed to hand the complex over to the Catholic Church, and to have the abbey restored. Work began in 1971 and the abbey was opened again as a parish church in 1975. What you see today dates mainly from the fifteenth century, built no doubt with the help of the rich offerings of the pilgrims who had flocked to this Suir-side monastery over three centuries to venerate the relics held there. The stonework is the finest of its kind for the period, particularly the rib vaulting in the roof over the chancel, the central crossing where the nave and transepts intersect, and the north transept. The carved stone window tracery, although not as light and feathery as in later periods, is flamboyant and wonderfully flowing. The complex is a remarkable survival from a period in Ireland when the destruction of such fine structures, deliberate or by neglect, was commonplace.

While the gracefulness of the fine vaulting of the roof and the robustness of the columns and walls were impressive, I found myself most taken by the little things, such as the numerous signatures of the masons carved on walls and columns and the wealth of little extracurricular flourishes of individual masons, like an owl perched high up on a column, the ram's head in a corner or triffid-like clusters of ivy leaves growing out of corbels. The finest piece of work in the abbey is the exquisite ceremonial seating for the priest and deacons beside the altar, called the sedilia. Roger Stalley, the expert on Cistercian monasteries in Ireland, commented: 'The most sumptuous of all Cistercian fittings, indeed the finest piece of church furnishing in medieval Ireland, are the sedilia in the chancel of Holy Cross.'

Local folklore suggested that underneath the sedilia lies the body of a prince of England, who was travelling through Ireland to collect alms, called Peter's Pence, for the pope, when he was set upon by members of a local clan, the O'Fogartys. He was robbed and killed. A blind monk at the abbey was drawn by a series of visions to where the prince's body was hidden, and when he found it, his sight was miraculously regained. A ring taken from a finger of the corpse identified the prince as a son of

King John and Queen Isabella, so after the body was buried with great ceremony in the abbey, the monk was chosen to take the ring to the Queen, now a widow, in London. In gratitude, the queen presented the monastery with a relic of the Holy Cross, presumably part of a gift from her husband's brother, Richard Coeur-de-Lion. A recent examination of the area under the seat of the sedilia turned up the remains of not just one burial, but disarticulated bones of 56 individuals, male and female, all packed into the small space.

West of the monastery is a Sue Ryder Home, a scatter of pavilions sensitively laid out in a parkland of young trees. Sue Ryder served during the war with the British Special Operations Executive, which Winston Churchill set up to co-ordinate the various resistance groups in occupied Europe. Her work brought her into contact in particular with the Polish resistance movement, and she was so influenced by the religious faith of the Polish men she met that she became a Roman Catholic herself. In 1953 she set up the Sue Ryder Foundation to assist the sick and disabled, and began to establish Sue Ryder Homes in Britain and Ireland. Around the same time she met and married Leonard Cheshire VC, an RAF bomber pilot and one of the most famous winners of the Victoria Cross. He had flown 102 hazardous missions over Germany before flying over Japan as the RAF observer of the apocryphal atom bomb raid, and his experiences led him to seek another path in life after the war. Cheshire became a Roman Catholic and in 1948 founded the Cheshire Homes, to provide residential care for elderly and disabled people, a venture that soon spread throughout Britain and Ireland. He died in 1992 as Baron Cheshire, and Sue Ryder died aged 77 in 2001 as Lady Sue Ryder of Warsaw.

The bridge at Holy Cross was built in 1626, and has a plaque bearing the Butler and O'Brien arms; it was built by James Butler and his wife Margaret O'Brien, and includes a Latin inscription asking the traveller to say a short prayer that 'both builders might escape the Stygian Lake'.

The Suir flows southwards from Holy Cross to where a small island at a place called Twofords divides it into two streams that flow under a pair of grand stone bridges, each of seven arches, clothed with herbs and lichens. Downstream, the Clodiagh river adds its waters to the Suir,

Seven-arched Twofords bridge

(*Right*) The elegant Longfield House, home of Charles Bianconi

before a long meander takes the river past gracious Longfield House, standing in terraced lawns high above the water. Built in about 1770 by the English Long family who had made their fortune in India, Longfield is a fine three-storey dwelling with bow windows at the front and the back, and three-sided bows at both ends. It is said that Charles Bianconi, the Italian coach entrepreneur of the early nineteenth century, noticed this house as a young man during his travels around Tipperary peddling framed prints. On his way to Cahir by way of the Suir, he lay down to rest on the slopes of an ancient motte. Across the river he spotted and admired Longfield and decided that one day he would own it. Forty-one years later, in March 1846, he bought Longfield and 1,000 acres of land for £22,000. He died there on 22 September 1875, two days before his ninetieth year.

Longfield House subsequently passed into the family of Daniel O'Connell, Bianconi's great friend. Bianconi's daughter married a nephew of the Liberator, and Longfield remained in this family until it was bequeathed to the Irish Georgian Society in 1968. The house now belongs to Coolmore stud.

After a series of tight meanders, the Suir passes the high motte built

Eighteenth-century Ardmayle church with its medieval tower

by Walter de Lacy from where Bianconi first glimpsed Longfield, and reaches the hamlet of Ardmayle. It is a quiet place today, but judging from the impressive assembly of historic structures scattered through the village and its nine-arched late medieval stone bridge, it was once a busy and important crossing point of the Suir. The church here was erected in the thirteenth century under the auspices of the Knights Templar. It was badly damaged in 1315 and again in 1581 during the Desmond rebellion. The church was replaced in the late eighteenth century, but the medieval tower was retained. The beautifully kept graveyard is used commonly by Protestant and Catholic, reminding me of some lines by William Makepeace Thackeray in his *Irish Sketch-Book*: 'In the old graveyard Protestants and Catholics lie together…where they sleep, and so occupied, do not quarrel. The sun was shining down upon the brilliant grass and I don't think the shadows of the Protestant graves were any longer that those of the Catholics.'

The medieval tower of the church has a delicate carved face on one of the dressed stone windows, and fragments of stone carvings that must have been built into the church wall, clearly upside down. In a field across the road are the remains of a robust early towerhouse with a narrow intramural stairs. Later on, when cannon began to be used, these stairs constituted a weak point in the wall, and internal spiral stairs were adopted. It is a bit of a scramble to reach them, but the climb to the grassy roof, from where the towers and pinnacles of Cashel to the south can be seen, is a rewarding one.

Below Ardmayle the river passes through watermeadows and marshlands and the undulating wall of the Galtee mountains seem to spread across the horizon ahead. As if unsure what to do faced with this barrier blocking its direct access to the sea just over 60 kilometres to the south, the Suir begins to weave through a series of long meanders.

South of Camus Bridge the Suir as far as the village of Golden is part of 35 kilometre-long Tipperary Heritage Way, and I took the opportunity to walk it. A sign warned that it is not 'open' between October to March, when long sections of the path are flooded, and this I knew, because on an earlier visit the river was clearly flowing well above its normal banks. I found it a most enjoyable walk through tall reeds, swaying stands of rosebay willowherb, fragrant meadowsweet and yellow flags, although rough and damp going in places even in July.

As the river swings west once again, it passes on the south bank a tall slated stone building that looks part house, part mill and part castle, all within a walled garden. This is Castlelake, which, as far as I could ascertain, was originally a mill on a tributary of the Suir, which underwent a number of alterations and additions to make it the beautifully informal dwelling it is today. On the opposite side of the Suir is one of the many towerhouses along its course, so remote from modern roads that, except for the farmer who owns the land and the passing angler, it is rarely visited. Ballinahinch Castle, formerly a Butler stronghold, has the remains of a bawn, two surviving corner towers and a fine arched gateway with a guardhouse over it. From the roof of the castle, which is reached up a narrow intramural stairway, a long reach of the river is visible. Nearby are the remains of an old church and a mausoleum of the Butler family, who lived in the castle until the early eighteenth century. In the midst of broken fragments of decorated stone from what was surely once a very fine little structure, a plaque on the ground states: 'Here lie the remains of the Butler Family since the year of Our Lord 1300'.

The waters of the river along here were slow-moving, and for the first time it looked as if the Suir would be easily navigable by large rowing and sailing craft. There were herons and swans in plenty along this stretch, and as I walked to the songs of reed warblers, glorious flocks of goldfinches flowed ahead of me over hummocks of thistles. After the Suir is joined by the Mulleen river it turns south, and I was relieved to reach a much-improved path, probably an anglers' path, which led me into the village of Golden.

It was here by the river in October 1172, at the eastern boundary of his kingdom, that Domhnal Mór O'Brien, King of Limerick, met with Henry II, who was staying at the time at Cashel. Domhnal was married to a daughter of Diarmuid Mac Murchu, and thus would have been a brother-in-law of Strongbow, the Earl of Pembroke, whose activities in Ireland had been one of the reasons for Henry's visit. During their meeting, Domhnal made his submission to the Norman king, and agreed the tribute to be paid, appropriate to the wealth of the kingdom of Limerick. Like other Gaelic chiefs, Domhnal kept on the right side of the Normans as long as it suited him, but by 1185 he was at war with them.

The island in the middle of the river at Golden has been developed into a public park, overlooked by part of a circular tower, the scant remains of Golden Castle. In the horrific wars of 1641, the castle became a refuge for a variety of Protestant planters, including a Scots dyer and a Welsh shoemaker, who were seeking protection from the depredations of the Catholic insurgents who were laying waste the countryside all around. The rebels laid siege to the castle

(Right) Ballinahinch Castle, home of the Butler family from the fourteenth to eighteenth century

for eleven weeks, and when they finally broke in, they buried some of the unfortunate settlers alive in a pit, threw an infant child into the river and killed a heavily pregnant woman. It was a time of vicious murder and retaliation, and it is recorded that Catholic armies were encouraged by their priests to massacre all English Protestants.[2]

Just over three kilometres west of Golden are the ruins of Thomastown Castle, once the seat of the Mathew family, who came to Ireland from Wales in the early seventeenth century. The Mathews were part of the small Roman Catholic 'New English' community in Ireland, and at Thomastown in about 1670 George Mathew, who was a half-brother of the Duke of Ormond, built one of the first non-fortified houses in the country. The Mathews were enormously rich, and entertained on a grand scale in their great house, which had forty guest rooms. Jonathan Swift stayed there in 1719 on one of his journeys through Ireland, and although only intending to stay a month, three months were to pass before he reluctantly left. The house was run like a luxury hotel: there was a bar and coffee room, a games room with billiard tables, and hunting and fishing trips could be arranged with the staff. Francis Mathew was made Earl Llandaff in 1797.

Father Theobald Mathew (1790-1856) the priest and Temperance crusader whose statue stands in O'Connell Street in Dublin, was son of one of Earl Llandaff's agents, and was born at Thomastown. He studied at Maynooth and afterwards became a Capuchin monk and worked with the poor in Cork, establishing a school for poor children. After twenty-five years of service there, convinced that much of the hardship that people endured in Ireland was caused by alcohol, he established in 1838 a society encouraging total abstinence from alcohol. Alcoholic drink is a central part of almost every form of recreation in Irish society today, and from this remove it is interesting to recall this man's remarkable achievements. Less than a year after he had started his society, nearly half the population of Ireland, mostly the poor it must be said, had given up drink. Records show that the tax intake on alcohol in Ireland during the period dropped from £1.4 million in 1839 to £0.8 million in 1844. After the success of his campaign in Ireland, Father Mathew concen-

2   *South Tipperary 1570-1841, Religion, Land and Rivalry*, David J Butler

trated on Britain, establishing temperance clubs and libraries there. Before he died, he had expanded his crusade to the United States with considerable success. Incongruous in its rural location on a triangular patch of grass at a crossroads near his birthplace in Thomastown, another statue of this remarkable man stands, erected on the centenary of the foundation of the Society for Total Abstinence.

Coincidentally, it is near the village of Golden that the Suir enters a region known as the Golden Vale, which stretches from Limerick through north Cork and south Tipperary, and which is famous in Ireland for the fertility of its soil. As the river surges under the bridge of Golden and reaches south, the quality of the land visibly improves.

A couple of kilometres downstream, the west bank is the site of one of the most picturesque of Ireland's many ruined monasteries, the Priory of St Edmund at Athassel. Judging by the extent of the surviving stone buildings, which would have formed only the core of the settlement, this place must originally have been

Priory of St Edmund, Athassel

(*Below*) Detail, Athassel

R.S.A.I.

extraordinarily extensive, truly a monastic city. It was founded by William de Burgo about 1200, and was occupied by the Augustinian order. They set about reclaiming and improving the surrounding lands and building a fortified monastery, moated for security and accessed across a bridge and through a guardhouse. Some of the stone that was used for decorative purposes is from Dundry Hill near Bristol, suggesting the Suir was navigable at the time at least this far upstream. At the centre of the monastery was a great church surrounded by cloisters, conventual buildings, the chapterhouse, storehouses and other secular buildings. Within a few years more lands were granted to the monastery, including an extensive area near Limerick, and the priory became very wealthy. The subsequent history of the place parallels that of most such settlements in Ireland. Inter-tribal strife and power struggles among Anglo-Irish and Gaelic lords led to the monastery and its surrounding town being burned in 1319: an elaborate thirteenth-century stone tomb-front discovered during excavations in 1946 displays heat damage from this event. The town was sacked again in 1329. The establishment survived through almost constant inter-church disagreements that involved excommunications, bloodshed, abductions and complaints to the pope until it was surrendered in 1541 during the dissolution of monasteries. Even at that late stage the Priory's property still included well over 1,000 acres of excellent land and 45 rectories. Although lying in ruin, a rich collection of fine carved stonework remains, including a tomb that may have contained the body of William de Burgo.

South of Athassel, I found another section of the Tipperary Heritage Way walking route, and followed a faint but very pleasant riverside path through meadows along the west bank of the Suir. Here the river is narrow and flows briskly, the east bank a dense jungle of mature trees that overhang the river, and some of which lie fallen, with their tops submerged in the rapids. Black-winged damsel flies flitted about great clumps of rosebay willowherb along the banks. As I walked, feeling the warmth of the sun and the power of the river, I spotted an animal about fifty metres ahead of me. It was dark, almost black, in the bright sunlight, and as it bounded along I realised it was an otter with wet fur. While I watched, another otter bounded up out of the water and gave chase to the first one until they were rolling about

(*Left*) Watercolour of the ruins of Athassel by Geoge du Noyer c.1850

playfully in the long grass. I kept getting closer and closer, trying to crouch down and move stealthily, but when I was within about 20 metres, one of the otters looked up suddenly and met my gaze. I froze, hoping to be ignored. The second otter, sensing a problem, stopped writhing in the grass and put its head up and looked at me. The three of us must have remained still observing each other for maybe a minute, and then the first otter turned its head and looked at its companion, and immediately after, took a couple of strides to the river's edge and slipped in without as much as a splash, followed almost in parallel by its companion. They left not a ripple in the fast-flowing water. Explosively, I let out my breath and realised I had been holding it for a long time.

Below an old weir that still causes great turbulence in the river, Suir Castle towers out of the trees on the east bank, built in a dominant position on an outcrop of rock high above the water's edge. A drawing by du Noyer dated 1840 shows a fine eighteenth-century house with bow windows beside the castle, but this has been

Suir Castle by George du Noyer, 1840

R.S.A.I.

reduced to a scatter of overgrown ruins. An overgrown track ramps down from the castle site to the river's edge, past an old well, referred to on the map as Cromwell's Well. The castle itself is of the usual pattern of others in this part of Tipperary: a narrow and steep intramural staircase, three timbered floors and then the vaulted roof. Apart from a number of spacious intramural rooms, it has two secret ones, stacked one over the other within the thickness of the wall. What I had not come across before is the timber spiral staircase leading from the top of the stone stairs to the attic or roof. Unfortunately, it was decidedly weakened by woodworm and rot, and I did not have the courage to try to climb it.

Below Suir Castle a constant roar of heavy machinery intrudes on the peacefulness of the riverside path from a major gravel quarry, thankfully hidden from the river by a great embankment. Beyond this, at New Bridge, the Tipperary Heritage Way walking route leaves the riverbank to take to the public road again.

On high ground west of the river and south of New Bridge is

View of Suir Castle from the west

(*Below*) Timber spiral staircase leading to roof of Suir Castle

Suirville, the birthplace of General Sir William Butler (1838-1910). He was a soldier and writer, and an illustrious member of a family that is remarkably widespread in Tipperary and Kilkenny, all descendants of, or connected to, the Norman lord William Marshall. William Butler was educated by the Jesuits at Rahan in County Offaly, and like many Irishmen in a period when there were few careers at home, he joined the British Army. Inspired by the grandeur of the landscape and the character of the Native Americans he came across during his six-year posting to Canada, he started a parallel writing career with *The Great Lone Land* (1872), a best seller in its day. After his sojourn in Canada he took part in the Zulu wars in South Africa, and in the British force that was dispatched to relieve General Gordon at Khartoum, and was knighted for his services in 1886. His literary career continued with a biography of Gordon and a number of travel books, and he retired with the rank of Lieutenant General to Bansha Castle, a few kilometres to the west. He was a strong and vocal supporter of the Gaelic League and Home Rule, and when he died was granted the request he made in his posthumously published poem of that name:

REQUEST

Give me but six feet three (one inch to spare)
Of Irish ground, and dig it anywhere;
And for my poor soul say an Irish prayer
Above the spot.

Let it be where cloud and mountain meet,
Or vale where grows the tufted meadow sweet,
Or boreen trod by peasants' shoeless feet;
It matters not.

I loved them all – the vale, the hill,
The moaning sea, the flagger-lillied rill,
The yellow furze, the lake shore lone and still,
The wild bird's song.

But more than hill or valley, bird or moor,
More than the green fields of my native Suir,

I loved those hapless ones, the Irish poor,
All my life long.

Little I did for them in outward deed,
And yet be unto them of praise and meed,
For the stiff fight I waged 'gainst lust and greed,
I learnt it there.

So give me an Irish grave, mild Irish air,
With Irish grass above it anywhere:
And let some passing peasant give a prayer
For the soul there.

Below the bridge the townsland on the east bank is called Ballyslatteen, or 'place of the osier rods', which suggests that the thick fringe of willows bordering the Suir along here has changed little in the last millennium. The willows decrease, however, as the river weaves its way through vast fields of nitrogen-rich grass scattered with prime cattle. Then swinging abruptly east and joined by the river Aherlow from the tranquil and remote Vale of Aherlow, the Suir skirts Slievenanard, the easternmost outlier of the Galtees, and races southwards towards Cahir.

At Knockgraffon, overlooking the meeting of the Suir and Aherlow, is a towerhouse, the ruin of a large church and a most impressive Norman motte. It must have been an important place in former times, and one can only imagine the many mud cabins and timber houses that were once gathered here which now are long returned to the earth. The motte is a simple but most spectacular oval-shaped mound, 17 metres high and 70 metres long by 55 metres wide. It is thought there was a ceremonial earthen mound at Knockgraffon long before the Normans arrived. Three Gaelic kings are said to have been buried there, including the first chief of the Eoghanacht, Eohgan Mhor. In 1192, when the Norman warlord Philip of Worcester was evicting the Eoghanachta or O'Sullivan clan and strengthening the Norman hold on the Suir valley, he constructed a motte and bailey on this site, sacred to the Gaelic clans, a symbol of the new order in the region. His men would have taken off the top of the original mound to create a level platform for the construc-

tion of a timber palisade, the 'bailey' of the typical Norman motte and bailey. In doing so, any trace of the former burials would have been destroyed. The Eoghanachta were forced westwards to the extremities of Munster and the Beara peninsula. There they remained, Gaelic in every way until the last of the Chiefs, Donal Cam O'Sullivan Beare, was forced to abandon the clan's lands and embark on an epic march northwards to his nearest ally, Tiernan O'Rourke in Leitrim. The mound features in many local stories. One tells of a hunchback from Aherloe falling asleep on the western side of the mound in the evening sun and waking in darkness to find himself in the midst of a party of the little people, singing and dancing. At first he was afraid, but then he got involved and ended up singing a few songs for them, which they much enjoyed. When he awoke in the morning his hump had gone.

Approaching the great motte, I was trying to conjure up from this great green mound some idea of its past, some sense of what went on here centuries ago. As I turned a corner in the road, I was suddenly confronted by a very large Clydesdale horse with great bushy gaiters, and could think only that this is the kind of horse that Philip of Worcester would have ridden. The horse was tied to the roadside fence in such a way that he could make full use of the 'long acre', the free grazing provided by the large roadside margin.

The panoramic view from the top of the motte was stupendous: the evening sun gleamed its reflection off the flooded Suir flowing southwards by way of long sweeping meanders and then turning to squeeze around the eastern foothills of the Galtys. The valley of the Suir stretched eastwards between Slievenamon and the Comeraghs, and the southern horizon was lined by the Knockmealdowns. To the southwest was layer after layer of the undulating grey-blue Galtys. In the foreground all round was the rich farmland of the Suir, a composition of brown ploughed fields and brilliant green pastures, some of those nearest the river silvered in flood waters. I am sure the richness of the lands bordering the river was also clear in 1192 to Philip of Worcester when he first stood here, lord of all he surveyed.

Below the motte is the church where in the seventeenth century, Geoffrey Keating or Seathrun Ceitinn in Gaelic, poet, historian and local priest, preached a sermon on sexual immorality that so

(*Left*) Towerhouse, local inhabitants and motte viewed from churchyard at Knockgraffon

angered the authorities that he had to go into hiding in the Glen of Aherlow. People came from far and wide to hear his sermons, and on this particular morning there was a married woman called Elinor Laffan in the congregation. A beautiful woman, she was thought to have had numerous extramarital affairs, and as the sermon proceeded, whether Keating intended it or not, the sentiments he expressed seemed to be increasingly directed towards Elinor Laffin. The rest of the congregation did not miss the point, and kept turning to see how she was reacting to Keating's admonitions. At the end of the service she left in anger, and made her way to one of her admirers, who happened to be Donough O'Brian, the Earl of Thomond and Lord President of Munster, and made a complaint about Keating. The Earl immediately issued orders for the priest's arrest, and a reward was offered for his apprehension.

Changing his name and disguising himself, Keating fled westwards into the Glen of Aherlow, which was still at that time covered in post-glacial wildwood, and a place of resort and shelter for rebels and priests on the run. It is said that during his sojourn there, in seclusion, he did the preliminary work on *Foras Feasa ar Eirinn*, his History of Ireland and the nation's first Gaelic history, as a reaction to previous biased histories by Edmund Spenser and Giraldus Cambrensis.

The old church is in a very ruinous condition, but the vestiges of a vaulted chancel and a few, partially eroded, decorative stones survive to suggest what an impressive place it was in its day. Nearby, guarded by a family of ravens, stands a towerhouse that was built in the early sixteenth century as a stronghold of the local Butlers.

Advertisement for a Cahir outfitters, late nineteenth century and similar façades in modern-day Cahir's main square

(Below) The impressive ruins of medieval Cahir Abbey

As it flows towards Cahir, the Suir, boosted by the Aherlow, broadens greatly, and for the first time can truly be called majestic. High up on the west bank in the northern outskirts of the town are the substantial but now almost forgotten ruins of Cahir Abbey, a priory of Canons Regular of St Augustine, founded around 1200 by Geoffrey de Camville, Norman Baron of Cahir and of Fedamore in County Limerick. Although little but the fortified church tower and the choir remains reasonably intact, the scale of these suggests the priory's importance in the medieval period.

P. J. BRODRICK,
ollen and Linen Draper and Outfitter,
The Square, CAHIR.

PARTMENTS.—Woollens, Hats, Blankets, Flannels, Shawls, Cashmeres,
Dresses, Prints, Baizes, Calicoes, Linens, Muslins, Handkerchiefs, Shirts,
dashery, Stays and Ladies' Underclothing, Boots, Millinery, Manties, Silks,
ta, Ribbons, Flowers, Hosiery, Gloves, Umbrellas.

GENERAL OUTFITTING.

loring managed by a Cutter of long experience and ability,
and none but really practical workmen employed.

Millinery and **Dress** Departments always replete with the
latest novelties.

First-Class Milliners on the Premises.

The Suir enters Cahir under a towering Victorian railway viaduct decorated with turrets and castellations. Completed in 1853, it was built from wrought iron and was fabricated in William Fairbairn's Manchester works; it is the only such bridge in Ireland to be still carrying traffic without additional strengthening. Downstream from this brilliant example of Victorian engineering, the Suir flows on over a great vee-shaped weir to reach Cahir Bridge and Cahir Castle.

The town of Cahir grew up around the great castle which is said to have replaced an Iron Age stone fort built on a rocky island in the river. Its original name was Cathair Dun Iascaigh, or 'the stone fort of the fish', from which the name Cahir is derived. By the twelfth century the Vikings were sailing their vessels up the Suir as far as Cahir, where they established a stronghold and an important link between their settlements at Waterford and Limerick. The present castle was begun by the Normans in the thirteenth century, but it was extensively reconstructed in 1375 when it came into the hands of the ubiquitous Butler clan. The

Cahir Butlers remained strongly Gaelic and Catholic, and somehow managed to hold on to their titles and most of their lands until the male line became extinct in 1858.

The castle has had a history as long and as eventful as the Butler family itself, and is the largest surviving fortification of its period in Ireland, with a tall surrounding wall enclosing two courtyards, a great hall and a strong keep. By the time it was completed in the sixteenth century, however, the use of gunpowder had already made it obsolete. During the Elizabethan wars it had become a gathering place and stronghold for the Catholic and Gaelic Irish of Munster, and whoever wanted to gain access to and control over the northern Suir valley had to reckon with Cahir. Unfortunately for the Irish, the first encounter with Elizabeth's forces was with the very determined Lord Lieutenant, the Earl of Essex, who brought the full force of a substantial and fresh English army south from Dublin to lay siege to the castle in May 1599. The defenders put up a strong resistance until Essex's great cannon arrived, and after a few days of terrifying bombardment the garrison fled downriver and the castle fell.

Less than fifty years later the castle fell again to the Lord President of Munster, Murrough O'Brien, and in February 1649 Oliver Cromwell appeared before the walls with the Model Army. I have always thought the horrors he is said to have visited upon the Irish during his short but bloody involvement in Ireland have been exaggerated. Warfare is always destructive to soldier and civilian alike, and it is certainly no different today. It seems to me that Cromwell's policy in Ireland was to avoid a long-drawn-out and murderous war, a continuation of what had gone through the previous decade, and rather, by being ruthless in the beginning, to bring his enemies to their senses and into the humour for negotiation. There was some initial resistance at Cahir, and a letter he sent to the castle governor as his army was drawn up under the walls of the castle tells a little of his hard but merciful military policy:

> Sir,
>
> *Having brought the Army and my cannon near this place, according to my usual manner in summoning places, I thought it fit to offer you Terms, honourable for soldiers: That you march away. With your baggage, arms and colours; free from injury or violence. But if I be necessitated to bend my cannon upon you, you must expect the extremity usual in such cases.*
>
> *To avoid blood, this is offered to you by, your servant,*
>
> *Oliver Cromwell.*[3]

The prudent governor duly surrendered and the castle was peacefully taken. In his report to Parliament Cromwell could not resist boasting that what had taken the Earl of Essex six weeks of hard fighting, he had achieved on behalf of the Parliament without loss.

In spite of this and other successful sieges, intrigues and bankruptcies, however, the castle remained in the Butler family almost continuously for nearly six hundred years. Although the male line became extinct in 1858, the ownership of the castle remained with female side of the family until 1961, after which the castle came into the ownership of the Irish people.

---

3   Thomas Carlyle, *Oliver Cromwell's Letters and Speeches: with elucidations*, Chapman & Hall 1924.

The Butlers were not all rich. When the 9th Baron Cahir, James Butler, died in France in 1786, the title and extensive estates passed to his brother Piers, who enjoyed them for only two years before his death. The title then passed to his nephew, James, who was living in an impoverished state in the East Indies. He never learned of his good fortune because he also died within weeks of his uncle. He had left his wife, a son and a daughter behind in Ireland, where they eked out a poverty-stricken existence in Cahir, his wife scraping a living by winnowing corn.[4] His twelve-year-old son now inherited the title and estates, but before news of his father's death reached Cahir, covetous relatives persuaded the mother to let them take the children to France and give them a good life.

Mrs Jeffereys of Blarney Castle was passing through Cahir at the time and heard the scandalous story at the inn there of the children's abduction. She visited the mother of the two children, who confirmed it but said she was powerless to do anything. Mrs Jeffereys had a daughter, Emily, in school in France, and when she was to travel to visit her she received permission of the authorities to bring the Butler children back to Ireland. This she did, after finding them 'in a miserable Garret all overgrown with hair'. The children were returned to their mother, and the family were properly housed and educated with Mrs Jeffereys's support. Richard, the new young Earl of Glengall and Baron Cahir, spent a lot of time with Mrs Jeffereys's family, and in 1793, when he was seventeen and Emily Jeffereys was sixteen, they married. The young baron seems to have seamlessly translated from poverty to riches and from poor youth to rich husband, and the young couple 'lived happily ever after', that is, until they were parted by death in 1819 when the Baron died at the young age of forty-four. Emily survived him by twenty years.

At Cahir I came across a theme that repeated itself often along the Suir: the relationship between the Quakers and the prosperity of the main Suir towns. The Fennel family were the first Quakers to arrive in Cahir, and John Fennel, who settled here in 1659, established a dynasty that lasted for eight generations up until the early twentieth century.

---

4   Dorothea Herbert, *Retrospections of Dorothea Herbert 1770-1806*, Town House 1988.

Within a hundred years the Fennells had been joined by other Quaker families, such as the Grubbs and the Goings, generating a powerhouse of entrepreneurial expertise and economic vision. The Quaker virtues of honesty, thrift and hard work, combined with exceptional business acumen, channelled them almost exclusively into manufacture and trade, and through their industry the town of Cahir expanded dramatically in the nineteenth century, the corn trade in particular. Not content to focus on corn and milling alone, they extended their business out in both directions, to farming and growing the cereals, then processing the results of their milling in beer manufacture and retailing.

The compact town of Cahir enjoys a heritage of fine buildings, including a number of good Quaker houses dating from the late eighteenth century. The central square was substantially rebuilt in 1840 to the designs of William Tinsley, the Clonmel architect who completed his career as a prominent architect in Cincinnati, Ohio in the 1880s. At the northern end there is a fine modern monument to legendary piper and composer Edmund Keating Hyland, who died in 1845.

St Paul's church was completed in 1818 in the Gothic-Revival style to the designs of the celebrated English architect John Nash, one of whose clients was George IV, and whose better-known works include the exotic Brighton Pavilion. St Paul's is extolled in tourist literature as the second most important piece of architecture in Cahir after the castle, and I suppose it is, being one of only three churches designed by Nash. Although it has some worthy features, there are problems of scale and proportion and the spire is overly heavy for the rest of the structure; indeed, it is said the church was not consecrated until two years after it was completed in order to be sure that the weight of the spire would not be too much for its foundations.

On some of my visits to Cahir, I stayed in the Cahir House Hotel overlooking the main square. It was built by the Butlers in the late eighteenth century when their Cahir home after the castle became too uncomfortable, and is mentioned in the wonderful contemporary gossipy memoirs of Dorothea Herbert:

> Lord Cahir gave a most flaming fete champetre in Cahir House where the company dined under marquees on the lawn and danced all evening.

Lady Cahir danced an Irish jig in her stockings to the music of an old piper. We had a superb supper in the three largest rooms all crowded as full as they could hold and we did not get home till eight o'clock next morning and so slept all day.

It became a hotel in 1927 and has enjoyed a good reputation since, looking after an interesting mélange of guests, including Jackie Kennedy, Mae West, Douglas Fairbanks, Eamon de Valera, Sir Anthony Eden, W. T. Cosgrave and Walt Disney.

The Suir slips by Cahir, its castle and old mills, and flows southwards through the castle demesne away from the town.

St Paul's church, Cahir, designed in Gothic-Revival style by English architect John Nash

(*Above*) Cahir House Hotel, built in the late eighteenth century by the Butlers

Chapter Four

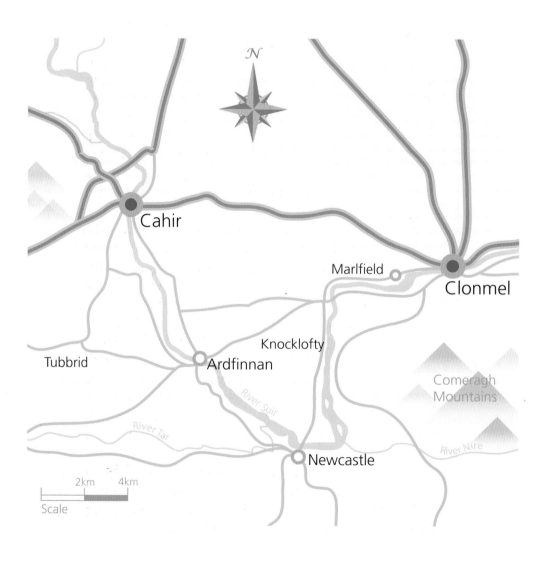

Cahir to Clonmel

AS THE SUIR FLOWS OUT of Cahir through the demesne of Cahir Castle, to the west only some walls and gates remain of Cahir Cavalry Barracks, constructed in 1811 as the headquarters of the South Irish Horse. It was very large establishment, with a parade ground covering 23 acres, and in its heyday in the mid-nineteenth century housed nearly 500 soldiers, their families and 280 horses. It was newly refurbished after World War I and was in excellent condition when the British Forces marched out of it in June 1922, but not long after, to deny it to the Free State army, it joined a long list of buildings and installations that were burnt down or destroyed by the Anti-Treaty forces during the Civil War.

Overlooking the Suir, about 2 kilometres south of Cahir, is the Swiss Cottage, built by the young Baron Cahir in 1810. It is one of the finest *cottage orné* of the period, not only in Ireland, but in these islands. At the beginning of the Romantic movement there was an increase in interest in the countryside and the picturesque, and it became popular for rich landowners to romanticise peasant life by laying out rustic gardens with quaint hovels, in which they sometimes paid suitably gnarled old men to live and gaze out rheumily at the rich perambulating by. In France, Marie Antoinette and her friends, it is said, would dress up as peasant girls and entertain themselves by playing at being milkmaids. In Ireland, rural poverty was anything but romantic and the condition of the Irish peasantry at the time was perhaps the worst in Europe. This did not deter the rich from emulating the French queen, and a number of teahouses masquerading as rustic cottages were built in private Irish demesnes where the ascendancy could relax and feel part of the countryside as they took tea. Notable examples were built at Marlay Grange in County Dublin by the La Touches, at Glengarriff in County Cork by Lord Bantry, and at Glena Bay near Killarney by Lady Kenmare. At Cahir, Baron Cahir and his wife Emily took part enthusiastically in the popular activity by building the Swiss Cottage, rustic *par excellence*, all crooked and cosy. It is possible that John Nash, architect of St Paul's church in Cahir, who had designed a village of similar cottages at Blaise Hamlet near Bristol, was persuaded to design one for the Cahir estate. The site chosen for the cottage was on high bluff overlooking the Suir: an old house, where the Quaker Fennells had lived, had to be demolished and an early Quaker graveyard cleared to make way for the new building and its grounds. Even before the Quakers had lived there, there had been a monastic settlement on the site, and the old yew tree to one side of the cottage is said to date from that time.

The survival of the Cahir Swiss Cottage, almost two hundred years old at the time of writing, is extraordinary. The fortunes of the Cahir Butlers waned towards the end of the nineteenth century, and in 1853 most of their lands in Cahir were lost through bankruptcy. Ownership of the cottage was regained in 1877 by Margaret, granddaughter of the Baron Cahir who had built it, and who had married into the wealthy English Charteris family. In 1961 the estate was taken over by the Land Commission, and the cottage was sold to Mr Heavey, its long-time caretaker, who continued to look after it until his death in 1980. The cottage was then in a poor condition and derelict, but it was rescued at the last minute by a collection of philanthropists allied with the Office of Public Works, the Georgian Society, Cahir Community Council, and The Irish American Foundation. This disparate grouping contributed the funds necessary to allow major expensive and necessary restoration works to be carried out, and after four years of reconstruction, the cottage was opened to the public in 1989. A tour of the cottage provides a glimpse of another world, and leaves one wondering at a destitute child who became a rich lord.

The Swiss Cottage stands at the northern extremity of a wooded limestone escarpment bordering the Suir. The woodland here, nine hectares in all in what is called Cottagehill Wood, consists of an ancient yew forest, one of only four such forests to survive in Ireland. Probably because of the disinterest of the Charteris family, the yews survived while many other Irish forests were felled and sold, but today the ancient forest

is threatened by the invasion of exotic species such as sycamore, beech, rhododendron and laurel. Natural regeneration of these threatens to swamp the yews, and with them the unique native ground flora that has survived under them – plants like wood avens, wood sanicle and enchanter's nightshade. Coillte, Ireland's largest forestry company, however, has come to the rescue, establishing a woodland restoration programme that involves the slow clearance of some of the foreign species and the restoration of the yew wood by using cuttings from existing trees. The yew is a slow-growing tree, however, and it will be some years before the results of this fascinating programme will be seen.

The Swiss Cottage at Cahir

On the opposite bank of the river to the Swiss Cottage, I sought out one of those whimsical Patrician sites one finds all over the country, in this case a stone in which St Patrick is said to have left the imprint of his knees when he prayed during his visit to the area. It was formerly

[97]

venerated by the local people and is sufficiently significant to be marked on the Ordnance Survey map as St Patrick's Stone. I searched to and fro along the road at Grange Moore where it is shown without success, until, standing at Grange Cross and just about to abandon my search, I realised I was almost standing on it. In the middle of the road was what looked like a small lozenge-shaped traffic island that had seen better days. Little pieces of kerbing surrounded a few cobbles with weeds growing between them, and protruding from the centre of the cobbles was a dumbbell-shaped bit of limestone bedrock with the depressions filled with mud and moss. It had at some time in the past been painted post office green. These were St Patrick's knee prints, and their condition clearly indicates the stature the saint enjoys in the Ireland of today.

As the Suir flows south over weirs and fords, the blue-grey conical summits of the Knockmealdown Mountains dominate the horizon ahead. They have such a presence, it must be impossible to live in the area without being somehow influenced by their existence, their powerful permanence.

A little more than a mile downstream of Cottagehill Wood, the Suir is overlooked by the large estate of Ballybrada House. The house, built in 1879, is a fine example of Victorian architecture and craftsmanship and was designed by the Belfast architects Otway and Watt. The estate includes woodland with fifty species of rhododendron and a rich variety of exotic trees, and one of the finest organic farms in Ireland, concentrating particularly on the production of organic cereals and wool. Wandering the narrow roads of the area one evening in July I had just passed a cottage gateway and had stopped to consult my map when a man appeared, seemingly out of nowhere, at my side, asking if he could help me. Dressed in a suit and wearing a baseball cap, he was probably in his late sixties. I asked him about Ballybrada, and in no time we were chatting about the Quakers of Cahir, and of the Malcolmson family, who had built up a great commercial empire in County Waterford. He was a mine of information, and unlike some who believe themselves to be local historians, there was a quiet, considered authority and accuracy about his comments and explanations.

He talked of the Fennels in Cahir and how they were the forbears of eight generations of the family in the area, which became prosperous in the milling business and multiplied until the last of them died in the 1920s. He listed the other Quaker families who joined the Fennels in Cahir, some of whom became the most important and successful business people in south Tipperary. I could have listened to this gentleman for hours, but he urged me to carry on along the road before it got too dark, to find the Ballybrada Quaker burial ground, established in 1738 as the last resting-place for the large Quaker population of Cahir and its surroundings. I thanked him and followed his instructions, and soon came to a dark, walled enclosure with a scatter of the standard grave markers the Quakers used. Although free of grass, weeds and undergrowth, it was clear that there had not been a burial here for quite some time, reflecting the disappearance of the Friends from this area.

The man with the baseball cap also suggested that I visit the birthplace of Geoffrey Keating, the important son of the Suir valley whom we first came across at Knockgraffon. On my way there I passed through the pleasant village of Ballylooby on the Thonoge river, about six kilometres west of the Suir. A picturesque ancient bridge spans the little river, beside which stands the church, originally erected in 1813 on the site of an earlier church, but almost completely rebuilt in 1929. Additional land was needed for the 1813 church, and 26 perches of land were bought from the neighbouring farmer, Patrick Burke, for it to be built. However, when the church was completed, Burke claimed that he had not been paid in full, and he erected a wall within the church along the original boundary. Writs were served on parishioners who crossed the wall, and it is said that the Burkes frequently threw stones at people going to mass. This comical situation existed for a number of years before the dispute was settled. Afterwards the Burkes could have no luck, however, and gradually the family left the neighbourhood. The last of them, nicknamed 'the Barrister Burke', presumably because of his insistence on sticking to the letter of the law, was found dead in a nearby quarry, thus confirming to all that it was not a good thing to go against Holy Mother Church.

A few kilometres south I came to the townland of Burges, where Geoffrey Keating was born about 1580. His forebears were of Catholic Anglo-Norman stock that had become more Irish than the Irish themselves, respectable people who, while not of the landlord class, were comfortably well off and lived in Nicholstown Castle at Garryroe, 8 kilometres east of Cahir. All that remains today is one tall ivy-covered wall, but locals proudly point it out as the Keating castle. Geoffrey's parents lived at Burges, where he attended a local bardic school and was educated in such subjects as law, medicine, poetry and music, taught through the medium of prose and poetry. Keating went on from the bardic school to a Latin school in Cahir, and eventually, around 1600, to a school of moral theology in Bordeaux. He also studied at Salamanca and Rheims, and did not return home until 1610, by which time he had been granted a doctorate in theology. On his return to Tipperary, he was appointed curate at Outragh, north-east of Cahir.

I had earlier searched for Keating's church at Outragh and, directed to Mortlestown, I believe I located it in a walled graveyard in the middle of a field. Little remains today other than part of a standing gable, covered with ivy. Under the Graveyard Enclosure regulations of the early nineteenth century, parishes had to build walls around local cemeteries. While the regulations prevented graveyards from spreading out into surrounding lands, they were probably responsible for the final destruction of many old churches, and I am sure that this is what happened here; there were stones bearing medieval tool-marks in the wall and gate piers.

At Outragh Keating quickly gained a reputation as a fine preacher, but also as a poet whose verses were critical of the Ascendancy and the authorities, which did him no favours later when, as a result of his sermon at Knockgraffon, he had to flee into the Glen of Aherlow. When Donough O'Brian, Lord President of Munster, died in 1624, however, Keating's famous sermon was forgotten and he was able to emerge from exile. He obtained support from his bishop to devote his time to researching *Foras Feasa ar Eirinn*, and spent the next ten years travelling Ireland seeking out and consulting surviving documents and annals in private hands and in what remained of the great monasteries. The great history was published about 1634, after which he returned home again as parish priest of Tullaghorton on the river Tar, a few miles south of his birthplace, where he continued to write poetry and essays on local history. In 1644 he erected a mortuary chapel at Tubbrid over the grave of another priest poet, Eoghan Ó Dubhtaigh, who had died a century

before, and when Keating died c.1644, he was also interred there. His burial place at Tubbrid is a few kilometres west of the Suir, in a large graveyard beside a roofless Protestant church, which, although in plan form is similar to the many rural churches built during the first half of the nineteenth century, has some remarkable features. At each corner of the nave are bulbous cylindrical buttresses with conical tops, and the tower has similar but octagonal corner buttresses. Completed in 1820, it opened its doors a mere two months after St Paul's church in Cahir, and one wonders if the vicar here, impressed by the work of John Nash, urged on his own architect to produce something a bit more elaborate than the usual standard First Fruits[1] church of the

The Geoffrey Keating mausoleum at Tubbrid

---

1   The Irish Board of First Fruits was established in the early eighteenth century to fund the building and repair of ecclesiastical buildings of the Established Church. In the late eighteenth century and particularly in the early nineteenth century the Board received considerable grants from the Irish Parliament to invest in a substantial building programme, during which some 400 churches were built throughout rural Ireland.

time. Tubbrid was, after all, one of the wealthiest Protestant parishes in the diocese, enjoying tithes from Protestant and Catholic alike in this rich agricultural region. By the early twentieth century, however, long after tithes had been abolished and the local Protestant population greatly reduced, the church was closed. The roof was removed in 1920, but the decorative wrought iron gateway, stamped with the name of a Clonmel blacksmith, just about survives and is a delight.

The mortuary chapel is roofless, and there are a lot of graves in the overgrown interior. At the east end, Keating's grave is marked by a large tombstone with a Gaelic inscription which, roughly translated, says: 'This stone commemorates Seathrún Ceitín, one of the greatest intellects in Ireland in his time, an authority on Gaelic and Latin, a devoted, virtuous, prayerful, and pious priest, with true wisdom and fine manners, he was an expert on doctrine and a guiding star to the Irish nation.' Some nice features of the chapel survive, including a much-

eroded sandstone holy water font just inside the little gothic door, and a limestone plaque dated 1644, above the door.

In the graveyard I met a man who had been living in Tubbrid for some years, and who, without much encouragement and in answer to a simple question about the church, asked 'Will I tell you a story?' I am always open to such invitations, and quickly agreed, but he went on to regale me with tales about the area which got taller as he proceeded. He also took time to give me a lesson in Gaelic, claiming that the name Tubbrid means 'settlement', and that there has been a 'settlement' here for two thousand years, and to underline his considerable knowledge of the language he told me that the name Tipperary, or Tubbrid Arann, meant 'settlement in Ireland'. I was amused that someone who patently knew so little would waste their time telling a stranger such nonsense.

⸺◈⸺

Sweeping on down to Ardfinnan, 87 kilometres from its source, the Suir

Ardfinnan geese

(*Right*) Ardfinnan Castle overlooking the Suir

divides again to form English's Island. The narrow southern stream, probably an old mill stream, is locally called 'The Half River'. St Fionan Lobhar (the leper) established a monastery at Ardfinnan in the 7th century, on the site where the early nineteenth-century Church of Ireland church stands high on the hill north of the river, 'The High Place of Fionan', which gives the place its name. Ardfinnan is a very ordinary village with a church, a modern primary school, a butcher's, a bar and a post office, all looking out over a riverside green to a wooded promontory and the photogenic Ardfinnan Castle. The green is inhabited by a large and picturesque flock of geese, which occasionally pester visitors for titbits. I was told that the flock was not just decorative but owned by the local butcher, and they all end up on dinner tables at Christmas!

The castle is thought to have been started by the Earl of Morton, or King John as he later became, during his 1185 expedition to Ireland. It has a strategic location on a promontory site overlooking the fording point of the river, where a bridge of fourteen arches was later built. The

keep is an oval shape with an attached circular stair tower: later a banqueting hall was built, and the two were surrounded by a curtain wall with rectangular towers. In the eighteenth century the banqueting hall was demolished and a three-storey house was built on its site. The battlements were added to the tower in the nineteenth century. Except for a number of decades after Cromwell's forces sacked the place in 1650, the site has been occupied continuously for over 800 years. In recent years, I was told, it was the home of the local postman.

The village was a busy industrial place at one time, with a woollen mill producing fine tweed until well into the twentieth century, and although Ardfinnan tweed was once much sought after, all that remains of the industry today are a scattering of derelict mill buildings near the bridge.

Ardfinnan has been an important crossing point since prehistoric times, and it is here that the ancient road, the Rian Bó Phádraig, connecting the monastic settlements of Cashel, Lismore and Ardmore, crosses the Suir. The name Rian Bó derives from a legend that tells of St Patrick's Cow grazing peacefully in the water meadows beside the Tar river with her calf. When her back was turned, the calf was abducted by a wily cattle thief from Kilwatermoy in County Waterford. As soon as the cow discovered her calf had been taken, she set off an angry galloping pursuit, during which she ploughed up twin trenches with her horns that stretched twenty miles over the mountains into County Waterford. There she caught up with the cattle thief and gave him a good trampling before returning north with her calf.

The route of the Rian was documented and traced out in 1905 by the Waterford historian and archaeologist Rev. P. Power, Professor of Archaeology at the University of Cork. Today the only section to survive much as it was is a stretch that crosses the Knockmealdown mountains, but the rest was traced by Power by way of myriad side roads, some surfaced, others overgrown and disused. Where there are interruptions, the route can often be followed along what must be ancient hedgerows to link up with the next apparent section.

Standing on Ardfinnan bridge at evening time, I tried to imagine St Patrick and his retinue, as tradition has it, crossing the Suir here, through the shallow waters over the ford. In Archbishop Healy's *Life of*

St Patrick, the author relates how the saint was not enamoured by the watercourses of the region, because his books were 'drowned' in some stream near Ardfinnan as he crossed a ford. He was on his way to Cashel, which at that time was the fortress headquarters of the Eoghanachta, rulers of the area, where he is said to have baptised their king, Aongus. During the ceremony the tired St Patrick leaned heavily on his crozier, which inadvertently pierced the King's foot, but believing this was part of the strange Christian ceremony, the King kept quiet.

Before that, it is likely that St Declan also crossed the old ford here on his way to Cashel, as described in a twelfth-century life of the saint. After St Patrick's time there would have been a constant flow of monks, traders and mule trains passing north and south, but the most impressive crossing must have been in the winter of 1171, with the clamour and colour of the great hosting accompanying the train of Henry II as he crossed on his way to Cashel.

On the outskirts of modern Ardfinnan, high above the river, is the demesne of an early nineteenth-century house called Ladysabbey which I came across when I was trying to find the route of the Rian Bó Phádraig

Ardfinnan bridge

south from the village. When I passed, the house was boarded up, its garden fenced off as the site office for a housing development that has sprung up over the last couple of years. The concrete paths and roads of this estate obliterate the Rian Bó Phádraig as it arrives in Ardfinnan, but in their midst I found a hedge-lined boreen, so wonderfully narrow that I knew I must have found the Rian.

I followed the lane out of the housing estate into the countryside, and soon came to the original Lady's Abbey, or *An Mainistir Mhuire*, marked on the map as a friary, and from which the nineteenth-century house had taken the name. It is a little gem, a miniature fourteenth-century friary standing beside the ancient road. Little is known about it, and it is not clear whether it was occupied by the Carmelites or by the Franciscan Third Order. A tiny chapel extending south from the main building is said to be the Lady's Chapel, and its gothic hooded window has a carving of the head of a woman with a medieval headdress beside a stylised rose. Opposite it, however, is an unusual carved image – that of the pagan 'Green Man', usually depicted with vines and leaves pouring out of his mouth, as is the case here. His origins are lost in the deep past, but he is said to represent a pagan deity, a spirit of the forest, and his cult dates to the time when the post glacial wildwood covered most of Europe. Depictions of the Green Man are very rare in Ireland, probably because they were more usually carved in timber, and few medieval buildings in Ireland have surviving wood. Images of the Green Man in wood and stone can be found as far away as India and Indonesia, and are very common in Britain, where there are few medieval churches in which his image cannot be found.

While little is known about the two centuries of the prayerful existence of *An Mainistair Mhuire*, there is documentary evidence that in 1537 the Prior was found by the Heads and Commoners of Clonmel to be living in 'flagrant, continued and open immorality', accusations that were not uncommon in those turbulent times, often used as the excuse to proceed with the dissolution of the establishment.[2] The ruined buildings and graveyard have been used for burials for the 500 years since the friars left, leaving the ground level a metre higher than the present

2   Patrick Power, *Waterford and Lismore: a Compendious History of the United Dioceses*, Cork University Press 1937.

interior floor level. Unfortunately, structural problems are developing: all the cut stone linings in one window have recently fallen to the ground, and the cracks in the tower, although they may have been there for many years, have large trees growing out of them. In addition, a shroud of ivy is at work, reaching to the very top of the tower and providing a perch for a yellowhammer who sang his sweet song – 'a little bit of bread and butter and cheeeeese'– all the while I was there.

Below Ardfinnan the Suir bends towards the south-east and flows between water-meadows in a stretch that was traditionally rich in salmon. Indeed, Ireland's record rod-caught salmon, a monster of 57lbs, was caught near here in 1874.

Downstream at Lacken I was excited to find what must have been a very old approach lane to one of the many fords shown on the old maps. It was the nearest thing I have seen in Ireland to what are called holloways in Britain; from the Anglo- Saxon *hola weg*. A holloway is a sunken path that has been in constant use for so long it has eroded down

to the bedrock and is recessed below the level of the surrounding countryside. The oldest holloways in Britain date back to the Iron Age, and there are none less than 300 years old. Another place I have come across them is on the Camino de Santiago de Compostela in Spain, where long sections of the cross-country route pass through deep woodland holloways.

The holloway at Lacken is almost hidden by the works recently carried out to the imposing entrance to a new house, but under the shade of overhanging trees I clambered down to discover this tiny old road, deep and dim, its earthen walls clothed in hart's tongue fern. It had an 'other world' ambiance, a piece of built environment fashioned over many hundreds of years by innumerable feet, hooves and cartwheels, to become what it is today, a three-dimensional, hundred metre-long record of the passage of people and animals to this particular ford on the Suir. As it emerges at river level, it is clear that the river has taken over and flooded the end of the path with water and reeds. Some vigorous ripples in the middle of the river suggest shallowness, and on the far side a stony, earthy patch indicates where the ford reached the east bank. There the road is subsumed below farmland, but a palimpsest of it exists as a hedge that leads from the water to an ancient church, from which there is a discernible track to the modern road past Neddans House. It was becoming clear to me that all the many fords of the Suir, most of which are today probably detectable only during high summer if they have not long ago been replaced by bridges, have in close proximity either a motte, a castle, a church or a monastery.

Examining my map, I saw that the next ford to the south originally led to Cloncully on the east bank, where in 1677 a diocesan synod was held in Cloncully Castle, which no longer exists. Near the ford on the west bank is a motte called Knockademsey, which may have been the ancient assembly place of the Dempsey clan. The modern side road leading down to the river, on the original line of the ford road, passes through and becomes a part of a farmyard, only to disappear in a field short of the river. I spoke to the farmer, who said that the ford has not been used for two hundred years, and no one passed that way now. This must be the case for many of the fords and the lanes leading to them, and no doubt before long none will remain. Thus, routes that were so important a millennium ago, will, unless protected, disappear from consciousness, memory and map.

As the Suir, swift-moving and deep, reaches the village of Newcastle, just over 100 kilometres from its source, it swings sharply away towards the east, as if it knows that it cannot tackle the foothills of the Knockmealdown Mountains, which begin to rise just a kilometre farther south. But the Comeragh Mountains fill the horizon to the east, and a little farther on, as if warned by the Nire river which joins the Suir from the Comeraghs, it swings determinedly north again.

Newcastle village is a busy service centre for the surrounding rich farmlands, and has no resemblance to the moribund, poor place I remember from my first visit about thirty years ago. The castle that gives

the place its name is ivy-covered and well camouflaged with elder and brambles. A few stones are all that remain of a great doorway, and ivy has been growing freely on this structure for so long that, without doubt, it would all collapse if the ivy was removed.

The old church is an unusually large structure with a triple-moulded gothic north door and opposite, a less ornamented south door. The roofless interior is packed full with tombstones dating from the eighteenth century up to the twentieth century. One of the more recent graves outside the walls had, in the midst of a field of plastic flowers, two solar-powered garden lights, which must bring a new dynamic to the graveyard at night!

Passing by Newcastle the Suir loops around the ancient site of Molough Abbey before it swings north and absorbs the Nire river. Here,

with the Galtys to the north, the Knockmealdowns to the south and the Comeraghs to the east, is a fine complex of ruins with tall gables. The Life of St Declan suggests that a nunnery was in existence here 1,500 winters ago, founded by the daughters of Cinaed, King of Deise. In the fourteenth century the Butlers founded an Augustinian nunnery on the site, and records tell us that Joan Powere, the last prioress, surrendered the house in April 1540, and the property was handed back to the Butlers.[3] Like many of the ancient sites in the area, the buildings here are in poor condition, and unless conservation work is carried out, they will not survive much longer. The ancient walls were clearly used for many years as a handball alley, a sport that has all but

The Knockmealdowns to the south

3   A. Gwynn and R.N. Haddock, *Medieval Religious Houses, Ireland,* Irish Academic Press 1988.

disappeared from the Irish countryside in the last few decades.

I carried out some of my explorations in this area with my friend Dick Cronin in a Landrover. This was just as well, because some of the many boreens were, owing to the wet spring and summer of 2008, almost impassable even on foot. One day we followed a grassy boreen that only barely accepted the width of the Landrover, and it seemed to come to an end at a cottage surrounded by pretty gardens and various out-offices. A text was painted on the gable of the cottage which I recognised as the English translation of a line from the song 'Guantanamera', sung by Pete Seeger in the heady days of the sixties:

> *El arroyo de la sierra,*
> *Me complace más que el mar*
>
> *The mountain stream,*
> *gives me more pleasure than the sea*

It was starting to rain and I got out and called at the cottage to enquire where we were. A man and a woman came to the door and greeted us. They were charming and friendly, not getting many surprise visitors in this remote little backwater, and in no time it transpired that they were, amongst other things, publishers, and we had mutual friends. Erica Van Horn and Simon Cutts run Coracle Press, and while it was an unusual place to come across a publishing company, Coracle Press is anything but usual.

On an Irish cross-country walk twelve years ago Simon and Erica cut their way through the tunnel of foliage that had grown over the ancient boreen and stumbled upon the derelict cottage and its gathering of outhouses. They had fallen in love with the surrounding area, what they called the 'quiet isolation and dishevelledness of Ireland', and over the next six years they repaired and refurbished the dwelling and developed the surrounding garden. It is an understated, informal garden, patches of lawn, flowers and vegetables informally separating the little gathering of buildings which now includes a studio and a print shed as well as the cottage. From this idyllic base, Erica and Simon produce pottery, artwork, and prints, and they also make many of their books by hand.

They must have been regarded with some puzzlement by their

neighbours when they first arrived: the local man who constructed the print shed told them that he had put the windows up high because he thought they were astronomers. Being the people they are, however, interested in everybody and everything, they soon became accepted and are on first-name terms with most of the people in this isolated and sparsely populated area.

Knocklofty House, erected in the eighteenth century by Richard Hely Hutchinson

We were invited in for a cup of tea, and we enjoyed a half-hour chatting about the area and their work before we reluctantly had to leave and continue on our way.

A little to the north, between Tullaghmelan and the Suir, lies the Knocklofty demesne. Knocklofty House was originally erected in the eighteenth century by Richard Hely Hutchinson, who inherited his mother's title and became Baron Donoughmore in 1788. The vast house has fine classical features, but what appeals most to me is the informality created by the meandering extensions to the original that were mainly carried out in the nineteenth century. The Knocklofty demesne is long and narrow, sandwiched between the public road and the river, so in the late nineteenth century, to gain more farmland, the Donoughmores bought the Kilmanahan Estate across the river in County Waterford, and connected the two by a steel lattice bridge.

The Donoughmore family had many distinguished members, including army generals, a lord lieutenant, a paymaster general, a president of the British Board of Trade and an Under-Secretary of State for War. The present 8th Earl of Donoughmore was one of those earls to fall foul of the Labour Party and lost his House of Lords seat in 1999: he lives today in Oxfordshire. His heir apparent is John Hely Hutchinson, Viscount Suirdale, but the family's connections with Ireland today are mainly in their names: they sold Knocklofty in 1985 and it has had a chequered existence since then. At one stage it was rumoured that Elvis Presley's daughter, Priscilla, was interested in buying it.

Before visiting the area, I looked up Knocklofty on the internet and was presented with an elaborate Knocklofty House Hotel website, where I would find, it said, 'a wealth of welcome, intimate tranquil atmosphere and people who care about your needs' [sic]. While researching the area by car with my wife, Teresa, we were feeling peckish and we decided to try Knocklofty for lunch. We drove through one of the fine gates of the demesne, passing through a parkland of ancient oaks of great girth and parked at the front of the house. There were very few cars about, and a small sign indicated a Leisure Centre, but there was no indication as to where the entrance to the hotel was. I asked a girl in a tracksuit who was coming out of the Leisure Centre, where I could find the hotel entrance and if they served lunch.

'I wouldn't know, I'm afraid,' she replied. 'I only go to the Leisure Centre.'

She got into a car and drove off, so we went to the main entrance door and tried the brass handle. It opened smoothly, and we walked into a narrow but finely decorated hall that led by classical-style doorways on both sides to rooms with shelves lined with books. The middle of the hall floor, was taken up with a stack of chairs piled high, which suggested that maybe the hotel wasn't open. I called loudly, 'Hello? Anybody there?', and repeated myself as I walked up along the book-lined room towards what appeared to be a reception desk, but even as I did, I realised that the place was definitely closed, empty, abandoned even, and there was little chance that we were going to get a 'wealth of welcome', and while, but for our rumbling stomachs, it was 'tranquil', there was no one to 'care about' our needs. As we stood there, at a loss to know what to do next, a young man came down a stairs into the hall. I told him we had come for lunch.

He replied in an eastern European accent that the house was closed, and had been closed since October, six months before. He assured me, however, that it would be open the next Sunday. I explained about the website invitation, and he said the hotel was not in that ownership any more, and that now there was a new owner. Our peckish feeling having developed into a hunger that would not wait until Sunday, we thanked him and made our escape, promising ourselves that we would stop for food at the next opportunity.

Downstream from Knocklofty bridge, a fine and elegant hump-backed bridge with three tall arches, the Suir sweeps around in an easterly direction and flows between meadows and parkland on the left bank, and a steep, treed escarpment on the right. We didn't cross the bridge, but took the more direct route towards Clonmel. A few miles farther on we saw another great mansion down by the river, which according to the map was called Marlfield. The hunger was obviously taking over and fogging our memories, and we made the error of think-ing that this Marlfield House was the famous Marlfield in Gorey, County Wexford, beloved of gourmets. With great anticipation, we drove through the fine Georgian gateway and along the drive through river-side parkland to the great house, hoping at least for tea and a sandwich. Again, there were few signs of activity: just a few cars parked outside the front of the house, but no sign of life. I went up to the front door, which was open, and walked in.

For the second time that afternoon I was presented with a fine classi-cal entrance hall, filled with stacked furniture. In a niche at the back of the hall a colourful religious statue stood. In front of this were two black marble columns supporting a classical pediment. This time the hall was occupied, by a man on top of a long ladder applying gold paint to details of the frieze.

'I suppose a sandwich would be out of the question?' I asked him, explaining that we were looking for a place serving lunch.

He seemed relieved at some diversion to his finely executed work, and he slowly climbed down the ladder to explain why I wouldn't get a sandwich.

'The mews is rented out as holiday accommodation, but this is a private residence.'

I still hadn't realised my mistake, and asked if the Bowes were still here, and he said he had never heard of them. Seamlessly the subject of our conversation moved to the intricacies of painting classical details at the top of a ladder.

'It's a devil on the neck and shoulders, this work. I'm painfully stiff at the end of every day,' he said.

I sensed that he would have been happy to talk more, but my sympathy lay elsewhere and I had to bring the bad news out to Teresa in the car, so I thanked him and left. We finally found lunch in Clonmel.

I found out later that Knocklofty House had been owned by businessman Denis English since 1989, and had during that time been run as a hotel by a number of management teams, and his residence in Tipperary is the nearby Marlfield House where I had sought a sandwich. He has undertaken considerable conservation works on the house, and put in place the development of a golf course on the beautiful 400-acre parkland demesne. English has persuaded Padraig Harrington to design the golfcourse, the first such design Harrington has carried out, and the theme is to minimise the impact of the course on the natural surroundings by making use of the existing landscape as much as possible.

Marlfield House was built by Colonel John Bagwell, a descendant of a Cromwellian planter, in the 1780s for a sum of £13,000. Bagwell was typical of large landowners of the time: he was commander of the Tipperary Militia and approved of the harsh treatment of dissidents by the authorities that ultimately led to the rebellion of 1798. After changing sides twice, he voted for the Union and benefited from the rewards it offered, buying the town of Clonmel in 1800, which put him in such a politically influential position that in 1801 he was returned as MP for Clonmel and then elected Mayor.

His son, William, built St Patrick's church in Marlfield, on the site of the Cistercian Abbey De Surio, founded about 1148 by Melaghlin Ó Phelan and re-endowed by the ubiquitous Domhnal Mór O'Brien in 1187. Not much of the abbey survives today, but it was an important

foundation: the abbeys of Fermoy and the more famous extant Corcomroe Abbey in County Clare were 'daughters' of Inishlounaght. The lands farmed by the monks included miles of fertile grazing lands along the Suir: the name of the place where Marlfield House now stands, Inis Leamhnachta, or the Island of the New Milk, harks back to that time. The abbots of De Surio were clearly well and widely connected: it was the Abbot Comgan of Inislounaght that persuaded St Bernard of Clairveaux to write the celebrated 'Life' of St Malachy.

When I visited the church, I expected it to be in a state of ruin like so many of the simple First Fruits churches around the country. Towards the end of a road leading to the river, I found the gateway, a fine cut stone Gothic-arched construction, mirrored on the other side of the road by another which gave access to the church from the Marlfield demesne. I walked down a long avenue lined with great chestnut trees to find that the building was intact and there were cars parked outside. A girl stood by the door smoking. I asked her if I could see inside.

A hungry heron wading across a weir

'Of course you can,' she said. 'We're only hoovering the floor and polishing the pews.' And then, as if she couldn't resist saying it, 'I'm getting married here tomorrow!'

She went on to explain that she lived just up the road, and since the church has been used by the Catholic parish for mass once a week, she decided she would like to be married here.

Inside, there was a fine collection of marble and bronze wall plaques, commemorating the members of the Bagwell and Gough families. Three of the Goughs, two brothers and one of their sons, achieved the rank of Brigadier General in the British Army in addition to winning the Victoria Cross for gallantry, two during the Sepoy Rebellion in 1857, and one during the Somalian war in 1903. The real treasures in the church, however, included a Romanesque doorway, part of a window dating from the original Cistercian Abbey of the early twelfth century and a beautiful east window, all built into the nineteenth-century church. They are remarkable survivals of a period when such work was regarded as being quite primitive.

North of Marlfield village is the celebrated holy well of Inislounaght. In the pre-Christian era springs were seen as sacred entrances to the underworld where powerful gods lived. Water emanating from such places, having originated in the underworld and been touched by the gods, was regarded as sacred and powerful, and its power to cure physical complaints no doubt goes back to that time. The Gaelic word for a spring well is *tobar*, and the great number of place-names with 'tobar' in them indicates the widespread importance of wells. Early Christian missionaries recognised the value of pagan observances, festivals and the sacred well culture and subtly took ownership of them, assimilating them into the new religion. Early saints consecrated wells and often the well was named after the particular saint, and festivities at the well would take place on that saint's feast day, or patron day. This practice, used so successfully by the early Irish missionaries, soon became the policy of Rome. In 601, Pope Gregory gave instructions, with regard to the evangelisation of Britain, that while Christian altars with Christian relics should be substituted for pagan idols, the temples that contained them should be retained and blessed with holy water. In this way, in a familiar building, the natives could more easily continue to worship.

I often think the Irish never entirely made the leap from paganism to Christianity. Gatherings at holy wells for celebrations and prayers were widespread until comparatively recently, and certainly in the eighteenth and nineteenth centuries, from which we have many eyewitness accounts, the popular devotions at holy wells and the beliefs on which they were based, seem highly superstitious. The reasons given by the Church for the faithful to visit holy wells was to do penance, give thanks for blessings received and to pray for further blessings. The populace in general, however, used prayers as hypnotic mantras, while proceeding through sometimes complicated and often masochistic rituals, and made offerings of a decidedly unChristian nature. The practice of clockwise perambulation, for instance, called *deiseal* in Gaelic and imitating the daily motion of the sun, has firm pagan roots. Devotees also expected, if they adhered to the specific rituals for a particular well, to be cured by its waters of a variety of ailments: Ireland's 3,000 holy wells are reputed to relieve the symptoms of upwards of 75 complaints. At Struell in County Down there is a complex of four holy wells, one for drinking water, one for eye complaints, and one each for men and women to bathe their limbs. On Midsummer's Eve, ailing pilgrims gather at a rock formation called St Patrick's Seat and circle it seven times before immersing themselves in the holy well. The practice of leaving rags tied to the bushes or trees about a well is still continued in some places, and is based on rubbing the diseased part of the body with the rag, thus transferring the ailment to the rag, which gradually leaves the body as the rag rots away.[4]

We do not know if there ever was a pagan 'temple' at Inislounaght, but it would be hard to believe that the spectacular upspringing of water in the dell there, fed by a subterranean aquifer under the limestone strata of the hills to the north, would not have attracted much attention and reverence in pre-Christian times.

Historians suggest that Patrick, as he passed through the region, was granted land on which to build a church at the sacred site of Inislounaght by the local Desii[5] chieftain, whose residence was at

4   Eugene Broderick, *Devotions at Holy Wells*, Decies No. 54.
5   Present-day County Waterford and part of Tipperary formed the territory of the Decies, inhabited by a tribe called the Desii in the early Christian period.

Loughtally, a few kilometres to the west. The spring well at Inislounaght was thereafter named after Patrick, and it has always been noted for its curative properties for 'sore lips, sore eyes, the scrofula and several other chronic diseases'.[6]

In 1619 Pope Paul V granted 'through our pious charity, out of the heavenly treasures of the Church, merciful in the Lord, full indulgence and remission of the temporal punishment of sin, to all the faithful of either sex who, truly penitent, having gone to Confession and Holy Communion, visit the Church of St Patrick of the Abbey of the Suir...on the feast of Pentecost or the feast of St Patrick ... the person so visiting to pray for peace among Christian rulers, for the uprooting of heresies, and the exaltation of Holy Mother Church'.

Pilgrims were still coming to this place in their thousands in the early nineteenth century, praying and wading across the pond and around the ancient cross that stands there.

My visit to St Patrick's Well at Inislounaght seemed to occur at a time when elements of paganism had returned there, if only temporarily. I followed a long, well-built stone-paved staircase that led down to the pond, which was surrounded by paving and well-kept lawns. Beside a statue of St Patrick a woman sat reading a Dean Koontz book while her young children played nearby. A little distance away, in full view, a couple lay on the grass in an intimate embrace. On the far side of the little pond stood the seventeenth-century church, and sitting on a wall beside it were two threatening-looking young men, drinking beer, with a plastic bag full of cans on the wall between them.

The couple on the grass ignored me, and as I passed them I noticed they were both female. I wonder were they there for a cure for 'sore lips, sore eyes, the scrofula and several other chronic diseases'?

———

After passing by Marlfield, the Suir, flowing slowly but strongly, swings north and then east, and passing by the Working Men's Boat Club, reaches the town of Clonmel.

The name Clonmel is thought by some to be derived from the lyrical

---

6   Monck Mason, *Survey of Ireland 1813.*

Gaelic Cluain na Meala, or 'meadow of the honey'. The town strad-
dles the Suir at the foot of the northern slopes of the Comeragh
mountains which rise steeply from the river valley to reach a height
of 520 metres at Lachtnafrankee, less than six kilometres south.
Clonmel is Tipperary's largest town and has had a busy and sometimes
turbulent history. It seems reasonable to surmise that its location at this
point on the Suir is owing to the cluster of islands that divide the river
here into a number of streams. They would have provided short fording
places and in earliest times some measure of security for settlements
established on them, and it would be reasonable to imagine a fishing
and farming community growing up here, initially on the islands, and
eventually spreading to the riverbanks on both sides. Clonmel's
existence as a settlement is not recorded until the early thirteenth
century, when the Norman Richard de Burgo was granted a fair here,
suggesting that it must have been a good-sized town by that time.

As the settlement developed into a town in the fourteenth century, the
produce of the rich lands around Clonmel found their way to the market
there, and much of it was exported downstream to Carrick and the port
of Waterford. Carriage up-and downstream in the early days was by

shallow draft, half-decked sailing craft with a crew of about six. Their shallow draft meant that they needed to be weighed down to sail safely, so a ballast of stones had to be employed when there was no cargo. When the medieval walls of Waterford were being repaired from time to time, an enormous volume of stones were required which must have led to a lack of ballast material along the river, and the shortage of suitable building stone for repairs during the sixteenth century was such that part of the admission fee for receiving the freedom of the city was two barges of stones. One can imagine that this scarcity must also have led to the disappearance of ruined buildings along the Suir.

Disagreements between Waterford and Clonmel in the sixteenth century, however, and probably the difficulties with piratical robber barons along the course of the Suir, led Clonmel to seek another port of exit for its exports. Attempts were made to take goods over the mountains to the small port of Dungarvan in west Waterford, but the

excessive charges made by the carriers with their packhorses soon brought about a switch to another small port, Youghal, on the Cork side of the river Blackwater. The two towns concluded a trading agreement in 1609, allowing goods to be carried overland to Cappoquin and then shipped downriver on the Blackwater to Youghal, before being exported.

The Main Guard, Clonmel, c.1675, now restored

(*Above*) West Gate tower

Downriver trade resumed in later centuries, and by the first half of the nineteenth century there were as many as one hundred small barges or yawls regularly sailing between Waterford and Clonmel. While it was easy to sail downstream, from above the reach of the incoming tide just above Carrick, teams of four or six horses were used to tow craft upstream. When steam-powered barges became available in the mid-nineteenth century, various schemes were devised to improve the navigation between Carrick and Clonmel by deep dredging of the river and by the construction of canals. Most of these proposals, at a time when Ireland was ruled from Westminster, came to nothing, and anyway the coming of the railways about the same time sounded the death-knell of inland waterways.

———〜〜〜———

In April 1650 Oliver Cromwell suffered what must have been the worst defeat of his career to that time, at Clonmel. The town was garrisoned by 1,200 men of Hugh Dubh O'Neill's Ulster army, and Cromwell did not expect to meet such a serious adversary at this little Suir town. He assumed that once his guns had breached the town walls, the battle would be over, but O'Neill, who had seen service on the Continent with the Spanish army, was an experienced soldier and tactician. He counted on Cromwell's powerful guns opening a breach into which the men of the New Model Army would pour, and he set up avenues bounded by ramparts of loose stone inside the walls where breaches were likely.

When the guns had finished their work, Cromwell's men, after some fervent hymn-singing, charged through the breach and found themselves hemmed in by walls on each side. As soon as enough men were through the breach, O'Neill's men appeared on top of the ramparts and opened fire with cannon and musket shot. Those at the front, before they died, shouted 'Halt, halt!', but their calls were unheard behind in the din of battle shouts and gunfire, and their followers continued to push ahead. It was a classic trap, and more than 2,000 of Cromwell's men were killed before a retreat was called. Cromwell himself was stationed in front of the main gate to Clonmel, waiting impatiently to be admitted by his men, when he was told the bad news. An eyewitness recalled that the commander was as vexed 'as ever he was since he first put on a helmet against the King, for he was not used to being thus repulsed'.[7] He ordered another assault immediately, and hundreds more were killed before he called a retreat and withdrew.

The successful defence of the town was not without cost: O'Neill's small force, although they had suffered very few casualties, were now nearly out of gunpowder. O'Neill knew that Cromwell's superior numbers would eventually prevail, and so, under cover of night, he withdrew his army, crossing the river to the south bank and marching to

---

7   Antonia Fraser, *Cromwell, Our Chief of Men*, Weidenfeld and Nicolson 1973.

Waterford. At dawn, the Mayor of Clonmel sent an emissary to Cromwell offering surrender on condition that the citizens would not be harmed. The commander of the Model Army must have been very much relieved, and accepted the terms the mayor had requested. When Cromwell did enter the town, however, he was furious to find that O'Neill had left, but as a man of his word, he stuck to the terms of the surrender.

St Mary's church, built in sandstone with many fine cut-stone details

The centre of Clonmel is a bustling, prosperous place today, with a wealth of surviving fine architecture of many periods, particularly of the late eighteenth and early nineteenth centuries, although some important buildings have become the victims of neglect or heavy-handed refurbishment. The jewel in the crown is surely St Mary's Church (Church of Ireland) and its graveyard setting, surrounded on two sides by long ranges of the medieval town walls complete with towers. Although the

church was altered and added to many times since it was first constructed, major work was carried out during the nineteenth century, when substantial parts of the complex, including the roof and supporting columns, were rebuilt. The result is a relaxed and pleasingly informal gathering of buildings in warm sandstone, with many fine cut-stone details. The east window of the church, in particular, is a blend of the exquisite tracery of the early sixteenth century and the rich reds and blues of its early twentieth-century stained-glass panels, made by Catherine O'Brien, who worked with the artist Sarah Purser.

The restored Main Guard facing O'Connell Street, completed about 1675, is one of the few relatively intact seventeenth-century buildings in Ireland. It is possibly the work of Sir William Robinson, architect just a few years later for the magnificent Royal Hospital in Kilmainham in Dublin. The building originally housed the courts of the Palatinate of the 1st Duke of Ormond, and who was to become Viceroy of Ireland in 1677. James II was received by the Corporation of Clonmel here in March 1689, and later in its history it was the seat of the court for the infamous trial of Father Nicholas Sheehy in 1766. Until comparatively recently, the

White Memorial Theatre, Clonmel

fine arcade on the ground floor was infilled with little shops.

The Franciscan friary and church in Abbey Street was built mainly in the nineteenth century, but it incorporates the remains of the fifteenth-century tower and the thirteenth-century north choir wall of an earlier friary. The church's particular interest for me is that it houses the tomb of Thomas Butler, 1st Baron of Cahir and his wife Ellen, dating from the 1530s. A number of subsequent barons were also buried here in the old friary rather than in Cahir, indicating a strong connection between the Butlers and the Clonmel Franciscans. The Butler tomb originally stood in the choir of the old Franciscan church, but after disappearing for a time, it was unearthed during nineteenth-century works and eventually placed where it can be found today, shoe-horned into a space under an arch of the fifteenth-century tower. On the top of the tomb are effigies of the baron in full armour, holding a sword in its scabbard, and his wife in a flowing gown. Traces of paint that were found on the tomb suggest that, similar to a lot of sixteenth-century stonework, it was originally decorated in many colours.

Parallel to Abbey Street is Dowd's Lane; local people love to tell of the exquisite aroma of apples that filled the air here from late summer to Christmas as the apple harvest was pressed to produce Bulmers cider.

The finest exhibit in the new County Museum near the County Council offices is surely the 30-foot-long racing skiff called the *Cruiskeen*, built for the Davin family in the 1850s. It had rested, dust-shrouded and upside down, in the rafters of a cowshed for nearly a hundred years, until rediscovered a few years ago. Organised racing of boats on the Suir began in the late eighteenth century, when prominent citizens entered boats that were rowed by their own employees. By the mid-nineteenth century the first independent boat clubs had been established, and they competed with each other in regattas at Waterford, Cappoquin, Carrick on Suir, Clonmel and New Ross. The long and low clinker-built *Cruiskeen* represents traditional boat-building at its finest, a local craft that has unfortunately almost died out, and with it age-old links between the town and the river Suir. The sweep of its lines somehow reminded me of the Viking craft that twelve hundred years ago made their way upstream from the sea to Clonmel and beyond.

The Court House in Nelson Street was designed by Sir Richard Morrison and dates from 1800: it was here that William Smith O'Brien, Thomas Francis Meagher and others were tried after the Young Ireland insurrection of 1848.

A visitor to the town could pass through without ever realising that Clonmel was founded on a great river, because it is a place of two parts: the vibrant and forward-looking town that boasts the Main Guard, St Mary's and the old town walls, and the town of the Suir, the old industrial milling centre based on four islands and a network of watercourses. Here, in the midst of the decaying remains of old mills, major construction works are in progress, building flood defences along the river. Beyond, however, much of Suir Island, the biggest of Clonmel's four islands, looks like a war zone.

Up until the end of the eighteenth century Clonmel was a quiet but prosperous county town, at the centre of a rich agricultural landscape. In the last years of the eighteenth century, however, a Quaker named David Malcolmson arrived in the town, and immediately recognised that the combination of Clonmel's riverine connection with the port of Waterford and the fact that the Suir here splits into a series of fast-flowing narrow

watercourses had enormous potential: within fifty years he and his family transformed Clonmel into Ireland's largest milling centre.

Suir Island and the Quays c.1900

Malcolmson was one of the descendants of a family of Scottish Presbyterians who were planted in County Armagh in the seventeenth century. He came south in 1784 as a penniless young man, but in a little more than twenty years he owned corn stores on the quays of Clonmel and a flour mill on Suir Island. His marriage to Mary Fennel of Cahir helped over the next hundred years to fund an expanding empire that was closely linked to the Suir in Clonmel, Carrick-on Suir, Portlaw and Waterford. I was to come across this enterprising Quaker family again farther downstream.

Local man Shay Hurley brought me on a tour of Clonmel's islands, and, although seriously threatened, it was clear that the essential character of this other, industrial, Clonmel tenuously hangs on. In his travelogue of Ireland, *Irish Miles*, published in 1947,[8] Frank O'Connor describes arriving here as follows:

> We re-entered the town by way of a footbridge and found ourselves in a complete suburb of eighteenth-century mills and warehouses all in ruin.

---

8   Frank O'Connor, *Irish Miles*, Macmillan 1947.

> As we stood by a tall rusty gate looking at a handsome old millhouse with weeds growing like thatch on its parapet, the bats swooped down on us...

Sixty years later this part of Clonmel is still a place of narrow winding streets, rushing watercourses, old stone bridges, tall warehouse walls with sandstone quoins and fine limestone archways. The narrow streets still wind, the watercourses still rush, but the bridges are under threat, the walls are overgrown with ivy, and the arches are filled in with concrete blocks. Most of the original mill buildings unfortunately have been demolished, and Suir Island is partly covered with their rubble, now thickly overgrown by a jungle of opportunist buddleia and Japanese knotweed. Still surviving, but only barely, is a collection of early nineteenth-century warehousing, an old Turkish bath, and an overgrown complex of culverts, sluices and watergates that served water-mills. Hidden in a shroud of laurels, draped with convolvulus and old man's beard, are the remains of a four-bay Georgian house with a slated gable, the 'handsome old millhouse' O'Connor mentions. Although roofless and fire-damaged, the walls and openings are sound, and this historic building, what Shay Hurley terms 'the only extant millhouse on an island in the Suir', is where a young girl named Margaret Power, who was to become Lady Blessington, spent her childhood.

Margaret's father, a corn and butter merchant, was an obnoxious, quick-tempered man who frequently terrorised his family, and young Margaret was not too unhappy when her father married her off at the age of fifteen to a Kildare landowner. Women were often regarded as chattels at that time, and before long, Margaret's situation deteriorated when her new husband began to beat her. She eventually ran away and went to live with relatives in Cahir. By now she had grown into a beautiful young woman, and in Cahir she met and beguiled Captain Thomas Jenkins, an English army officer, who took her away with him to Dublin, and subsequently to his home in Hampshire. There she lived a relaxed and luxurious life, and discovered and fell in love with books in the extensive library in the house. Over the following five years, with the aid of the library, she put herself through a personal course of education. She greatly impressed visitors to the house with her knowledge and beauty, including Charles John Gardiner, 2nd Viscount Mountjoy, who had

(*Top left*) Dereliction and heritage in danger at Suir Island and on the Quays

[133]

known her in her Clonmel days. Gardiner was very wealthy, with valuable lands and property in Ireland and a London residence in St James's Square. When he was created Earl of Blessington in 1816, he came to a financial arrangement with Jenkins, and whisked Margaret away to London where, after her first husband's death in 1818, he married her.

As mistress of a great London house, the beautiful Lady Blessington threw rich and lavish parties, and gained a considerable reputation for hospitality. In 1822 the Blessingtons embarked on a luxury Grand Tour of Europe which lasted for six years, during which they lived for periods in Genoa, Florence and Naples. During their tour it is said, with the knowledge of her husband, Lady Blessington had a number of lovers, including, possibly, Lord Byron.

Drawing of Lady Blessington's house in Clonmel by George du Noyer

(*Right*) A reburbished mill on Suir Island

When the Earl died in 1829, Lady Blessington found herself on a much reduced income, and resorted to editing popular women's journals such as *The Book of Beauty* and *Keepsake for a living*. In addition to writing magazine articles, she became a prodigious producer of novels, one of which, *The Repealer*, she wrote in not much more than a month. She eventually moved to Paris, where the cost of living was less than that of London, and there she died in 1849.

R.S.A.I.

The pool in the river to the south of the roofless house is still called Lady Blessington's Bath: it is said that the young Margaret used to swim there.

Nearby, over a tiny stone bridge, which I believe is scheduled for demolition, and opposite a little bar known locally as 'The Floating Pub', I found a terrace of old cottages being cleared by a bulldozer. Nearby a late-eighteenth-century house with a slated gable and a coach house lies burnt out and roofless.

This hidden Clonmel was an eye-opener, for its richness of heritage and for its looming destruction. Apart from the seeming indifference of the powers-that-be to the potential loss to Clonmel's built, industrial and social heritage by the continuing destruction of the old buildings and installations on these islands, there seems to be inadaquate concern about what lies concealed beneath the eighteenth- and nineteenth-century developments. I understand that some trial holes have been dug and reported upon, but I wonder if this is just paying lip-service to the conservation lobby, rather than a serious attempt to seek traces of the original pre-Norman founders of Clonmel.

(*Left*) Clonmel Quays from the new bridge

Burnt out 18th-century building destined for demolition

Chapter Five

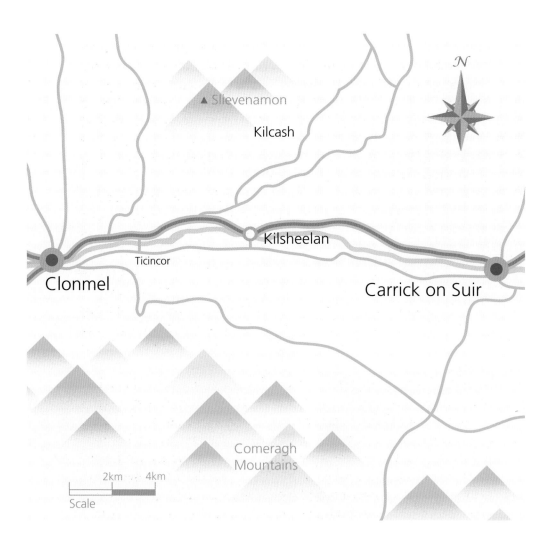

Slievenamon

Kilcash

Kilsheelan

Ticincor

Clonmel

Carrick on Suir

Comeragh
Mountains

2km 4km

Scale

Clonmel to Carrick on Suir

THE SUIR LEAVES CLONMEL, flowing strongly under a three-arch stone bridge, but a long line of stately old chestnut trees that graced the banks the last time I passed, a dozen years before, have been replaced by a riverside apartment block. The old towpath from the days when barges plied between Carrick and Clonmel can be followed all the way to Carrick. It is paved for the first four kilometres, but thereafter, except for a few stretches, it is grassy and overgrown in places until it comes near Carrick.

Between Clonmel and Carrick, the Suir is bordered by pastureland to the north and tightly hemmed in to the south by hills, the remains of a geologically ancient eastern wing of the Comeraghs, greatly reduced during the last Ice Age. Besides the different topography, there are other contrasts between the north and south banks. Within a four-kilometre zone of the river are the ruins of 21 churches on the north bank, while only six exist on the south side, which has seven prehistoric standing stones and three ogham stones, compared to just one standing stone on the north bank, evidence that the Suir was always a major cultural boundary.

The south bank is heavily wooded at first, while the north bank has a Celtic Tiger sprawl of pristine, shining steel-sided boxes serving as outlets for the sale of furniture, carpets and kitchens. Bursts of St John's wort with glittering golden stamens are in abundance along the river, overhanging the path and lining the bank. Although the establishment has warned of its dangers, the plant is still sold in 'alternative medicine' shops for treating a variety of complaints. The blood-red spots that mark its leaves in autumn are supposed to appear on 29 August, the day that

St John's Wort (above) and Himalayan balsam found in abundance along water's edge

St John the Baptist was said to have been beheaded. The traditional uses of the plant were widespread: a French name is *la tout saine*, or 'all-heal', and it was used to treat ailments of the mind that today might be termed depression: its stamens were called *Fuga Daemonum*, or devil's flight, alluding to the driving out of demons, and an old Italian name is 'devil-chaser'.

Himalayan balsam is another plant that thrives at the water's edge, standing in places over two metres high on leafy stalks, offering its pink blossoms to the sky. It is said to have come from the Orient as seedlings woven into jute sacks, the plastic bags of the nineteenth century, and is now relatively common in Ireland along navigable rivers where the seeds found sanctuary. Another alien that has taken hold in places along the riverside here is Japanese knotweed which is spreading wildly throughout Ireland and which in time will prove to be very difficult to eradicate.

It was introduced into these islands in 1825 as an ornamental plant, and was described in a gardening magazine in 1875 as 'a plant of sterling merit'. It is now illegal to plant Japanese knotweed in Britain.

Ticincor Castle, c. 1637, built originally for the Powers but confiscated in 1641

As the Suir weaves out into the open Long Hill, a northern foothill of the Comeraghs looms on the horizon, while a little farther east, the pinnacle of Raven's Rock, backed by the dark Knockanaffrin ridge, is easy to identify above the forest line. To the north-east, fabled Slievenamon can be glimpsed between stands of willow.

Just before the narrow eighteenth-century Thomas Bridge are the extensive buildings of St Joseph's School, founded by Arthur Moore, MP for Clonmel from 1874 to 1885 and an actively militant Catholic. Created a papal count in 1877, he used his personal wealth to assist in the building of churches, hospitals and schools, including this school, founded for the poor children of Tipperary. Run by the Rosminian Order until 2002, it is now managed by the Department of Education and Science, and caters for boys between ten and sixteen who have been referred there by the courts or by the Health Service Executive. The boys have their own bedrooms in units of homely scale, and are encouraged to help out with the housework. Metalwork, pottery and arts and crafts are taught in parallel with academic subjects, and the boys have available to them a fine sports complex, which includes a swimming pool and a gymnasium.

On the south side of the river below Thomas Bridge is Ticincor Castle, which was standing here in 1654 and was described then as 'a faire stone house, an orchard and a goodly garden, but all decayed'.[1] It was probably built around 1637 when the lands on the south side of the river were amalgamated with those on the north side, to form the Manor of Powerstown. A few years later, however, in the great changeover in land ownership after the 1641 rebellion, the lands were confiscated from the Powers, and came into the ownership of the Osbourne family, who let the castle fall into disrepair. In his description of his tour of Ireland in 1779, Arthur Young praises landowners like the Osbournes who enabled peasants to develop the marginal land above Clonmel by building cottages for them, placing families there and providing fertilizer and loans to allow them to obtain stock. Young is very dismissive of owners of other mountain land who leave it as they found it, using it only for foxhunting and grouse-shooting, calling them 'lazy, trifling, inattentive, slobbering, and profligate ... shame on such spiritless conduct!'[2] How times change; today a landowner who leaves the wild places undeveloped is praised as being 'eco-friendly'.

If one ignores the lack of a roof and the bungalow tucked up against its walls, Ticincor Castle, with its tall gables and chimneys, cannot be much different from what it looked like in its heyday. It is a good example of a dwelling of the fortified house type, which became popular in the relative peacefulness of post-medieval Ireland. The new type of house used a larger plan, which allows for a greater number of private rooms, usually separated by timber-panelled walls, lit by generous

1   *Survey of Waterford* 1654.
2   Arthur Young, *A Tour in Ireland*, Cambridge University Press, 1925 *Reprint.*

windows and heated by the many fireplaces that give this type of building its characteristically tall and often elaborately decorated chimneys.
Many Irish towerhouses have been refurbished and turned into fine
dwellings, but I have yet to see one of these fine Jacobean fortified
houses restored to its former glory.

East of Ticincor on the north bank, providing apples for the production of Bulmers cider, are 250 acres of orchard. The harvest here is
augmented by supplies of apples from growers all over Ireland, and
from County Armagh in particular. A short distance north of the Suir is
the Bulmers plant, a great Clonmel success, producing enormous
quantities of cider, mainly for export to Denmark, Australia, the United
States and Japan. The factory, with its vast collection of silos, was opened
by Seán Lemass in 1965, but the original plant was established in 1935
in an old brewery in Dowd's Lane, Clonmel by William Magner. It has
since been in the ownership of the English firms of Bulmers and
Showerings, and is today a subsidiary of Cantrell and Cochrane.

On the opposite bank of the Suir is the extensive, walled parkland
demesne of Gurteen le Poer, the erstwhile home of the Catholic branch
of the aristocratic le Poer or Power family, who, up until early in the
twentieth century, claimed ownership by ancient right of the lands of
the Beresford Poers farther south at Curraghmore. The le Poers were
descendants of Sir Robert de Poher, to whom Henry II granted a large
amount of land in east Waterford in 1177, but during the ensuing
centuries politics and religion split the family. Subsequently the Protestant wing, which held the most land, ran out of male heirs and it passed
into the hands of the Beresfords when Lady Catherine Power married
Sir Marcus Beresford in 1717. Sir Marcus arranged to succeed to the
earldom of Tyrone, a title that had previously belonged to the Powers.
The Powers of Gurteen, the remaining direct male line, actively sought
justice regarding the true lineage. A nearby roadside cross commemorates Edmund James, Count de le Poer, 'de jure seventeenth Lord la
Poer', who died in 1915. Their claim was eventually heard by the British
House of Lords in the early 1900s, but was rejected.

Today the le Poers are gone from Gurteen le Poer, a much turreted
and castellated Tudor style mansion erected in 1866 to the designs of
Samuel Roberts. It was sold some years ago to an Austrian artist named

Gurteen le Poer | Gottfried Helnwein. In 2005 he hosted the wedding of Marilyn Manson and Dita Von Treese, which was attended by such stars as Madonna, Lisa Marie Presley, Johnny Depp and Guy Richie. Manson, in spite of his name and the fact that he wears dramatic eye- shadow and lipstick, is male: his real name is the less startling Brian Warner. His bride, whose real name is Heather Sweet, is variously described in the media as a 'model', a 'burlesque dancer' and a 'stripper'. She is reported to have 'vowed' that the ceremony would out-do the marriage feasts of

both Britney Spears and Jennifer Lopez, and it is said to have cost 700,000 euro. The 'theme' of the wedding, designed by young Tipperary designer Fiona Leahy, was 'Wilde/Victorian', and the guests feasted on spit-roasted pig, lobster, salmon, crab and oysters. They spent the following day engaged in falconry and shooting, followed by a slap-up meal of steak and kidney pie with roast potatoes and hot whiskeys.

Kilsheelan bridge

The bridge at Kilsheelan is a fine construction, but was yet another

Kilsheelan bridge from afar | victim of the Civil War: the Anti-Treaty forces blew it up in 1923.

Downstream the robust walls of the old quay can still be seen, where barges from Carrick or Clonmel discharged or collected cargoes; the quayside today is covered in a pleasant grassy sward. After a swim with my family here one sunny afternoon, we watched an otter emerge from a drain and slip into the river without a ripple. He was there and gone in only a matter of seconds, and we waited to see if he would appear again. We were just about giving up staring out across the river when we heard a cacophony of duck calls and the flapping of wings in the reeds at the far side. A pair of female mallards came bursting out of their cover, scooting across the water, and then a third, all quacking loudly. They took quickly to the air, and as they did so, the otter swam swiftly from the reeds in their wake, looking up disappointedly at the duck as they disappeared over the bridge. He swam about seemingly aimlessly for a few minutes before disappearing back into the reeds.

Kilsheelan is a pleasant place strung along the main Carrick to Clonmel road, and is a past winner of the Tidy Towns competition. The ruins of an early thirteenth-century church overlooking the river suggest

that there has been a settlement here for many centuries. In the churchyard is a fine collection of tombstones of the eighteenth century, including some with naïve carved representations of the crucifixion scene and associated emblems. In the Middle Ages meditation on the passion of Christ was encouraged by the church, and to assist the illiterate general populace, pictorial depictions of the emblems of the passion were frequently used. The tombstones here are examples of a popular local revival of this devotion. Surrounding the primitive figure of Christ on the cross are representations of the cock that crows when St Peter denied Christ three times, Christ's seamless robe, the dice thrown by the soldiers for it, the thirty pieces of silver paid to Judas, the spear, the sponge with water and vinegar, and even the hammer and nails. The earliest of these stones in south Tipperary dates from 1721.

At the bridge in Kilsheelan is a fine motte, what remains of one of the first fortifications to be built to control the river here by the Norman knight William de Burgo in the twelfth century. Its conversion into a Marian shrine some decades ago has helped its survival. A cave-like,

Kilsheelan motte

(*Above*) Ruins of early thirteenth-century church at Kilsheelan

[145]

stone-lined grotto with a statue of the Virgin Mary has been constructed in the east flank, and the rest of the great mound is covered with tightly mown grass and decorated with flowerbeds. A sign that could have been put there by de Burgo himself says 'Danger! Please don't climb this motte'.

The Suir has always had a good reputation as a salmon river, and the fish weirs constructed to catch the salmon were a feature of the river. The earliest known such weir in Ireland was found in 1999 on the river Fergus in County Clare and has been dated to the sixth century. Ancient Gaelic laws frequently refer to rights related to weirs. By the medieval period, the technology of weirs was well developed, and ownership of such installations was a valuable asset. The Franciscan brothers of the friary in Clonmel possessed a significant set of weirs in the Suir, important enough to be recorded in 1541 during the dissolution of the monasteries. By that time weirs had become so dense on the Suir that they seriously obstructed trading vessels plying between Waterford and Clonmel and a regulation had to be enacted to ensure free passage and forbidding damming more than one-third of the river, leaving what was called the King's Gap.

With the enormous amount of industrial and urban pollution that must have drained unheeded into the river from the sugar factory, the mills, breweries, meat factories and creameries from the eighteenth century until comparatively recent times, it is surprising that any fish survived in the Suir. Even when these industries all but died out, their place as polluters was taken up by modern intensive agriculture. Is it possible, I wonder, that the environment is a lot sturdier than we think? When I walked the river from Kilsheelan to Carrick in September 2008, I passed about a dozen salmon anglers. One of them told me that there had been a lot of salmon caught along that stretch in the previous few days, but by law all catches of salmon had to be returned to the water. I asked another angler if they really obeyed this law, or did he have a few fish hidden in the nettles along the bank, and he replied with a grin, 'I don't tell lies, so I'll say nothing'.

Poaching was always common on the Suir, particularly for those many families who eked out a living fishing the waters in earlier times. In the early twentieth century it was customery to catch a few fish before

the season opened in order to pay for the licence to fish, and the so-called 'Blackberry Haul' after the season had ended was a popular poaching period.

Fifteenth-century Poulakerry Castle, built by the Butlers on a bend of the river

Downstream from Kilsheelan at a bend in the river is Poulakerry Castle, built by the Butlers in the fifteenth century and still occupied. It is surrounded by an exotic garden that stretches down to the riverbank, which consists of a robust stone wall, probably the remains of a harbour that once served the castle. The river is narrow here, and during one particularly lawless period in Ireland's history tolls were demanded from passing merchant galleys, a practice that led to these particular Butlers and others Suirside landowners being dubbed 'robber barons'. On the cheerful sunny day that I last passed here, it was difficult to imagine one of Poulakerry's more violent days, when in 1650 the occupants of the castle put up some resistance to a force of the Cromwellian New Model Army under Adjutant General Sadler. In the words of Cromwell himself in one of his reports, Sadler 'stormed it, putting thirty or forty of them to the sword, and the rest of them remaining obstinate were fired in the castle'.

North of the Suir is the soft, rounded shape of Slievenamon, an isolated and therefore significant mountain, forming a western prow to a range of hills that stretch between Fethard and Mullinavat. Although only 721 metres high, it seems to be cloud-capped quite often, presenting an ever-changing and sometimes brooding appearance. Amhlaoibh Ó Suilleabháin, the Callan schoolteacher who has left us in his journal well-observed comments on rural Kilkenny and Tipperary between the years 1827 to 1835, frequently describes the appearance of the mountain from his home as 'most glorious at sunset', 'a beautiful sight under a cap of cloud', or 'hidden in heavy black clouds like a dark oak wood'.

On the lower slopes of Slievenamon nearly five kilometres north from the Suir stand the ruins of Kilcash Castle, the subject of a song that has survived for centuries. Most people of my age would remember learning the song 'Kilcash' at school, which started with the lines,

> Cread a dheanfaimid feasta gan admadh,
> Ta deireadh na coillte ar lar...

It translates:

> What are we going to do without timber,
> the last of the woods is laid low,

and refers to the sale of the remaining timber from the fine woods in the demesne after the demise of the great period of Kilcash and passing of the Gaelic way of life with the death in 1744 of Lady Iveagh Butler.

The sentiments expressed are the opposite of those in 'Carden's Wild Demesne'; in the song 'Kilcash' the departure of the 'earls' and 'the lady' are lamented, and their return prayed for. With lines describing the gates that have been taken away, the avenue overgrown and goats in the garden, the ballad is an apt description of a decayed demesne, something that was to become far too typical in the following centuries.

Ruined Kilcash Castle is a five-storey towerhouse with a seventeenth-century extension. The original castle was built in the middle of the sixteenth century by a strain of the Butler family who, like the Butlers of Cahir, had remained Catholic until the mid-eighteenth century. Thomas Butler fought with the Jacobites at the Battle of Aughrim in 1691 and was lucky to survive; nearly half his battalion were killed or wounded, and the Jacobite army lost 7,000 men in all. He had his horse shot from under him, and was taken prisoner: he was later pardoned, however, owing to his close relationship with his cousin, the powerful 2nd Duke of Ormond.

At the level of the Ascendancy, power and influence in the late Middle Ages and well into the modern period were still held and shared through intermarriage by a few dozen premier families, often irrespective of the Protestant-Catholic divide, and the Butlers at Kilcash were no exception. Their complex primary inter-relationships provide a good example of what was common at that level of society at the time. While Thomas Butler's cousin was the Protestant Duke of Ormond, his brother Christopher was the Catholic Archbishop of Cashel. His wife, Countess Iveagh, was the daughter of William Bourke, Earl of Clanrickard and Chief Governor of Galway, and apart from her marriage into the Butlers, she already had a connection with that clan through her maternal grandmother, who was sister of the former Viceroy, James Butler, 1st Duke of Ormond.

The seventeenth-century extension was a three-bay house that probably replaced the banqueting hall that was a common part of many Irish towerhouses, and by 1677 the combined castle and house were grandly referred to as 'the mansion house of Kilcash'. Guests of all stations were entertained with great hospitality, and it is recorded that excellent hunting was to be had on the estate, where in winter a shooter could bag 'a dozen and a half woodcock in a couple of hours'.[3] Looking at the

---

3   David Butler, *South Tipperary 1570-1841*, Four Courts Press 2006.

Suir towpath near Ballydine

ruins now, it is hard to picture the place as it was at its best in the early eighteenth century, when the buildings were surrounded by colourful and fruitful gardens and a mature woodland stretched from the house down to the Suir.

The castle is, at the time of writing, in state ownership and undergoing conservation. It has the distinction of being one of the few tower-houses in Ireland to have come under artillery fire; as late as August 1922 it was fired upon by Free State forces using an eighteen-pounder field gun, when it was suspected that Anti-Treaty forces were occupying the castle.

Of the five fine houses that overlooked this stretch of the Suir at the end of the eighteenth century – Suir Lodge, Lindville, Bally-dine, Coolnamuck and Landscape – only Landscape remains, a fine Georgian house embowered with specimen trees, presenting a bow front to the river. Along the towpath I found two overgrown brick-vaulted boathouses that served one of these estates, possibly Ballydine, and the extensive walled gardens of Coolnamuck are all that remains of a large house that was once reached from the public road by an avenue of lime trees. It is said that one of the owners of Coolnamuck in the early days lived so extravagantly that it led to his bankruptcy. He avoided the embarrassment of his situation by loading his family into his coach

Landscape House, a fine Georgian house on the south bank

and driving it to Tramore and over the cliffs there.

At Ballydine, a massive industrial complex is hidden away behind a security fence north of the river. This is the Merck, Sharp & Dohme plant, an American operation producing ingredients for pharmaceuticals, including medications for high blood pressure, high cholesterol, angina, asthma and osteoporosis, established in 1976. The facility employing about 350 people, has a mission statement that the company says 'extends beyond the commercial aspects of the business and encompasses safety, environment and the local community'. Their founder, George W. Merck, is said to have stated: 'We never try to forget that medicine is for the people. It is not for the profits. The profits follow, and if we have remembered that, they have never failed to appear.'

Across the Suir from Ballydine and a kilometre from the river is a tiny wooded valley called Glen Poer. Up until the eighteenth century, a famous fair was held on the Feast of the Ascension on the riverbanks below the Glen, where a ferry operated. The fair was immortalised in a traditional air called 'The Fair of the Glen', but nothing of it remains today, not even in the memory of a couple of local people whom I asked about it.

A little distance downstream at Churchtown, overlooking the Suir from the south bank, is an old cemetery with some interesting graves. With the name Disert Nairbe, it was formerly a monastic settlement founded by St Aidan of Ferns, also called St Mogue, who lived between the mid-sixth and the early seventh centuries. The historian Canon Power said it was 'a notable place in pre-Invasion times', but nothing now remains of the old monastery, and only an ivy-covered gable survives of the post-penal church. Among those buried here are the Roche family of Glen, including Colonel James Roche, who was known as the Swimmer Roche. The Roches were supporters of Charles II, and their estates in County Cork were confiscated when they went into exile with him in 1651. James Roche's father commanded a Flemish regiment on the Continent, and like many others shared the pay he received with the exiled king. When Charles was proclaimed king in May 1660 and returned to England, many of his supporters, including the Roches, were forgotten and abandoned. James Roche followed his father into the army, and when years later he was invited to join forces with a large Irish contingent of soldiers to support Charles's son, James II, he

HERE LYETH IN
BENEATH THE DECE...
OF THE FAMILY OF COL[ON]EL
ROCH OF GLYN. HIZ S[EL]HE
HIMSELF SUSANA HIS FIRST
WIFE W[M] HIS ELDEST SON
AND ANNA MARIA WIFE TO
HIS SECOND SON JAMES
WHO DIED THE 9 JULY
1725 THE S[D] JAMES
CAUSED THIS MONUMENT
TO BE ERECTED IN MEMORY
OF HIS S[D] RELATIONS.

Plaque commemorating the Roche family in Churchtown cemetery

remembered how the Stuarts had treated his family, and instead threw in his lot with the forces of William of Orange.

As a colonel in the Williamite army of General Kirke, which was awaiting reinforcements before going to the relief of Londonderry, under siege by the Jacobites, he volunteered to slip through the lines with a message of encouragement to the citizens of the city. After a day and night struggling through undergrowth and swimming the river Foyle, no mean feat in itself, Roche made it into Derry with his message. Swimming back at night with a reply for Kirke, he was intercepted by a boat full of Jacobite soldiers, and pulled aboard after his jaw had been broken by the blow of a halberd. When he came to his senses, however, he slipped out of their grasp and dived into the river again. In spite of being struck by three bullets as the Jacobites opened fire, Roche made it

Cornfields near Coolnamuck

(*Right*) The Davin family plot

back to Londonderry, and there he remained as he recovered through the remainder of the siege. He managed to keep up communications with Kirke by means of signals from the church steeple, and was a great encouragement to the garrison. After the siege was lifted, the Swimmer Roche, as he was now known, was rewarded for his bravery by William III with a grant of the rights to all the undisposed-of ferries in Ireland – a very valuable asset at a time when there were relatively few bridges across Ireland's larger rivers.

One of the ferries he obtained the rights to was that at Glen, which had been confiscated from the local owners. Roche settled down at Glen Castle with his family, and here he lived until the end of his days. It is said that Seamus na Srona, a local Gaelic poet, gave such a vitriolic eulogy over his grave that it split his tombstone! I found no split tombstone but did ascertain that Roche is buried in a family vault beside the wall of the church: a plaque commemorating Roche, his wife Suzanna and his family can be seen on the remains of the church gable.

In a corner at the back of the graveyard, overlooking the river and shaded by venerable lime trees, the Davin family plot can be found. Maurice, co-founder of the GAA, and Pat, who is said to have held six world athletic records at one time, are among the members of the family buried here.

While the Davins were popular, they were of the wealthy Catholic class, and had plenty of detractors amongst the poorer members of their own religion. They owned the salmon fishing rights on stretches of the river, and had very effective weirs which the ordinary fishermen believed substantially reduced their chances of catches up- or downstream. The Davin weir below Kildroughtan was frequently robbed of fish, to such an extent that the family had a guard tower built to watch over it. The family's nationalist credentials and involvement with the GAA was eventually no protection, particularly at a time of general chaos in the country: in 1921 the weir was wrecked and the roof blown off the tower. The roofless tower survives today as a picturesque riverside sight.

As the Suir nears Carrick on Suir, the riverside walk is paved, and the river enters the town past a pleasant park overlooked by a row of limestone menhirs or standing stones. Public sculpture in Ireland has had a mixed success, both in the quality of the sculpture and in the level of its public appreciation. A few years ago some evangelist managed to persuade the powers-that-be that there was need for local authorities countrywide to provide for more public art. Some councils, including Tipperary County Council, decided that one percent of the money spent on sewage and drainage schemes would be used to pay for the design and installation of artwork in public places. I have noticed, however, that although competitions are often held to find a suitable piece of work, the winning designs are not always chosen by an appropriately qualified panel of judges. In some situations, I have heard of local officials attempting to have their name immortalised in the installation, and in others the process has resulted in very poor work that subsequently has been badly maintained.

Although the scope of this standing stone project, by Tipperary man Tony O'Malley, is impressive, some of the finer detail leaves a lot to be desired. The sculptor used disjointed, paraphrased excerpts from the poetic work of Michael Coady to characterise the Suir, Carrick and its people, together with images, some very good and some disappointing, carved onto the individual stones.

As the Suir sweeps into Carrick, a dramatic change begins to transform

Standing stone sculpture, Carrick on Suir

(*Right*) Traditional Suir cots

the river, in poet Michael Coady's words, 'from pastoral to esturial, anticipating its own imminent transfiguration and consummation – along with its sister rivers Nore and Barrow – within the cosmic continuum of "salt, estranging sea" beyond Waterford Harbour'. If Clonmel owes its location to a cluster of islands in the Suir, similarly it is likely that Carrick was sited where it is because of the existence of a large island and since this is where the Suir becomes tidal. Twice a day the moon commands the waters of the open sea to stretch their salty influence 50 kilometres inland, interrupting the flow of the river, and making it possible for ships to navigate up as far as this place, endowing the town, surrounded by rich farmland, with considerable commercial potential.

The original settlement at Carrick, known as Carrickmagriffin after the early Norman occupier, Raymond fitzGriffyn, developed on the island. The river along the northern side of the island was very shallow and was eventually filled in while the stream flowing south of the island was as broad and deep as it is today, and was bridged in the fifteenth century. This old bridge, at the west end of the modern town, survives, although damaged during the Civil War, and has all the qualities of the picturesque. Besides the flickering of reflected light from the river surface, which always give bridges a special aura, the structure is built of clearly ancient masonry that is dressed, in summertime, with thick herbage and the pink frothy flowers of valerian. This great structure has stood, braving the weather, the river and man's use and abuse for nearly six hundred years. Building a bridge across a large river is never a simple task, but in this case having to deal with the twice-daily movement of tides would have made the work even more difficult, and Carrick Bridge must have been a unique engineering feat when it was constructed under the orders of Edmund Mac Richard Butler of Ormond Castle in the mid-fifteenth century. Michael Coady's description of the place is a succinct blend of the ordinary and the amazing:

> Salmon wait for the tide
> To still the weir.
> Boys are fishing from a bridge
> Built before Columbus raised a sail.[4]

Carrick and its people came close to being at the centre of a major national revolution in 1848, an uprising that would have most likely ended in great carnage and failure. When the government demanded in that year that the Young Ireland movement should give up its arms, John Blake Dillon, Thomas Francis Meagher and William Smith O'Brien decided to fight before such a thing could be allowed. Although they were greeted enthusiastically by crowds everywhere they appeared, they were not successful in finding a place in the country with sufficient numbers of enthusiastic would-be revolutionaries to rise up: rural

---

4   From the poem, 'Still-Life from a Hill over a Town', *Two for a Woman, Three for a Man*, The Gallery Press, 1980.

Ireland was, after all, still reeling from the murderous effects of the Great Famine, the memories of 1798 were fresh and there can have been little stomach for war. They tried to inspire the people of Enniscorthy, but failed to find support for revolution, and in Kilkenny, where the town's garrison had been strengthened, they found the people poorly armed and their leaders reluctant. When they arrived in Carrick, however, on 24 July, they found a population ready for a fight, as Meagher later wrote:

> A torrent of human beings, rushing through lanes and narrow streets... whirling in dizzying circles, and tossing up its dark waves, with sounds of wrath, vengeance and defiance...eyes red with rage and despera- tion...wild, half-stifled, passionate, frantic prayers of hope, curses on the red flag; scornful, exulting delirious defiances of death...
> It was the Revolution, if we had accepted it.[5]

The population of Carrick on Suir at the time was around 11,000, all crammed into a town with half the footprint of the town today, and proba- bly swelled with many refugees from the country areas in the wake of the Famine. It was not a happy population, and was ripe for revolution. For some reason that even the principals could not later explain, the moment was not seized, and their efforts came to a half-hearted and pathetic end five days later at Ballingarry, to the north of Carrick. There, armed with a few muskets and pikes, a band of half-starved men who had been inspired by a small group of wealthy, well-fed idealists, were routed by the Royal Irish Constabulary in what was called 'the cabbage-patch revolt', refer- ring to Widow McCormack's garden where most of the action took place. In the aftermath, O'Brien and Meagher were captured, and eventually sentenced to transportation to Van Diemen's Land.

Michael Coady showed me a book that provided an interesting insight into that turbulent period, and provided a connection with a doomed post-war industry in Carrick. It is a volume published in the early nineteenth century relating to the travels of the poet Byron, of no particular antiquarian value, but the signatures and the handwritten dedication written in the front endpapers make it unique. At the top of

---

5   Arthur Griffith ed., *Meagher of the Sword*, M.H. Gill & Son 1917.

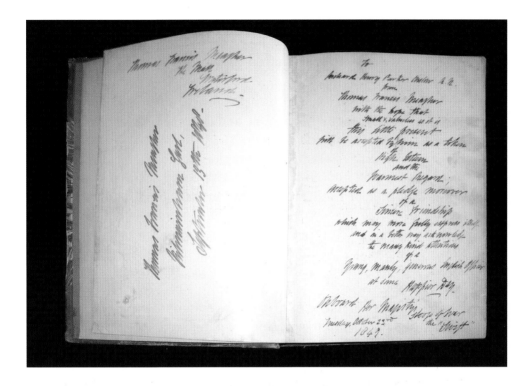

one of the endpapers is the legend 'Thomas Francis Meagher, The Mall, Waterford, Ireland'. Below this is another note 'Thomas Francis Meagher, Kilmainham Goal, September thirteenth 1849'. On the facing page is written:

Dedication by Thomas Francis Meagher to Richard Onslow of the Royal Navy

> To Richard Henry Parker Onslow, RN, from Thomas Francis Meagher with the hope that, small and valueless as it is, this little present will be accepted by him as a token of high esteem and earnest regard; accepted as a pledge, moreover, of a sincere friendship which may more fully express itself and in a better way acknowledge the many kind attentions of a young, manly, generous English Officer at some happier day. On board Her Majesty's sloop of war the 'Swift', Tuesday October 3rd, 1849.

Richard Onslow was probably the great-grandson of Admiral Sir Richard Onslow, an intrepid Royal Naval officer who served during the busy naval jousting years of the late eighteenth century, and was personally instrumental in the defeat of a Dutch fleet at the battle of Camperdown in October 1797, an action which effectively eliminated the risk of a Dutch invasion of Ireland during the subsequent 1798 Rebellion. When he died in 1817 at Southampton, he left instructions that not more than £120 was to be spent on his funeral, and that 'the funeral of a brave and honest sailor costs a much less sum'.

Thomas Francis Meagher, although a Catholic, was of a wealthy family and would not have had to endure being chained in the stuffy, unhygienic hold of a ship for the duration of the hundred-day voyage to Australia, as was the fate of thousands of poorer Irish that went before him. Instead, he occupied, with three companions, a spacious 'saloon, in which we breakfasted, dined, took tea, read, wrote, and got through a variety of agreeable pursuits,' such as playing backgammon. They enjoyed the service of a manservant, and the best food that such a sea voyage could offer at the time. It is interesting to see how, no matter what Meagher's quarrel with the Crown might be, he could appreciate friendship with an educated and 'young, manly, generous English Officer' without betraying his political beliefs.

How this book, which Onslow must have brought to Australia, came back to Ireland and to Michael Coady's bookcase within twenty miles of the Mall, Waterford, is a mystery. A Clonmel industrial story probably holds part of the answer. In December 1950 an Englishman named Sir Richard Onslow established a new industry in Carrick on Suir, involving the manufacture of prefabricated houses from precast concrete components. Based on a three-foot module, the system consisted of twin wall slabs placed between posts, creating a cavity wall that could be erected much faster than by the traditional method using bricks or blocks. In January 1951 production got underway in a small factory east of Dillon Bridge which employed 45 workers. Gravel for the concrete was provided from the vast gravel banks in the Suir, particularly near Piltown, and for which Suir boatmen received one shilling and sixpence a ton.

The first scheme of houses using the system was built at Castle Park in Clonmel, and soon after, the Mayor of Cork expressed interest in having 300 houses in Cork City built with the Onslow method. With a bright future promised for the industry and post-war employment in

Clonmel, it seems that Onslow began to experience considerable hostility from traditional builders and, it is said, also received anonymous threats. This situation must have become very serious because after only a year, Onslow had to sell the business and, I understand, he returned to his home place in Cornwall. It seems possible that, somehow, his ancestor's gift from Thomas Francis Meagher came to Ireland with him in 1950, and when he left again, it remained in Carrick.

After Onslow's departure, the prefabricated house business, now called Unicast, made a compromise agreement with the Irish Builders Federation. They agreed not to tender directly for housing schemes, but instead to provide the materials and components for sale to building contractors. Traditional contractors were still hostile to the system, and when some trades unions refused to handle the Unicast products, the industry was forced to close. With a little vision and proper support, Unicast could have become a very large industry: it had considerable export potential a few short years before the housing boom of the 1960s began, and could have transformed Carrick on Suir. It seems to me that small-mindedness, the worst kind of protectionism and the inability of government to look to the future, let down the town.

After the Young Irelanders' visit, the next political upheaval to occur in Carrick on Suir happened during the summer of 1922 when the town was occupied by Anti-Treaty forces. They isolated the town by destroying the incoming railway lines and, during the demolition of Dillon Bridge, were stoned by a local mob. Dan Breen, the commander of the Irregulars, gave out to the mob and told them that they were now paying for voting for the Free State.

Eamon de Valera came and went to the town a few times during the occupation, and it was reported in some newspapers that the Irregulars were 'commanded by Mr. de Valera in person'.[6] The workhouse and hospital were commandeered as the Anti-Treaty HQ, the patients being removed to Clonmel and to the fever hospital close by. Soldiers were billeted on residents of the town, and in a few cases where people were

---

6   *The Irish Times*, 28 July 1922.

unable to supply beds they were billed for the accommodation of the men in local hotels. The Anti-Treaty soldiers also seized clothing, boots and foodstuffs, including cattle and sheep from the outskirts of the town, which were slaughtered in the fields and the carcasses driven into town in commandeered motor cars. They asked in each case for a bill for the goods seized, but very little was ever paid back.

In August the town briefly hosted a group of top Republicans, including Eamon de Valera, Seamus Robinson, Erskine Childers, Countess Markievicz and Dr Kathleen Lynn until, on the approach of the National Army, they made themselves scarce, followed not long after by all 200 of the occupying Irregulars. As they went, they set charges to blow up Carrick's fifteenth-century bridge after them. I am told that a man named Mullins lay down on the northern end of the bridge to prevent its destruction, and after he had been given assurances and gone away, one arch of the bridge was blown anyway. Carrickbeg, the part of the town on the south bank, remained cut off until 1925 when the bridge was repaired.

In May 1934 Carrick experienced a taste of the Fascist movement that was becoming popular in Europe. When General O'Duffy, leader of the

Blueshirts, came to Carrick campaigning against the government, he was met by four marching bands, 6,000 blueshirt-clad men and 1,000 women and girls wearing blue blouses, and the parade was led by one hundred horsemen. There was at least one horsewoman: Mary Shee, in her ninety-first year when I talked to her, told me of how her father dressed her up in a blue blouse and she rode her pony in the parade. She well remembers the excitement of the affair, and the huge crowd that eventually assembled to hear O'Duffy speak. It must have been a popular movement to attract such a large turnout, although it is said the crowd came from the surrounding areas of south Kilkenny, east Waterford, and south Tipperary, as well as from Carrick. At a time of dullness and stagnation in Ireland, the Blueshirts organised dances and picnics, providing a bit of excitement for the young people of the time. My mother and father, who were certainly not followers of O'Duffy, first met at a Blueshirt fundraising dance in Waterford. On that night in Carrick, O'Duffy had a bodyguard of twenty men all over six feet tall, and he was joined on the platform in the centre of town by the Mayor of Waterford. O'Duffy complained that a meeting of Blueshirts in Drogheda the previous week had been disrupted by 'native and imported rowdies', and that if de Valera did not take steps to suppress the disruptive elements, blackguardism and Bolshevism let loose in the country, what had happened in the Soviet Union and Spain would happen in Ireland, presumably suggesting that Ireland was in danger of a communist revolution.

— ⁓ —

For centuries Carrick on Suir was a busy river port connecting the rich agricultural lands of the Golden Vale and the town of Clonmel with the port of Waterford, and it continued as a terminal for commercial river traffic to and from Waterford until the middle of the twentieth century. The last of the steam-driven tugs on the river, the 300-ton *Rocksand*, operated between Waterford and Carrick up until the mid-1960s, and continues in retirement to serve as a floating jetty for the Galley Restaurant at New Ross; it can be seen just north of New Ross bridge. The last sailing ship to sail up the river to Carrick was the *Mary B. Mitchell*, which used to visit from Wales until the 1920s. There was a substantial importation of coal into Carrick from Swansea, and coal vessels from the

Welsh port sailed up to the town to unload at the Coal Kay. Sometimes, prevented from getting into Carrick by a low tide, they would berth temporarily below the town, and be immediately descended upon by small scale merchants with asses and carts, who could buy the coal cheaply. The skipper kept an eye on the rising tide as the coal was sold, and as soon as there was sufficient depth, he would continue on up to the town.

Another commercial activity that stopped some years ago is the dredging of gravel and river sand, much of which was transported to Waterford building works via Carrick. There were a number of sources in the river for such material, including a bank nearly a mile long, known as the Purtoga, between Turkstown and Darrigal.

River trade was completely dependent on the movement and rhythm of the tides until the 1880s when a steam tug called the *Father Mathew* was purchased by the Suir Steam Navigation Company, and was used to tow cargo lighters or barges. Goods of every kind were carried, except alcohol, because the company was owned by J. Ernest Grubb, a Quaker, who also insisted that his skippers be tee-totallers: this in a town where in the 1870s there were 83 licensed premises.[7]

In 1912 mill owners Edward J. Dowley and Co. purchased the *Knocknagow*, a steam tug that could draw 120 tons, and in 1930 the larger *Knocknagow II* was introduced to the river. These were broad, low-slung craft with only a timber wheelhouse rising above the deck, and were still serving in the 1950s. Leslie Dowley related to me that in those pre-Health and Safety days it was not common to have safety equipment such as life jackets or flares on board river craft, but in spite of the intensive use of the river, there were very few incidents of crew members being injured or drowned. He told me of one voyage of the *Knocknagow II* down to Waterford when he was a boy. They unloaded on the north quays, but they were running late, and the skipper was concerned to get under the bridge, which they usually negotiated without it being raised, before high tide. When the unloading was finally complete, they headed back upriver at speed to squeeze under the bridge, but as they hurtled towards the middle span, it became clear that they would not make it, so the

7   Patrick C. Power, *Carrick on Suir Town and District 1800-2000*, Carrick Books, 2003.

skipper shouted for everybody to get out of the wheelhouse. Moments later the wheelhouse was swept away into the river: Leslie told me the weather was fine and sunny that day, and so they continued happily on to Carrick without much comment.

The *Knocknagow II* was eventually sold to Roadstone and was used by that company for drawing gravel until it was sold for scrap in the 1970s. It was saved from destruction by a County Wexford farmer, Richard Miller, who converted it into a houseboat, with accommodation for up to nine people. He sold it to writer Brian Goggins who turned it into a luxury barge, and is still using it to cruise Ireland's inland waterways.

The railway and the increasing transport of bulk loads by road brought about the ultimate demise of the commercial boats on this stretch of the Suir. Leslie Dowley commented that the barges were relatively small in terms of their capacity and he also said that their efficiency was impaired by the tidal nature of the route. Bad weather could cause delays of a number of days: when the time came that a lorry could transport more than twenty tons of cargo to or from Waterford in thirty minutes, it was clear that the days of the river trade were numbered.

Like Clonmel and many other old river towns, Carrick turns its back to the river, which would have originally been lined with docks and warehouses, the remains of which are being given new life as Celtic Tiger apartment blocks. The town is a place of two parts: that of the town, with its bustling main street and the West Gate tower, which almost ignores the Suir; and that of the river, a place of old warehouses, apartments and a new marina. Although a couple of streets provide physical links to the quays, as once did a larger number of slypes or narrow alleyways, one could easily pass through Carrick without glimpsing the river.

The largest building in the centre of town is what I first thought was a hotel, and then a convent, but from the clusters of Coca-Cola bottles and cosmetics lining some of the windowsills, I knew this couldn't be so. On enquiry, I found it is a former convent that is now a refugee centre, where upwards of 140 immigrants in family groups live until the immigration authorities can decide on their cases.

The Heritage Centre occupies the old Church of Ireland church which as a roofless ruin was rescued some years ago by a group of Carrick citizens and converted into a community-supported Heritage Centre, and here you can see a rich collection of artefacts, photographs and papers relating to the history of the town. I have a particular fondness for this kind of museum, which says so much more about a place than a formal, official museum filled with glass cases. I visited the centre during the week following the first Clancy Brothers Festival, and I was interested to see on exhibition memorabilia related to these famous Carrick sons. While I was there, Tom Grace, a local photographer who was looking after the place for the day, introduced me to Mary Clancy, the widow of the ballad singer Paddy Clancy. Still a beautiful woman in her late sixties, she was happy to chat about her husband and the halcyon early days of the singing group.

Two of the brothers, Paddy and Tom, emigrated to the United States in 1947, and lived in Greenwich Village in New York, working from time to time as actors and putting on plays in the Cherry Lane Theatre there.[8] When their theatrical work wasn't enough to pay the bills, they put on concerts, singing Irish songs and engaging other folk singers, such as Pete Seeger, Jean Richie and blues performers Sonny Terry and Brownie Magee.

---

8   Nuala O'Connor, *Bringing It All Back Home*, BBC Books 1991.

When their younger brother Liam joined them a few years later, they formed a singing group with Liam's friend Tommy Makem, and were surprised at the instant success they found. The sheer enjoyment they exuded as they performed and the drama they introduced into their music, combined with tin whistle, banjo and guitar, went down well with American audiences. True professionals, they rehearsed thoroughly, with even seemingly spontaneous jokes and banter being carefully crafted. The songs they popularised in Ireland in the early 1960s, and the way they sang them, was as far from the old standards such as 'When Irish Eyes are Smiling' as you could get, and appealed particularly to the rock and roll generation, to which they introduced a proud Irish dimension. Against the background of a rising of awareness of Irish identity at home and the popularity of folk music internationally, there is no doubt that Irish traditional music in every form was swept forward on the wave created by the Clancys and Tommy Makem. They were in part responsible, at the end of a dark period in Ireland of unemployment and emigration, for a rise in national confidence that was to be echoed on a much greater scale less than thirty years later by Riverdance and Ireland's success in world soccer.

I had the pleasure of spending a few hours in Carrick with Michael Coady, a poet whose work I have been constantly coming across over the last two decades. Although I am not one who takes to poetry easily, what he says, and the way he says it, always gets through to me. He is a gentle, quiet-spoken man, a quietness that belies his vehemently passionate feelings about many matters. Michael seems to know everybody in the town, and they seem to know and obviously like him. I felt envious of the sense of place, the sense of being rooted, that he seems to enjoy: he sees the ordinary with lyrical eyes, and immortalises it in poetry. A small town can be a prison to some and a universe to others. Michael clearly can do the interstellar travel needed to appreciate and make art from the particular universe he occupies.

We were joined down the town by Jim Power, an active enthusiast for the town of Carrick and a founder member of the Carrick Boat Club. They brought me to meet Patrick Drohan, who has a fishing and angling emporium down one of the streets leading to the river. He is a man of many occupations, including electrical goods salesman, bandsman,

undertaker, fishing tackle salesman and historian, and his shop, just two doors away from the old bridge, is a treasure trove of angling riches. There are charts depicting varieties of fish, a rack displaying rods, wicker baskets hanging from the ceiling and glass cases full of reels, lures and lines.

We talked of fishing on the Suir, and Patrick told me that he believes that, owing to agricultural pollution and the legislative changes that have taken place relating to the catching of salmon, we have all but seen the last of the fish on the Suir. Salmon were so plentiful in the river up until recent decades, and the fishermen of Carrick so efficient at catching them, there was a period in the late nineteen fifties when Mullins's chip shop were selling a fish and chip supper with salmon steaks. Apart from increasingly infrequent seasons when salmon numbers are up, Patrick said they will never again achieve the levels of the mid-nineteenth century, when, apart from fish sold in the Waterford and Dublin

markets, nearly 21,000 salmon caught in the Suir were exported annually to Bristol. Trout are also under threat, he says: phosphates leeching into the river create a moss-like carpet on the gravel beds where the fish used to bury their eggs: the vegetation prevents the eggs being deposited under the gravel and they are soon washed away. It seems also that eels have declined dramatically in recent years, with very few elvers or young eels in evidence coming up the river annually.

A view across the river of Carrigbeg

(*Above*) Detail of gothic arch in honey-coloured, decorated Dundry stone

Another environmental change that Patrick talked about was the enormous increase in mink along the river valley: these vicious little carnivores prey on the young of many species, and in some places water hens, formerly plentiful, are now absent because of the mink's depredations. Swans have been driven downriver after having lost many cygnets to the little black marauder. The otter, Patrick claims, is the only animal that predates the mink, and the otter population is one that has has not decreased in recent years. He says the otter is an opportunist, and when all else is lost, has no problem feeding from the bins in the town.

———

Down the street from Patrick's shop and across the old bridge is Carrick-beg, where the land immediately climbs away from the river towards forested hills. Towering high over the river is St Molleran's parish church, built in 1828 upon the ruins of St Michael's fourteenth-century Franciscan friary: part of the north wall, and the tower dramatically corbelled off it, is original, as is the west entrance, a large gothic arch in honey-coloured, decorated Dundry stone.

Peter Walsh of Belline, the much-respected agent to the Bessborough estate near Piltown in the 1820s provided the timber for the church roof, which was donated by the estate. He oversaw the measurement on site and the calculation of the timber required and had twelve great pine trees, valued at £60, felled on the estate for the project. The transportation of the timber to Carrickbeg was a problem, but local farmers solved it by volunteering their labour and horses and carts. On the day arranged, a procession of thirty-six timber-loaded carts, led by a band, left Piltown, with a piper sitting atop the first load of timber playing Irish airs. A great concourse of people followed waving leafy branches. The whole party paused halfway to Carrick at Walshe's house at Belline where he had laid on refreshments, before continuing on the journey, gathering additional helpers along the way. By the time they got to the town, the streets were full of music and cheering: they paraded down Main Street, through Bridge Street, across the bridge and up to the church site where the timber was unloaded, and the volunteers were hospitably entertained by the local populace.

A limestone plaque built into the great retaining wall between the church and the street has the following sad statement carved in naive lettering:

> This wall was built in 1846
> A year memorable by the failure of the potatoe crop
> And the consequent scarcity of food
> Revd Patrick Gaffney PP Michael Fogarty John Dee Curates

At the eastern end of the town, almost without warning, you come across Carrick Castle, an exquisite Tudor house and a very rare building in the Irish context. You will find many houses similar to it in England, particularly in the Cotswolds, and the rest of Europe has plenty of domestic buildings of the same period. This Ormond manor house is, however, our only example of a Tudor high-status dwelling house, and in the context of turbulent Irish history, particularly in Munster, it is a miracle that it has survived intact into the present century.

Built around 1568, it was the brainchild of the 10th Earl of Ormond, known as Black Thomas, who had grown up surrounded by similar fine Tudor architecture. As a result of an English royal policy initiated in the time of Henry VII to gently encourage the Anglo-Irish aristocracy to assimilate England's language and culture, knighthoods and earldoms were dispensed, chieftain's sons were invited to London to be provided

Carrick Castle

[171]

Carrick Castle as painted in watercolour by George du Noyer in the 19th century

with the best in modern education, and there were even attempts to seduce Gaelic men and women with the latest in English fashion. Sir John Perrot, Elizabeth's lord deputy in Ireland, gave presents of English clothes, causing the Irish in receipt of such generosity to complain about the tightness of the trousers, that 'embraced like fetters': they presumably preferred the loose look. In spite of the difficulties the crown had with the rebel 15th Earl of Desmond, Elizabeth kept warmly in touch with Eleanor, his wife. When Eleanor sent a half-dozen pine marten skins to the queen as a token of her goodwill, Elizabeth reciprocated by dispatching a rich fashionable gown to the Countess. It was one of her own, and it is reported that before being sent, food stains were found on the front of the gown and a piece had to be cut out and replaced.[9]

Black Thomas was in this way reared and educated in London, growing up with the English royal family of the time, including the

9   Peter Somerville-Large, The *Irish Country House, A Social History*, Sinclair-Stevenson 1995.

future Elizabeth I. He was the first Ormond to be raised a Protestant, and it is said that he had a notion at one time of marrying Elizabeth. His assimilation into English ways was partially successful, and on his return to Ireland as the powerful Earl of Ormond, he brought many English ideas, including that which gave birth to the new architecture of Ormond Castle. Local tradition has it that it was built as a home for him to share with Elizabeth, should she marry him, or at least to provide a suitable place for her to stay in Ireland. There must be considerable truth in this: in the magnificent long gallery on the first floor, amidst the finest and rarest Elizabethan plasterwork in Ireland, is a decorative medallion depicting the queen with sceptre in hand.

At his Carrick home Black Thomas was the perfect English gentleman, entertaining like-minded neighbours at elaborate banquets in his spectacular house: the unaccustomed sunny brightness provided by the large windows was much commented upon, as were the novel wax taper lights used at night. Although he carried out modern improvements on his great castle at Kilkenny, including the insertion of wide Tudor windows, when residing there he played the part of the Gaelic chief, entertaining in the traditional way with blazing fires, flagons of wine and heaps of meat and fish strewn on great tables.

In his old age Black Thomas lived most of the time in the comfort of his Carrick home, and he died there in 1614. The house was also a favourite in his younger days of the twelfth Earl, who afterwards became the Great Duke of Ormond. Although looted by the rebel Earl of Desmond during one of his plundering forays along the Suir valley, even he must have been very impressed by the building because he spared it from the torch. Sometimes occupied and at other times derelict over the succeeding centuries, the house escaped the widespread 'improvements' that assailed many other houses after the Act of Union, and was robust enough to last into the twentieth century and be rescued by the Office of Public Works. It is now well protected and a popular visitor attraction.

The present population of Carrick on Suir is about 6,000, a comfortable number, and the place is so compact that you can walk from one end of the town to the other in a short time. Other than at the refugee centre, the town has not seen the great influx of outsiders that more commercially successful Irish towns have. Everyone in Carrick knows

everyone else, and the streets are full of the voices of neighbours, friends and acquaintances greeting each other as they pass by.

I was concerned to see that the quality of the old building stock of Carrick on Suir seems undervalued and has not been matched by modern developments. One large and fine eighteenth century slate-fronted house in the town centre has had all its slates stripped, its windows altered and insulted with flimsy concrete sills, thus losing its traditional character and the fine proportions that would have made it a boon to the town had it been appropriately refurbished. Cheap plastic signs and pastiche shopfronts abound, and the destruction of the old

limestone street pavings is almost complete. One hopes that this
state of things is temporary: it is clear that the town is blessed with
a small but vocal cohort of civilised and visionary citizens, and although
I get the feeling that they are weary of dealing with the constant attacks
on all that is worthwhile about the place, I am confident that their
passion for Carrick will eventually win out. I left the town with a fasci-
nation, a sense of mild wonder, and not a little envy for its most impressive possession, its people, their sense of belonging and pride, their
character, and their freely offered friendliness.

The marina, Carrick on Suir

Chapter Six

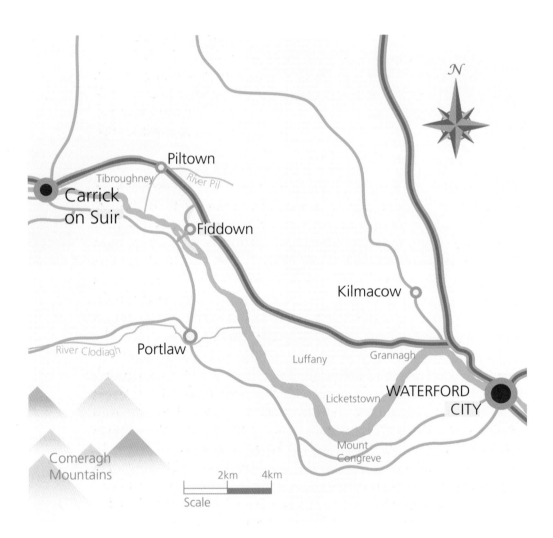

Carrick on Suir to Waterford

T HE SUIR FLOWS OUT OF CARRICK, weaving its way eastwards towards Waterford Harbour, hemmed in on the south side by high ground rich in prehistoric remains, including standing stones, chamber tombs and a gallery grave. On the north it is bordered by fertile grasslands so densely scattered with the remains of ancient villages, churches, castles and holy wells that it is clear it has been a well-populated landscape for millennia.

Up until recent years the catching of salmon by snap-netting – using two cots with a net between – was the popular way to catch the fish, a method that is mentioned in records that go back nine hundred years and more. It seems reasonable to imagine that long before any written records were kept, Ireland's prehistoric ancestors might have used similar methods and indeed similar craft to keep rich food on their tables. Recent European Union regulations brought all this to an end and the remaining cots are either lying derelict and rotting away on the banks of the river or are used as pleasure craft: I got the impression that all self-respecting Carrick men owned or shared the ownership of a river-worthy cot on the river.

Although the waters lapped right up to its walls in the sixteenth century, today a fringe of willows separate the castellated towers of Ormond Castle from the river. Below the castle the river is adorned with a necklace of willow-covered islands dividing it from Carrick's suburbs as it flows down to Roches Quay, one of the little harbours resorted to by pre-steam age commercial traffic when the tide prevented them getting boats up into the town. At one time there was a gaol here where prisoners who had been condemned to Van Diemen's Land were gathered to await shipment to Waterford and from there to the other side of the world.

The elegantly restored interior of Tibroughney Castle

A couple of kilometres east of Carrick the Lingaun tributary joins the Suir, and, about 135 kilometres from its source, the river finally flows out of the county of its birth, Tipperary, and continues as the border between the counties of Waterford and Kilkenny, and the provinces of Munster and Leinster. Downstream on the Kilkenny side, near an overgrown pier where I watched a young heron catch and swallow, with considerable difficulty it seemed, a large eel, stands Tibroughney Castle. Tibroughney is a very ancient and important site on the river Suir: scattered but scant remains of a monastic settlement are to be found here, the patron of which was St Mó-Dhomnóg of Bremor near Balbriggan in County Dublin. The only significant, upstanding remains of the settlement are those of a small, much later church standing in an old graveyard, in which can also be found a metre-high fragment of a high cross decorated with carved zoomorphic

Tibroughney Castle

(*Above*) Depiction of a
centaur on the Tibroughney
cross shaft

animals and sets of spirals. Nearby is Tober Fachtna, a holy well
dedicated to St Fachtna, a late sixth-century bishop who died at
Piltown in 590 AD, and from whom the name Tibroughney is
derived. An early nineteenth century description of the well says it
was formerly 'esteemed ... but is no longer so. This idle supersti-
tion of well-worship, derived from Scythian idolatry, and forbidden in
England by Saxon laws, may at last wear out in this country'.

Until the late seventeenth century there was an important river ford
here, one of the last such on the Suir before it reached the sea. It was of
such strategic importance that it was fortified about 1185 by the
construction nearby of a motte and bailey, part of Prince John's efforts
to protect the approaches to Norman city of Waterford. Not long after
that, Tibroughney was the site of a battle in which Domhnal Mór
O'Brien, king of Limerick, claimed a great victory over 'the people of the

son of the king of the Saxons, in which many foreigners were slain, along with the foster brother of the son of the king of the Saxons.'[1] The son of the king of the Saxons was Prince John, Earl of Morton, and his foster brother was son of Ranulf de Glanville, one of the Normans to whom John had granted the region of Ormond. Excavations carried out in 1856 during the construction of the nearby railway line exposed many human skeletons, no doubt some of the victims of Domhnal Mór.

The remains of the motte that Prince John built here can be found across the road from Tibroughney Castle, which itself was built about 1460. The density of remains of early buildings in the area suggests that this was once a busy place: the *Statistical Survey of the County of Kilkenny* of 1802 states that the foundations of a small Danish town were found here. This comment might not have been taken seriously by historians up until recently, but the discovery of a large early Viking settlement 15 kilometres downstream at Woodstown might put it in a different light.

Tibroughney Castle, with a modern house attached, stands in a large farmyard, and I was hovering about the gateway attempting to get a photograph of the castle, when a pretty young woman steering a wheelbarrow came along. Before I could apologise for my intrusion, she called 'Hello. Are you interested in the castle? Would you like to see it?'

She introduced herself as Daphne Dowley as we walked in towards the castle door, and hurried off to get an information sheet on the castle's history, leaving me in the company of a genial-looking Doberman pinscher. On a long chain, the dog proved to be as genial as she looked, and her only threat was her need to show affection for me by standing up on her hind legs, placing her front paws on my shoulders, and licking my face. As I tried to escape her friendly attentions, she circled me excitedly, threatening to trip me with her long chain, and so I danced about in a kind of Tibroughney version of the sword dance. I was mildly relieved when Daphne came back and ushered me in through the low, gothic-arched door of the castle, and via a tiny lobby into the ground floor room. This medieval chamber had been used as the kitchen of the nineteenth-century house that adjoins the castle up until recently, and it has been only a few decades since the rest of the castle was in

---

1. *Annals of Lough Cé* at Trinity College, Dublin.

domestic use. Daphne and her husband Louis have taken on the gargantuan task of refurbishing the castle and Louis had done most of the work himself, restoring the roof and rendering the external walls in lime render. As Daphne explained, it is still a work in progress. They are committed to the restoration of the castle, not because of its investment potential, but out of a sense of responsibility for a historic structure of which they found themselves the caretakers.

I have some experience of the restoration of medieval buildings, and was very impressed at what the Dowleys had achieved, while aware of the considerable additional work they face to finish the building to a modern residential standard without compromising its character. The rooms in the castle were generous, albeit mostly only one per floor, accessible by a narrow stone spiral staircase. Other than the fourth floor, which is vaulted in stone, and a tiny room on the third floor that looked as if it might have been a chapel, the floors are of timber, and are in very good condition. From the roof there was a great view all round – the Walsh Mountains line the horizon to the north-east: the adjacent ruined church and its tiny graveyard are hidden in a grove of trees close by. At low tide, a 'great rock', said to be the meeting point of the counties of Waterford, Tipperary and Kilkenny, is visible from the roof, exposed in the centre of the river.

I went down through the farmyard to see the ruins of the old church. It was much bigger than I had expected, and the overgrown graveyard is quite extensive. In its south-east corner I came across the carved 'pillar' that is described in some accounts of the place. It is clearly the bottom of the shaft of a high cross, and the archaeologist Etienne Rynne claims that it is an early one.[2] The carved decoration depicts deeply cut spiral designs on one face and stylised animals on the other. As I waited for the sun to give me some depth of shadow on the west side for a photograph, I noticed that one of the images on that face is clearly a naive depiction of a centaur, holding a sword in one hand and an archer's bow in the other. I was surprised at this because I hadn't noticed such an image on an Irish stone before. Later research told me that depictions of centaurs

---

2. M. Monk and J. Sheehan, eds., *Early Medieval Munster, Archaeology, History and Society*, Cork University Press 1998.

are rare in Ireland and for the best parallels for this particular image one must look to Pictish sculpture in Scotland, where centaurs are more common.[3] One wonders at the connection between this little church-yard in south Kilkenny and the enigmatic Picts, who seem to have disappeared from contemporary records in the early medieval period after five centuries of military and political power in Scotland.

Beside the Suir at Tibroughney until the late seventeenth century there was an extensive swamp until it was reclaimed, it is said, by a Colonel Axtell, a Cromwellian who was granted a large area of land here. Tall embankments, willow-crowned today, were built to hold back the river, and extensive green fields were created from marsh. The project was radical and very advanced for its time, and probably the first attempt at such reclamation work in the south of Ireland.[4] Some of the original marsh remains between the fields and the river, and I am told the remoteness and inaccessibility of this makes it a great wildlife habitat. Close to the nearby former hamlet of Ardcloyne is an old Gaelic place-name *Clais na nAlbanach*, or the Dyke of the Foreigner, which must refer to Axtell's work.

Ardcloyne was one of a number of fisher folk's villages along the Suir here, but today only a few of the old cottages are extant, and in such ruinous condition that it looks as if they will not last long. Replacing them is a small industrial estate of steel-clad factories.

⸻

Ireland was always a convenient battleground for English intrigues, and even England's War of the Roses reached over into the Irish countryside to this place in 1462. John Butler, 6th Earl of Ormond, was a supporter of the Lancastrian side in the war, and he brought a large contingent of English troops to Ireland to create a diversion and open a new front in the conflict that were raging across England and Wales. He increased his forces considerably by joining with Edmund McRichard Butler, and together they captured Waterford, where, to flush out Thomas, 8th Earl of Desmond, they made a prisoner of Garrett, his son. Their ploy was

3. Peter Harbison, *The High Crosses of Ireland*, Rudolf Habelt 1992.
4. *Statistical Survey of the County of Kilkenny 1802.*

effective, and the two sides agreed that, to settle the matter, they would have a pitched battle – an arranged contest between both armies drawn up in formation. The site agreed for the encounter was near Tibroughney, in Butler territory: the opposite bank of the river, across the ford, was Desmond territory.

Cottage at Ardcloyne

The date agreed for the battle was a Monday in August 1462, but when the time came, it emerged that the English soldiers whom the Earl of Ormond had brought over were not accustomed to fighting on a Monday, or indeed in the afternoon on any day. Ormond, realising that without them he would be fighting with a much reduced force, prevailed upon McRichard to postpone the battle, but McRichard refused.

The two opposing forces lined up near Rogerstown Castle, about a mile north of the Suir. As they clashed, the Butler force, without its English allies, gave way immediately. The Desmond forces drove the Butlers eastwards to the river Pil, a tributary of the Suir, across which there was at the time a narrow bridge. By this time the Butlers were in full rout, but couldn't get across the bridge fast enough: many were slaughtered while more, weighed down by their body armour, drowned in the little river. What remained of the Butlers fled towards the north-east and the Walsh Mountains, but they left nearly 500 dead on the field of battle. It is interesting to note that another, better-known battle, the battle of the Boyne, which took place 200 years later, was delayed for 24 hours because William of Orange was determined never to undertake anything on a Monday, and rejected the advice of his military men to attack the Jacobite forces across the Boyne on the evening of Monday, 30 June 1690.

Downstream from Tibroughney, as the river broadens and swings around a wide, majestic bend, the south bank rises steeply, a scattering of fields and farmhouses reaching uphill to a ridge covered with conifers. Fringed again with a thick curtain of willow, the Suir sweeps down past the meeting with the river Pil, which was navigable at one time up to the village of Piltown, a little more than a kilometre to the north. It is a place of substantial buildings that suggest a former importance, including Anthony's, a well-known hostelry that has been doing business here for more than two hundred years, and is still serving refreshments in comfortable surroundings.

The early name for the Piltown area, now reused in the name of the agricultural college here, is Kildalton. Sir John Ponsonby, another of the Cromwellian grantees of rich, fertile land along this part of the Suir, got a large estate north of the village of Piltown in return for raising and commanding a company of horse soldiers for Cromwell's use. Ponsonby changed the name of the area to Bessborough in honour of his wife Elizabeth, attracting the scorn of Jonathan Swift who railed about naming houses and estates after people's wives. Ponsonby, however, did well in post-Cromwellian Ireland, and by the time of his death had accumulated 6,500 acres of land: his great-great-granddaughter was Sarah Ponsonby, one of the two ladies of Llangollen.[5]

Bessborough House was designed by the Clare architect Francis Bindon and built in about 1744 in blue Kilkenny limestone. Like so many other great houses, it was burned by Anti-Treaty forces in 1923. Subsequently, partially restored, it was taken over in 1944 by the Oblate Fathers and converted into a seminary. Today it is an agricultural training college. One of the last of the Ponsonbys to live at Bessborough was

5. In 1776 Sarah Ponsonby and Lady Eleanor Butler formed an intense relationship and 'eloped' from Ireland to Llangollen in Wales, where they set up home together, inspired by Rousseau, seeking to establish a rural idyll. Witty and cultured, they entertained there many distinguished guests, such as William Wordsworth, Edmund Burke and Sir Walter Scott.

Myles Brabazon Ponsonby, born in 1881, who went to France in 1915 as a major in the Grenadier Guards. A memorial in the graveyard of Piltown church states that Ponsonby died there at the battle of Loos in September 1915, while 'gallantly leading his men'.

The rolling coutryside of the Curraghmore demesne

Opposite Piltown the south bank of the Suir rises steeply over 200 metres above sea level to Tower Hill, which overlooks the estate of the Beresford le Poers and the great house of Curraghmore, the home of the premier marquess in the peerage of Ireland, the Marquess of Waterford. Known locally as Lord Waterford, John Hubert de le Poer Beresford, 8th Marquess of Waterford, also holds the titles Earl of Tyrone, Viscount Tyrone, Baron Tyrone, Baron le Poer and Baron Beresford. His family has lived at Curraghmore since the twelfth century, and until 1999 he sat in the House of Lords.

The house at Curraghmore has grown out of a medieval towerhouse,

the old home of the Norman le Poers, and mainly dates from 1700, although there have been numerous alterations and additions over the years. With a central tower of five storeys flanked by a pair of two-storey wings, it is a tour-de-force of tiered pilasters, balustrades and parapets, a building one would not be surprised to come upon in France or Italy rather than Ireland. The estate, a typical English parkland of woods and hills, is 7,000 acres in extent, 4,000 of which are within the demesne walls. The gardens, which boast a wonderful shell house decorated in 1754 by Catherine le Poer, Countess of Tyrone, and the tallest tree in Ireland, a 50-metre sitka spruce that was planted in the 1830s, are open to the public, but the house, which has magnificent interiors, unfortunately is not.

Ponsonby Mausoleum at Fiddown

Downstream from Piltown, at Fiddown, a four-acre island divides the river. It was used until recently for the planting and harvesting of willow whips for cot-building and basketry. Today it is a wildlife reserve, providing asylum for a number of relatively uncommon birds, such as the elusive and secretive water-rail, small numbers of which breed in Ireland. Except for its long, sharp red beak, it is a bit like a corncrake, and until the 1950s used to be almost as common.

Opposite the eastern side of the bridge that spans the river and the island are the remains of a thirteenth-century church built on the site of a sixth-century monastery founded by St Mo-Medog, another well-travelled early Irish saint, having served in Scotland and France before coming here to the banks of the Suir. The old church was partially demolished in the mid-nineteenth century to create a mausoleum for the Ponsonby family. The funerary monuments commemorating the family in the mausoleum are particularly fine, but because the place is locked up one can get little other than a glimpse of them through grimy glass. In the graveyard is an obelisk marking the grave of Peter Walsh of Belline, who organised the roofing of the Friary at Carrick.

Below the bridge at Fiddown is Morris's oil depot, to which tankers used sail upstream to unload until 2007 when the construction work on Waterford's new bridge commenced. The route was discontinued temporarily for safety reasons, but some of the locals feel that it may not be reinstated when the construction work has been completed, and consequently the commercial use of the Suir above Waterford may have come to an end.

At Fiddown, 140 kilometres from its source, the Suir widens appreciably to become a broad waterway bordered by a thick forest of willows fronted in places by reeds which get more plentiful as the river proceeds towards Waterford. Like all rivers, the Suir has been much changed in the past century by the expansion of the built environment on land. In the old days much of run-off rain water – that is, water being shed off roofs and roads and paths – just ran into the ground, which slowly released the water into the river. Today all modern buildings, roads and carparks are connected to storm drains, which deposit water directly and immediately into the river, which can lead to weather-related flooding. Periodic discharges of large volumes of water like this have heavily eroded the riverbanks and washed away islands. One such island, downstream from Fiddown, has disappeared in recent decades.

A kilometre below Fiddown is Turkstown, the name of which may have originated as a term of derision directed at the planters who were settled there.[6] A famous and prodigious builder of fishing cots, Thomas Cuddihy was born at Turkstown in 1881 and carried out his craft here and at Piltown until his death in 1944. He left a marvellous legacy in the notebooks he filled with details of the construction of his craft,[7] and since there are relatively few records of the activities of the Suir cot

6. Owen O'Kelly, *The Place Names of the County of Kilkenny*, The Kilkenny Archaeological Society 1985.
7. Published in 2004 in facsimile form by Coracle Press under the title *Boats, Cots, Punts & Wherries*, through the offices of Shay Hurley.

Ruined gate lodge of
Mayfield Manor House

fishermen or their craft, these notebooks are a unique and marvellous resource. His father and uncle had been salmon fishermen,
but they were also known for the building and repairing of cots,
and Thomas and his brothers followed in their wake. Thomas expanded
his repertoire to include racing cots, punts and what he refers to as
pleasure boats, and has made a very large number of craft over the years:
his cots cost £4 each in the 1930s. He combined boat-building with
fishing and cot racing, and won the title of Champion of the Suir, Nore
and Barrow at the Waterford Regattas in 1909 and 1910.

Riverquarter and Clonmore on the Kilkenny bank are both sites of
old riverside villages, of which there were once many along this reach of

the Suir. Opposite Clonmore the manicured lands of the large estate of Mayfield or Rockett's Castle reach down to the river on the south bank. The picturesque five-storey round towerhouse at the river's edge is said to have been erected in the early thirteenth century on land that was assigned by King John to a Fitz Norman de la Rochell – hence the name Rockett. The story is told that Rockett's Castle was the base of an infamous pirate of the same name, one who robbed the rich English and gave to the poor Irish. A famous gallows tree on the Yellow Road in the south-west outskirts of medieval Waterford, where he is said to have been executed, was called Rockett's Tree.

The original manor house of Mayfield was established by the Cromwellian Algernon May of Sussex; it was close to the nearby town of Portlaw, which itself was originally called Mayfield. I am told that a previous owner, a Russian gentleman, extensively refurbished the house and grounds, establishing a lake between the house and the river. This estate is currently the home of Thomas and Rosemary Driver.

Below Rockett's Castle the wide Clodiagh river joins the Suir. The industrial village of Portlaw, founded by the Malcolmson family in the early nineteenth century to serve a cotton spinning industry is 2 kilometres upstream. The industry started small, supplying shops in Waterford and Clonmel, but the product was of such high quality, and the Malcolmsons' business acumen so enthusiastic, that within a few years they were exporting large quantities of finished cotton and calico to China, the United States, India and the colonies in general.

The Malcolmsons laid out a model village to accommodate their mill workers made up of housing blocks on a triangular plan, with the apexes of the triangles meeting at a large public plaza, a formal design more usually found, on the far larger scale albeit, in great cities like Rome or Paris. Beyond this plaza was the town's industrial centre. A bell was rung each morning at 6 o'clock to summon the workers, and it must have been quite a sight to see them coming down the radial streets, converging on the public space and moving together down to the factory. While it is a layout that owes much to city planners such as Hausmann, who laid out nineteenth-century Paris, it is interesting to note that such a plan allowed one policeman standing in the public plaza to monitor almost all movements in the town.

(*Left*) Rockett's Castle

Malcolmson's ideas for the town were based on the theories of Robert Owen, a Welsh ex-mill owner and social reformer, who encouraged a holistic approach to the establishment of manufactories that would cater for the health of the workers, their profit-sharing participation in the venture, the education of children, male and female, and thrift and cleanliness among all. The Malcolmsons believed in their workers being well looked after and sharing in their prosperity: a resident doctor was employed to serve the community, an early version of social insurance was set up, and after-hours educational facilities were provided for the mill workers.

The early houses built for the workers were two-storied, but later single-storey houses were used, each with four rooms and a dry closet privy at the back of the dwelling, a somewhat revolutionary modern convenience for working people at the time. What made the Portlaw houses unique were their curved roofs, made of a tar-covered fabric stretched over a wooden lattice structure: the tar was a by-product of the village gasworks. Their construction was so well thought out and practical that a large number of them are still in use today.

The factory complex the Malcolmsons erected, at the centre of a complex network of canals, weirs, water mills and weaving sheds, was an engineering wonder of its time. It is said that the roof of the main building, some 80 metres in length by 12 metres in width, was also a water reservoir: a flat structure achieving this kind of performance was certainly a spectacular feat of engineering.

The business thrived between 1825 and 1856, when 1,600 people were employed in Portlaw, and at its height, the factory was manufacturing 6 million yards of calico annually. Raw cotton, imported into Waterford, was barged up the Suir, the Clodiagh and then a short canal to the factory, and the finished cloth was barged downstream to Waterford for export. The shortcomings imposed on Ireland by the Westminster government, however, meant that the goods had to be shipped from Waterford to Liverpool first before being exported around the world.

Early twenty-first century globalisation, with its positive and negative influences on local economies in Ireland, is nothing new. A century and a half ago the American Civil War had a detrimental effect on the Malcolmson industrial empire, which, in addition to milling and linen, included shipping, ship-building and coal-mining in Germany. Malcolmson's ships had to run a naval blockade to obtain raw cotton from the southern states of America, and to continue to supply finished cotton. For much of these exports, particularly those involving the American southern states, the Malcolmsons were never paid, and when the Civil War ended, they were left with very large bad debts. To make matters worse, the United States then placed tariffs on cotton imports, and since Malcolmson was unable to compete with the much larger Lancashire mills, his main market disappeared. These and many other financial problems led to the bankruptcy of the family empire in 1874, and overnight everyone in Portlaw was plunged into unemployment: some of the workers, having been offered a financial interest in the business, had bought shares, and they lost their savings as well as their jobs. A great exodus of the menfolk took place to the Lancashire mills, where there was still plenty of work, and many never returned to County Waterford.

There was a brief reprieve for the town when a company called the Portlaw Spinning Company took over the factory, but when this closed in 1904, the population rapidly declined and grass grew in the once-bustling streets. Waterford historian Patrick Power stated in 1910 that the town's 'former prosperity is difficult to conceive by those acquainted only with its poverty of today, when the merry shuttle's song is replaced by the song of the wind through the tenantless streets'.

Portlaw remained in an impoverished state until a tannery was opened in the refurbished factory in 1935. The population increased again, and the town was a hive of activity for the next forty years. Then history began to repeat itself: tariffs and the global economy wore down the Irish leather industry, and in 1983 the workforce was hit again by redundancies. Many of the workers had no choice but go to England to try to find work. One woman remembers not being able to get used to the quietness, after decades of the early morning din of the hobnailed boots of the men going to work.

In spite of its history, there is a strong community spirit in the town, which is a bright and cheerful place today. Although many of the original houses have been refurbished in recent years, I was sad to find that, close by, the factory area, with its fine gatelodge and ironwork gates and what remains of Mayfield House, are in a pathetic state. Added to this is

a concern I heard voiced that the considerable amount of chemical waste, which was never disposed of after the tannery ceased operations, may be leeching into the Clodiagh river and the reservoirs that supply water to Waterford city. In architectural and social history terms alone, Portlaw deserves to be declared a heritage site, and concerted efforts should be made to save what is possible. It has sufficient characteristics to attract appropriate European funding, and its location at the centre of a handsome landscape should give it considerable tourism potential. Unfortunately, the state of national finances as I write suggests that there is little chance for a resurrection of Portlaw soon.

Downstream of the Clodiagh are the extensive Coolfin and Darrigal Marshes, reclaimed land that is very wet in wintertime and provides feeding for some of the largest flocks of greylag geese in the country. Opposite is Portnascully, an other-world cluster of old farm buildings around an ancient graveyard of large, leaning tombstones in serried rows. At Ballygorey, below Portnascully, the river swings southwards to pass around a hill that reaches 80 metres above the water, from where there are extensive views upstream which show what a majestic river the Suir is at this point. Ballygorey and its neighbouring hamlet, Luffany,

Thatched cottage at
Luffany

have a delightful collection of traditional thatched cottages: Luffany was formerly two hamlets, in one of which the farmers lived and in the other the farm labourers, and the Doyles and Dunphys of the neighbourhood were the backbone of Mooncoin hurling teams.

Opposite Moonveen, the most southerly point of County Kilkenny, is the townsland of Knockanagh, which Canon Power translates as 'Place abounding in hills'. It is a good description of the Waterford side of the river along here, which includes the demesne of Mount Congreve. The Congreves first appeared in the area in the middle of the seventeenth century, and in about 1721 Mount Congreve, a large three-storey, seven-bay house with three-bay wings, was built by John Congreve, High Sheriff of Waterford in 1755. The house was much remodelled in the nineteen sixties by Ambrose Congreve, who was born in 1907, educated in Eton and Cambridge, and served in the British Army in World War II. He became interested in gardening at the age of eleven, and except for his absences at college and in the war, has been hard at work developing the gardens at Mount Congreve ever since. The estate comprises over 700 acres, 100 acres of which Congreve has, with the assistance of his late head gardener, Dutchman Herman Dool, transformed into one of the finest gardens in Europe. Sixteen miles of paths weave through this garden landscape, much of it a woodland of great trees planted in the eighteenth and nineteenth centuries. Included is the largest collection of magnolias in the world, and there are 3,000 varieties of rhododendron and 600 of camelias. More than a hundred people are employed in the nursery attached to the estate, and 66 acres, the most important part, will be left to the nation on Ambrose Congreve's passing. He seems to be in no hurry, however: at time of writing he is 101 years of age.

After Mount Congreve, the Suir passes into the Long Reach (or as it is wryly known in bad weather, the long retch), which runs downstream as far as Grannagh Castle and which can be very difficult in certain weather conditions, particularly when the tide is rising in its mid-range and the wind is from the east. At Mount Congreve, although the Suir is, as the crow flies, within ten kilometres of the sea at Tramore, it has more than 30 kilometres to flow before it reaches the Atlantic. In the area between the river and the sea, stretching from Waterford Harbour west towards the Comeraghs, there is much evidence of considerable human settlement in prehistoric times, the earliest dating from about 7,000 years ago during the period called the Late Mesolithic. The Neolithic and early Bronze Age periods are represented by an unusual density of fine Megalithic tombs built over a period of millennia when the area was densely inhabited and cultivated by a people who were organised and secure enough to have the time and resources to build these non-essential structures. Similar tombs found in the Scilly Isles suggest that the same people occupied both places at one time.

At the Long Reach the Suir swings around through almost ninety degrees and flows north-east, forming a triangle of land bounded on two sides by the river and on the third by the main Limerick road, the N24. The remote nature of this triangle ensured that it was slow to progress into the twentieth century, and it managed to keep much of what was good about its vernacular farms and cottages. A century ago there were four extensive farm villages in this triangle, Portnahully, Ballygorey, Doornane and Licketstown, that were made up of clusters of small farmhouses at right angles to each other, creating enclosed courtyards. Although of the others only fragments remain, at Licketstown much of the traditional farmstead layouts survive, reinforced in recent years by the influx of a new generation of young people who value the traditional architecture.

At the time of writing, both banks of the Suir bordering the Long Reach were like a great building site, while roads serving the new bridge were being constructed. Large orange and yellow road-building machinery crawled over the landscape like great insects as clouds of dust rose from gargantuan excavation works. At one stage in June 2008 this frenetic progress was briefly interrupted by a happening straight out of Kitty the Hare stories in the *Our Boys* magazine. In the Mullinabro district, north of the river, locals were kept awake at night by the terrible screeching of a banshee: the *Munster Express* reported one frightened resident as saying, 'One night last week the screeching was so terrible that my skin crawled and the hair stood on the back of my neck'. Local folklore tells of a young man named Jones returning home from a night's drinking in Waterford, finding the gate to his home locked, and attempting to jump it on his horse. The horse refused, and the man was thrown and impaled on the gatepost. His heartbroken sister declared that the gate should never be opened again, and vowed that if it were, her spirit would come back to haunt and torment the area. Apparently the cursed gate remained locked and overgrown until construction workers building the new road started to bulldoze it out of the way. The *Munster Express* reported that, on being told the story by locals, the workers stopped work, but a few days later, another team came and removed the gate and the copse of trees near it called Jones's Wood. A member of the nearby golf club told the newspaper: 'Most people, including myself, would laugh at such stories and at the superstitious people who believe in them. That said, after what I experienced the other night, I wouldn't walk home from the club after dark on my own. I still don't believe in banshees, but there are some things best left alone.'

During the course of excavation work on the new roads here, a major Viking settlement, predating the city of Waterford, was discovered at Woodstown. In the ninth century the broad estuary of Waterford Harbour provided a safe haven for plundering Scandinavian seafarers, and when they sailed upriver they found that the Suir, Barrow and Nore rivers gave them entry deep into the interior. The Viking longship was a masterful design. Fast and light and with a very shallow draught, it was not only eminently seaworthy, but capable of sailing inland to explore every river and shallow tributary in search of wealth. The northerners carried out their plundering campaigns during the mild and calm days of spring and summer, usually returning home to enjoy their spoils through the winter. Eventually, however, they began to establish settlements so that they could winter in Ireland rather than undertake the long voyage northwards, and Woodstown was probably one of these winter havens. From such settlements, which they fortified with timber palisades, the Vikings sailed their craft each spring to sea again and also farther inland to continue their business of pillaging wealthy and defenceless monastic settlements.

For a century or more, the old Gaelic monasteries were terrorised by raiding Scandinavians seeking slaves, gold and silver; valuable books that were looted were usually torn out of their jewelled covers and dumped in the sea. This little quatrain written by a monastic scribe in the margin of a ninth-century manuscript portrays the fear engendered by the raiders, and the comfort monks found in stormy weather:

> Fierce and wild is the wind tonight,
> It tosses the tresses of the sea to white;
> On such a night as this I take my ease;
> Fierce Northmen only course the quiet seas.

As years went by, however, the Scandinavians became more settled, marrying into the local populace, and eventually peaceful trading took the place of violent robbery. From the late ninth century onwards, they became commercially involved with the indigenous rural population as they bought and sold goods, and socially as they intermarried and formed familial links.

From the archaeological digs that have taken place since the discovery of Woodstown in 2004, it is clear that it was once a busy place, but it seems that it was abandoned about the year 1050. After a few centuries, the existence of the settlement was even lost to local folklore and memory, and remained so until it was discovered during road-building.

———

As the Suir sweeps around another sharp bend and flows towards the

south-east, it passes Grannagh Castle on the Kilkenny shore. Located where it is, with a clear view of three miles of the river to the west and a direct line-of-sight to the walls of the medieval city, the castle would have been a first line of defence of Waterford from enemies to the west who might approach on the river. The old name of the site on which the castle was built was Dun Bhrain, or Brann's Fort, and it was common for the Normans to build their fortifications over earlier Gaelic forts, either because of the strategic location or to emphasise the establishment of the new order. The three great drum towers of Grannagh reaching out of the waters of the Suir suggest an early thirteenth-century date, but we know that the central keep was erected towards the end of the fourteenth century, probably by James Butler, 3rd Earl of Ormond. Perhaps the most famous of its inhabitants were Piers Butler, a claimant of the Earldom of Ormond, and his wife, Margaret Fitzgerald.

Grannagh Castle

As we have seen, being a Butler did not necessarily mean wealth. The early married life of Piers Butler and his wife, in the last years of the fifteenth century, was beset with difficulties: Margaret's father, the Great Earl, was in the Tower of London accused of treason, and Piers, in his attempts to establish his claim to the Ormond title, came into conflict with Sir James Ormond, the illegitimate son of the 6th Earl, who committed him to gaol. Even after his release, Sir James hounded and hunted the couple, and they found themselves, with Margaret pregnant, penniless and on the run. However, one day when Piers was out searching for food for his wife, he met Sir James travelling on horseback without his bodyguard, and without hesitation he charged and ran him through with a spear. With his persecutor out of the way, things immediately improved for Piers and his wife, with Piers being made a Royal Commissioner, then Seneschal (representative of the crown) for Tipperary and eventually, in 1538, he became the 8th Earl of Ormond. While Piers was making his way gingerly through the enormously complicated and very often dangerous minefield that was succession in those days, Margaret, known for her man-like stature and 'stoutness', was kept busy. She was a remarkable woman for her time and took a central role in the building of Ballyragget Castle and Balleen Castle, the rebuilding of Gowran Castle and the refurbishing of Grannagh Castle, in addition to founding Kilkenny Grammar School and beautifying Kilkenny Castle, for which she imported craftsmen from Europe. There is a possibility that she was instrumental in the donation to the clergy of Waterford of a spectacular set of sixteenth-century embroidered High Mass vestments which were rediscovered in Christ Church cathedral in the city in 1774. In an interesting ecumenical gesture for the time the then Protestant bishop of Waterford presented the vestments to the Catholic dean of Waterford.

While they had many homes, Grannagh seems to have been a favourite of the Ormonds, and they are said to have entertained there in a grand manner in the great hall of the castle. Its proximity to one of Ireland's busiest trading ports made it an important seat, because a large percentage of Piers's income came from wine imports. For centuries Grannagh also controlled a valuable ferry service to the south bank, one of the main entries to Waterford City from the north. Sessions of the feudal manorial court were held in the castle, when the seneschals and sergeants of the manor sat in judgment on a wide range of crimes. Tradition has it that Margaret personally supervised the sentencing to death of a group of rebels, and the sentence was carried out by hanging them from a window of the castle. Piers and Margaret are buried in a fine tomb in St Canice's Cathedral in Kilkenny, where their effigies seem to suggest that she was as tall, if not taller, than her husband.

Grannagh Castle was reduced severely during the wars of the seventeenth century, and, according to its owner in 1837, George Roche, 'despoiled ... by the thoughtless neighbouring peasantry'. He did some repairs at that time, and it has changed little since, remaining a most picturesque ruin. It has some good surviving details, including an oriel window with decorative carvings, and the stone plaque erected by George Roche, which someone, maybe one of the 'neighbouring peasantry', felt so strongly about that he censored it by chisel.

Just below Grannagh the great new road bridge across the Suir was under construction at the time of writing, and the lofty concrete pylon that would eventually carry the cables suspending the bridge looked like some War of the Worlds monster just about to stride across the river. Below the bridge the river Blackwater joins the Suir from the north. On its way south through County Kilkenny, the Blackwater gathers a series of strong tributaries, and it seems certain that mills were established on the river as far back as the seventh or eighth century. By the eighteenth century there were fourteen watermills on the Blackwater, mainly at Kilmacow, 3 kilometres north of Grannagh. Kilmacow and the surrounding area sit on a bed of limestone close to the surface, and this fact, together with easy access to the Suir by way of the Blackwater made this limestone a valuable commodity. The rock was extracted from as many as 43 separate quarries, supplying lime to Waterford and Wexford for fertilizer, whitewashing and limestone blocks for building. Towards the end of the nineteenth century there were as many as 300 people working in the quarries in this area, and more involved in the transportation of the limestone by river: the busyness of the place at the time gave it the name 'Little America'.[8]

North-east of Grannagh is the hamlet of Dunkitt. In the overgrown

---

8.   Kathleen Laffan, *The History of Kilmacow*, private, 2005.

Tombstone in Dunkitt graveyard

churchyard there you will find a tombstone of 1733 with a fine cruci-fixion scene, and the burial place of the antiquarian John O'Dono-van, whose influence and learning is still felt today in Irish scholarship. He was born into a poor rural family in 1806 at Attaeemore, nearly 6 kilometres north-east of Dunkitt. When he was eleven, his father died and he went to live with an older brother, William, who worked a small farm nearby. William must have regarded education as important, because, although poor, he managed to send John to school in Waterford. Inspired by what he learned there, John returned to his native place at the age of sixteen, and set up his own hedge school. A couple of years later his brother took a job in Dublin, and John went with him, and there attended a school of classics. At the age of twenty-one he got a job working with the Commissioner of Public Records, where his grasp of the Gaelic language was found to be very useful. When Thomas Larcom, one of the most influential organisers of the Ordnance Survey of Ireland, was seeking a tutor to teach him Gaelic, O'Donovan, in peasant garb it is said, turned up at his home to give him lessons. His contact with Larcom was greatly important for his career: at the age of twenty-six, encouraged by Larcom, he joined the ground-breaking topographical department of the Survey of Ireland, and it was there he began his enormous contribution to Irish historical research.

O'Donovan travelled all over Ireland collecting information on place-names, traditions, topography and antiquities, and reporting back to headquarters in a series of letters, which, assembled, are called the O'Donovan Letters, probably the most comprehensive extant body of Irish topographical information. He was outgoing and humorous, and had little difficulty striking up conversation with rural people and eliciting topographical information without encouraging suspicion.

O'Donovan published many works on a wide range of subjects, but his greatest was probably his translation and editing of the *Annals of the Kingdom of Ireland*, published in 1848. The original Annals, which recorded events of significance that occurred in Ireland from earliest times to the seventeenth century, were assembled and compiled in Gaelic by a group of monks in the 1630s. O'Donovan is said to have commented: 'we live in such an atmosphere of antiquarianism that one thousand years seem like the other day'. John O'Donovan's energy and output were prodigious, and when he died aged fifty-five in 1861, he left a legacy in Irish topography, history, language and genealogy that has never been surpassed.

———

A short distance below the new bridge is the second last bridge on the Suir, locally known as the Red Bridge, a steel-girdered railway crossing built in 1906 to connect the Rosslare to Waterford line with the Dungarvan line. Its name derived from the red lead that it was painted with to

prevent corrosion, but today its red colour has bleached to a rusty grey, it is and long disused and without a centre span. Here the Suir narrows to a little over 200 metres, to pass through a gap it has carved between two hills that reach to over 60 metres above the water.

That on the south bank is called Gibbet Hill, for it is to this eminence, a suitable distance outside of the city, that prisoners sentenced to death by Waterford courts were brought to be executed. This name is forgotten in Waterford today and the eminence is widely known as Bilberry Rock. The hill on the northern bank is known as Mount Misery, the origin of which is lost in the mists of time. The tops of both hills are crowned with tall steel pylons carrying high tension electricity cables across the river from Leinster into Munster.

The Suir enters the city of Waterford between these two hills, passing the sheds of the old foundry and a ship's graveyard that is a study in corroding dereliction. Modern Waterford is heralded by the gleaming, curving façade of the Guinness plant on the southern bank: the new railway station planned on the north bank opposite it will be just as modern when it is eventually built. Passing these, the Suir flows under the last of its many bridges, and in the words of the poet Spenser, 'adorns rich Waterford'.

(*Top, previous page*) New Waterford bridge behind the oldRed Bridge and derelict diesel engine

(*Above*) The new Waterford Bridge under construction

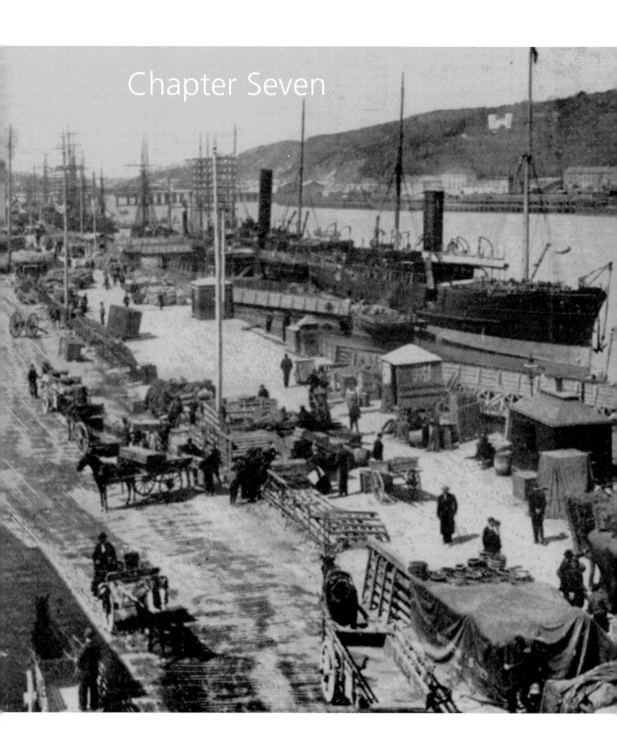

Chapter Seven

The Suir at Waterford City

TRAVELLERS ARRIVING at Sallypark, on the north bank of the Suir just above Waterford Bridge, are presented with a classic view of the city. The gleaming silver curved façade of the Guinness plant leads the eye to the low-slung bridge, and on to the pleasant scale, informality and colour of the houses and shops spread along its mile-long quays, which locals name in the singular as The Quay, and which historian Mark Girouard claimed in *Country Life* in the late 1960s was 'the noblest quay in Europe'. In those pre-prosperity days, there was a tired grandeur about the Victorian façades, and traffic and parking was slight, but it must have been hard to ignore the jumble of dock buildings and the container cranes that lined the river. French traveller the Chevalier de La Tocnaye commented on the paraphernalia of the port when he wrote in 1798, however, that the Quay 'might be a very ornamental feature had the authorities not thought fit to place some boat-building yards on it, along with several tasteless sheds for the public service'.

When Waterford Port moved downstream and out of the city in recent decades and a marina was established with pleasure boats and yachts replacing the cargo ships along the Suir, there was for a brief time an opportunity to transform the former docks, the margin between the road and the river, into a wonderful urban riverside park. But no, the motor car god had to be bowed to and celebrated, and the riverside strip was turned instead into a lucrative carpark, and so it will remain until the day, maybe not so far in the future, when the oil runs out.

At the bridge of Waterford the Suir is 300 metres wide, and has

(*Left*) The busy Quay at Waterford, c.1900

flowed 165 kilometres from its source in County Tipperary, negotiating routes around three mountain ranges and gathering many tributaries along the way. The river does not flow through, but majestically by the city of Waterford, because the bulk of the city lies along its southern bank. With the exception of a small enclave called Ferrybank, the land to the north of the river is in County Kilkenny. Until very recently Kilkenny County Council did not seem inclined to either hand over land to Waterford or go to the expense of providing the kind of infrastructure that would be required for a city the size of Waterford to expand naturally. With difficult topography west of the bridge, the city, therefore, has had to expand, awkwardly, to the south and east.

The history of Waterford, Ireland's first true city, it is said, is a long and chequered one, and the Suir has always played a central role in it. It is likely that the Vikings established a winter haven on the triangle of land between the Suir and its last large tributary, St John's Pill, some time in the ninth century. Before long the place became a permanent settlement which they called Vedrafjordr, from the old Norse meaning 'stormy weather haven'. It seems that this settlement was fortified by 860, when the Gaelic clans the Eoganachta and the Araid Cliach had a pitched battle nearby with the Scandinavians, during which they were driven back into what the annals describe as 'a small place with strong fortifications around it', which the Irish called Port Lairge or Loch Dacheach.[1] It may well be that engagements of this kind made the territory west of Waterford untenable, and caused the previously mentioned settlement at Woodstown to be abandoned. By early in the tenth century, Waterford was well established and there are frequent references in the annals to Waterford Scandinavians carrying out raids into Ossory and as far away as Kildare, Dublin and Meath.

It is likely that the town was fortified with masonry walls by the eleventh century, a sign that it was becoming wealthy enough to be a target itself for raiders, and that by this time the Scandinavians had established Waterford as a significant commercial and trading centre. As the closest ship haven to Wales, the south of England, France and Spain, Waterford became one of Ireland's principal ports.

The fortifications of Waterford, in which the Suir played a major part, made it a difficult city to take, but in 1170 the Normans, after two failed attempts, burst through a breach in the walls and took the city after a bloody siege. They recognised early the strategic and commercial importance of the city and Waterford Harbour: the Barrow could be followed into the heart of Leinster, and the Suir would take them through the fertile lands of north-west Munster to the borders of the kingdom of Limerick. Soon after the Normans had established themselves in Waterford, they extended and strengthened the walls and fortifications and reconstructed the iconic Reginald's Tower, on the site of a tower built by Reginald the Dane in the eleventh century.

Although it relied on the country to the west, accessed easily by way of the Suir for its raw materials, Waterford was physically cut off from the rest of Ireland by the same river. For the early centuries of the conquest,

---

1   Joan Radner, ed. *Fragmentary Annals of Ireland*, Dublin Institute for Advanced Studies, 1978.

heavily fortified, it operated much like an island city state, and certainly commerce with England and the Continent would have been far more influential to the development of the city than that with Dublin and the rest of the east coast of Ireland. The leading citizens of the medieval city were highly educated and cosmopolitan, travelling frequently to culturally and technologically advanced places such as Flanders, Portugal and Spain, as well as to England. Their experience of these other cultures must have had an important influence on the development of Waterford.

The view of Waterford from across the river of about 1370 is a copy by the artist du Noyer of an illustration in the fourteenth-century Waterford Charter Roll, and shows a substantial, colourful city surrounded by fortified walls. The fish depicted in the river are clearly salmon, and of the four ships shown, two, those with forecastles, are probably warships.*

The loyalty of the citizens of Waterford to the English crown was well secured by the fifteenth century: the inhabitants by that time were mainly Irish, English or of English or French descent, and although the English were dominant, progressive Irish well knew that co-operation with the English would ensure their own prosperity. By the end of the fifteenth century the Irish formed the backbone of the city's trade as craftsmen, artists, artificers and merchants, with names such as Teig Carroll, who founded the Weavers' Guild of the city, and Teig Breack, who founded the Shoemakers' Guild, and Donogho O'Fyne, Master of the Incorporation of Guilds clearly show.[2] Such was the desire of the authorities to encourage the Irish that laws were passed which even included a fine of thirteen shillings and fourpence to be imposed on anyone who cursed, defamed or despised any person of Irish birth. In addition, the Irish population seems to have been allowed its own courts and judges. This liberalism helped to ensure a supply of essential raw materials and labour from the Irish-held hinterland, but dealing with those whom the crown regarded as traitors, to provide the wherewithal to export goods to the crown involved treading a diplomatic tightrope.

A copy by du Noyer of a detail on the Waterford Charter Roll depicting the city and river in the fourteenth century R.S.A.I.

---

* George Vincent du Noyer (1817-1869) travelled widely during his work for the Ordnance Survey and the Geological Survey of ireland during the mid-nineteenth century, and produced a prodigious amount of drawings and paintings of people and places..

---

2   Alice Stopford Green, *The Making of Ireland and its Undoing*, Macmillan 1913.

Enshrined in the laws of the city was a fifteenth-century version of a mission statement, declaring the city 'consisteth, and always did consist, of traffic and merchant trade...',[3] and certainly the Waterford of the time was successful in trade: it became widely famous for its cloaks and rugs, and its linen and woollen goods were generally regarded as the best produced in Ireland.

Being a seaport, the openness of Waterford to international trade meant that it was vulnerable to the various plagues and diseases that were rife in Europe in the Middle Ages. The Corporation often blamed these afflictions on another characteristic of a typical seafaring town: prostitution. At one stage in the sixteenth century this belief was recorded in the civic records as 'the maiestie of Almyghtie god might be most offended whose iust indignacion and plague is most commonly provoked by the filthy dissolute life of such as abandon them selfe to that abhomynable trade of horedome...' It was further decided that the problem essentially arose from the use of serving women in the wine taverns, who were often 'nawtie corrupte women', and an ordnance was enacted to exclude 'any woman maide wife wench or wyddowe' owning or serving in such taverns.[4]

Two incidents at the end of the fifteenth century confirmed the loyalty of Waterford to the crown. In 1487 Lambert Simnel, who claimed right to the English throne, landed in Dublin with an army of 2,000 men. When his Irish supporters had him crowned Edward VI on 24 May in Christ Church in Dublin, there was a strong reaction from Ireland's second city. John Butler, the Mayor of Waterford, sent a messenger to Dublin with a letter refusing allegiance to Simnel, and declaring that all those who supported him were traitors. The messenger was hanged, an action that is said to have led to the coinage of the phrase 'killing the messenger'. Thus rebuffed, however, Simnel sailed to England and was defeated in battle on 16 June. Ten years later, when another pretender, Perkin Warbeck, who claimed to be Richard IV, tried to take Waterford in a backdoor effort to consolidate his power in Ireland in 1497, the citizenry soundly repulsed his forces. These two expressions of loyalty gained the

---

3   Alice Stopford Green, *The Making of Ireland and its Undoing*, Macmillan, 1913.
4   Niall J. Byrne, ed., *Liber Antiquissimus Civitatis Waterfordiae*, Irish Manuscripts Commission, 2007.

gratitude of Henry VII, who gave the city its motto Urbs Intacta Manet Waterfordia, which means 'Waterford remains the untaken city'.

In the early sixteenth century, at a time when English influence and power was at low ebb in Ireland, Waterford contrived to retain its loyal reputation while doing its utmost to shake off royal influence and power in its affairs and striving to retain its autonomy. As the authority of the English crown began to be impressed on Ireland under Elizabeth I, the continued existence of almost autonomous enclaves such as Waterford was frowned upon by London, particularly if they were unwilling, as Waterford was, to support the crown by providing soldiers for the continuing war against the Irish. When Sir Henry Sidney, Elizabeth's Deputy in Ireland, came to Waterford and asked for 300 men for his army, he was royally entertained to a rich banquet by the mayor and corporation, but left with no soldiers. In spite of all, Waterford continued to be a very busy port and by the late sixteenth century handled most of Munster's trade, and even took overland goods from Limerick and Galway.[5] Sir George Carew, Elizabethan soldier and administrator, wrote in the 1590s that 'there is more shipping in that harbour than in any part of Ireland.'

As time went on, however, a succession of mayors were accused of bad governance, selling wine to the rebel Irish and allowing Papists, 'the most arrogant Papists that live in this state' as a later Lord Deputy claimed, to practise their religion in public. The crown found many means over time to indicate its displeasure with Waterford, including the persuasion of English merchants to avoid trading with Waterford, and the city began to decline.

Aided by 500 Ulstermen, led by Owen Roe O'Neill, the citizens of Waterford repulsed Cromwell's first attempt to take the city in November 1649: his troops were wet and miserable and weakened by disease, and the failure must have been partly instrumental in Cromwell ending his first visit to Ireland when he lifted the siege after eight days and sailed out of Waterford Harbour to return to England. He came back to Ireland the following May, and again failed to take the city, but the siege dragged on until August when the citizens of Waterford finally surrendered to General Ireton on honourable terms. Cromwell appointed commis-

---

5   C. Brady & R. Gillespie, eds., *Natives and Newcomers*, Irish Academic Press, 1986.

sioners to govern the city, but by the end of the Cromwellian wars, commerce was almost non-existent, and it remained moribund for the next couple of decades.

After the many wars of the seventeenth century, the eighteenth began peacefully for Waterford, and trade began to increase again, particularly in wool and butter. Up until that time the shipping quay had extended from Reginald's Tower west as far as the clock tower, divided from the city by the old medieval defensive walls. The only surviving footprint of this riverside city before the wall came down can be found in Coffeehouse Lane, a narrow street just behind the Quay, its name redolent of the time at the end of the seventeenth century when coffeehouses were enjoying great popularity.

The Quay was extended westwards about 1700, and a sign of how optimistic its citizens were for the future was the demolition in about 1711 of the old defensive walls along the river, opening up the city to the Suir for the first time. The rubble was used as a foundation for a new

Remains of an Elizabethan window, Waterford

(*Above*) Fisher's view of Waterford Quay from the East (Courtesy of Peter Carroll)

40-foot wide, paved Quay that stretched the length of the city, faced on the river side by a substantial harbour wall. A new Exchange building was erected where the business of the port could be transacted, and conduits were laid conveying fresh water to the quayside for the provisioning of the ships. An engraving by Giles King depicting the Quay as it was in 1746, from Charles Smith's book on Waterford of the same date,[6] shows the river lined with a variety of fine merchants houses, some four-storied, some with Dutch gables and other with Jacobean features. Half way along the Quay is the colonnaded Custom House, behind which the domed tower of the Exchange can be seen. It is clear that Waterford had by this time become the most impressive port in Ireland: the agriculturalist Arthur Young, on his tour in Ireland in 1776, described the Quay as: 'the finest object in this city – it is an English mile long, and unrivalled by any I have seen'.

In the days of sail, with no radio communications and total dependence on favourable winds, travel by sea was very often a hazardous

6   Charles Smith, *The Antient and Present State of the County and City of Waterford*, 1746.

affair. Laconic columns in the local news section of the *Waterford Herald* of the late eighteenth century give a vivid picture of the uncertainties brought about by spells of stormy weather and by the wars with France, for seafarers and also for their loved ones at home.

Many ships simply disappeared, with the loss of all hands and passengers, in winter storms, and even for those who avoided death, their experience of bad weather at sea cannot be imagined. A newspaper report of 1792 referred to the Ponsonby Packet, the regular mail and passenger boat between Milford Haven and Waterford, enduring a rough passage across St George's Channel which ended with what must have been a terrifying four hours beating three miles up Waterford harbour from Hook to Duncannon into an ebb tide and a gusting headwind. The report stated that the passengers, who included the Herberts from Carrick, parents of Dorothea Herbert, had to be put ashore at Duncannon because of the conditions, which suggests that they must have been very sick indeed. In favourable weather, however, there were times when mails were carried at such speed that a letter posted in London could be delivered in Waterford as little as sixty hours later.

The war with France and the activities of privateers – privately owned warships licensed to capture enemy shipping for profit – hunting the shipping lanes for defenceless merchant ships were added hazards during the 1790s. Ships captured by a French privateer were usually given a scratch crew and sailed to ports in France, where the surviving crew and passengers were ransomed. There are many reports of ships leaving Waterford but not reaching their destinations, and whether a ship had been lost to the sea or to the French might not be known for some time, as these two reports in the *Waterford Herald* of 1792 make clear:

> April 27 The *Triton*, Captain Richardson, sailed from this port for England several weeks past, has not been since heard of – It is generally apprehended that she has fallen into the hands of the French.

> April 30 The *Triton*, Captain Richardson, from this port to London, we are sorry to find has been taken and sent into Dieppe, by a French Privateer of eight carriage guns and 33 men called the *Ami de Loix*, Captain Scorry ... the *Ami de Loix* likewise took, on the fourteenth, a transport called the *William* of and from Dublin, bound for Chatham, having on

board 112 soldiers, 9 women and 18 seamen...the privateer was, on April 22, captured by *The Hound* Revenue Cutter, and sent into Shoreham.

Engraving of Waterford from 1746

In spite of such hazards, the last decades of the eighteenth century saw a great increase in shipping activity at Waterford, and increasing prosperity for the city came in its wake. An indication of the level of urbanity of the better-off populace of the south of the country at the time is suggested by a list of the wines available from one Waterford importer in 1791, which included 'Claret, Port, Methuen, Red and White Hermitage, Sparkling and Red Champaigne [*sic*] Burgundy, Madeira, Paxeretta, Sherry, Lunel, Sauterne, Frontiniac, Carcavella and Vin de Grave'. Exports being shipped out of Waterford at the same time to London, Liverpool and Newfoundland included pork, beef, bacon, rye and butter.

In 1783 a Quaker uncle and nephew, George and William Penrose, established a glass factory at the west end of the Quay. The quality of the glassware they produced made the name of Waterford known world-wide. They invested nearly £10,000 in setting up the business, an astonishing sum for the time, and brought in upwards of fifty glass-makers from England to work in their factory. Within a couple of years the fame of Waterford lead crystal was such that the factory was visited by Prince William Henry, the future George IV, the first of many tourists, and he watched two very elaborate chandeliers being manufactured for the Irish House of Lords in Dublin.

Plain glassware was made, as well as lead crystal, and the export figures from the Penrose factory are an example of what Irish industry could do without British protectionist tariffs. By the 1790s, glassware was being exported to places such as Madeira, Portugal, Jersey, Newfoundland, France and Barbados: in 1793, 11,200 drinking glasses were exported to the Canadian Hudson Bay Company, and 36,000 sent to New York. Five years later annual exports to Pennsylvania came to 57,000 glasses and to Virginia 73,000 glasses.

The Penroses sold their factory in 1799, and it continued under new ownership to greatly expand its exports in plain and ornamental glassware. In 1825, the British parliament enacted excise regulations which sounded the death-knell, yet again, for Irish glass manufacture and export. The Waterford factory struggled on through different ownerships until it finally closed in 1851, the same year that its crystalware won several gold medals at the Great Exhibition in London.

In 1950 the Waterford Crystal brand was revived by 1916 veteran and entrepreneur Joe McGrath. He took part in the rebellion in 1916 and was subsequently jailed in England. Back in Ireland, he was elected for Sinn Féin in the 1918 general election. In the Free State government he served as Minister for Labour and Minister for Industry and Commerce, but resigned in 1924 and went into business. Initially he worked as an advisor to Siemens, the German firm that built the Ardnacrusha hydroelectric scheme, but is best known for his involvement in the setting up of the Irish Free State Hospitals' Sweepstake in 1930. The Sweep, as it became known, was a national lottery that supplied much-needed finance for the development of Irish hospitals, and it was enormously successful, particularly in the United States and Britain, where lotteries were illegal. In my youth, winning the Sweep was everyone's ambition, and the prizes amounted to life-changing amounts of money. Large sums were collected from abroad, where countless Irish emigrants had tickets supplied to them from home. McGrath and his partners were spectacularly good at marketing the lottery and giving it great respectability, and by 1932, in the middle of the Great Depression, the annual income to Ireland from the Sweep was higher than the national income-tax receipts, and before long McGrath was earning the equivalent of £1 million per year from the business.

In 1950 McGrath brought Czech artisans to Waterford to give a boost to his glass bottle factory there, and to pioneer the techniques in glass manufacture and decoration which had been lost for over a hundred years. Before long the brand was again internationally known, and a good foothold was established in the US, but exports there expanded dramatically when Jacqueline Kennedy, who was staying at Woodstown House in 1967, visited the factory and ordered chandeliers for the Kennedy Centre in New York. In recent years, however, the fall in value in the dollar is one of the factors that has led to the reduction in production of crystal in Waterford, and an increase in the Czech Republic, the home of the original artisans, and at time of writing the future for the Waterford plant looks poor.

Another export from Waterford at the end of the eighteenth century was people – Irish men and women and children who were leaving Ireland for England and the New World to escape poverty. There was a large, seasonal exodus of young men to Newfoundland where they could earn good money in the fishing trade. Arthur Young reported in 1776 that upwards of three to five thousand such workers were shipped out of the harbour annually. The rich fishing grounds of the Grand Banks, east and south of Newfoundland, had been discovered in the sixteenth century, and had attracted fishing fleets from Britain and Ireland, and particularly from Waterford. Fishing fleets would set sail westwards in April of every year to harvest the glut of fish and return in the autumn, but on occasion fishermen wintered over in Newfoundland. Many of them settled there, working at gutting and drying cod or acquiring a small farm of land and carrying on the farming they had been brought up to. Today, 85 percent of the citizens of Newfoundland of Irish descent can trace their roots back to Waterford, Wexford, Kilkenny or Tipperary, and certainly up until recently, older residents still spoke with the accents of these counties.

By the 1790s, as would befit a prosperous riverine city, the Corporation had built a ceremonial barge which was used for special occasions such as the annual boat races, when rowing boats owned by local worthies raced on the Suir for valuable prizes. There were two main races in this regatta: one for four-oared boats and another for six-oared boats; the first prize was a silver cup valued at seven guineas and the second a cup valued at three guineas, not insignificant money at the time. The specifications for the competing boats were strictly set in terms of construction and dimension, and the details overseen by the City Water Bailiff.

The races took place in the afternoon over two days in high summer and were enormously popular, attracting great crowds of spectators, visitors as well as locals, who lined the Quay and the parapets of the buildings along it and the moored vessels at the quayside. The fields on the Kilkenny side were filled with country people. Before the races, the Corporation barge, carrying the Mayor, the Corporation and a military band sailed majestically up and down the river, the band playing martial airs. After the races, the festivities on Waterford's Quay continued into the evening, when a fireworks display took place on the river, 'before a prodigious concourse of people, who swarmed like bees along the Quay, while the windows to the top of every house were crowded with spectators'.

By the early nineteenth century, nearly 150 sailing ships were registered to Waterford owners, and half of Ireland's bacon exports and about 60 percent of its flour exports, originating in the Malcolmson mills in Clonmel and Portlaw, were being shipped out of Waterford. Gaslights were installed along the Quay in 1817, the same year that saw the first steamship to visit the port, *The Princess Charlotte*. In 1832, 1,347 ships passed through the port, nearly twice the number that had come and gone in the 1820s.

Prime among Waterford's most important exports was pork meat. At the time, pork was cured by soaking it in brine, but this was not always successful because the salt often did not penetrate into the centre of the meat, which rotted from the inside out. To overcome this problem, Waterford butcher Henry Denny invented techniques that revolutionised the country's meat exports. He cured pork by compressing it between blocks of dry salt, producing bacon and hams that were successfully

exported to Britain, France and America. By cutting pork into long thin strips before salting it, Denny invented the rasher, for which the company is still well-known today. Unfortunately Henry Denny's company introduced their techniques to the trade in Denmark in 1894, and today that country is Ireland's largest competitor in the field.[7]

Another culinary invention that belongs to Waterford and is closely associated with the city's maritime character is the cream cracker, which was first produced in Bridge Street in the bakery of the Jacob brothers. The biscuit was the result of experimentation on recipes for biscuits that

Shipping at the Quay c.1900

7   Mary Mulvihill, *Ingenious Ireland*, Town House 2002.

would stay fresh on a long sea voyage. The original cream cracker was made by flattening and folding dough many times, creating a multi-layer biscuit, a product that today is sold all over the world. After the company left Waterford for Dublin, Jacobs created the Mikado biscuit in 1888, to celebrate Gilbert and Sullivan's operetta, and in 1893 the Kimberly, to celebrate the diamond mine of the same name in South Africa.

A Waterford recipe that remained in Waterford is that of the small round batch loaf called the Blaa, a light floury bread that is said to have been brought to the city by a French Huguenot family around 1685, the name blaa being derived from the French word blanc.

———∿∿∿———

For more than a thousand years the Suir was the lifeblood of Waterford and provided protection to a considerable length of the city perimeter. There is some evidence that Cromwellian forces erected a rudimentary timber bridge across the river during the siege of 1650, a structure subsequently strengthened and reused by the forces of William III during his siege forty years later. Until 1794, however, when the first proper bridge was built, the width and depth of the Suir's strongly flowing waters separated the city from the rest of the south-east of Ireland almost as effectively as if it were an offshore city state, which might explain the independent character of Waterfordians which has lasted to this day.

In 1770 Thomas Covey[8] published a book attempting to draw attention to the anomaly of a modern city 'confessedly ranked third Port for Trade in the United Kingdom' continuing to exist without a bridge to connect it with the rest of the country. Amongst the problems that previously had held up progress on the provision of a bridge were the legal rights of the Waterford ferry-owners. By the 1790s, however, confidence and enthusiasm for the future imbued by the golden age that Ireland was enjoying while it had its own parliament encouraged the Corporation and principal citizens of Waterford to look again at the possibility. In December 1792, the ferry rights were bought out for £13,000 'in their patriotic pursuit of building a bridge across the river Suir', and a consortium of Waterford entrepreneurs led by the banker Simon Newport,

---

8   Thomas Covey, *A Scheme for Building a Bridge over the River Suire at the City of Waterford*, 1770

The wooden toll-bridge
'Timbertoes' in 1890

invited the American architect Samuel Cox to prepare plans for a bridge. Construction began in April 1793, and the first commercial bridge to connect the city to the north bank of the Suir was completed in January 1794. The provision of the bridge was without doubt one of the most significant events in Waterford's history. The inscription on the foundation stone reads as follows:

> IN 1793
> A Year rendered sacred to national prosperity
> By the extinction of religious divisions
> The foundation of this Bridge was laid
> At the expense of associated individuals

Unaided by Parliamentary Grants
By Sir John Newport Bart
Chairman of their Committee
Samuel Cox, a native of Boston, Architect.

The 'associated individuals' clearly saw the project as a valuable investment, although the capital cost, without government assistance, must have been considerable.

The bridge, christened Old Timbertoes by Waterfordians, was a considerable structure of forty feet in width, built from American oak. It earned between 10 and 12 percent return annually on the original investment for the families of the investors for 114 years in all. Tolls varied from 2 shillings and 6 pence for 'every Coach, Breslin, Calash, Chariot, Chaise or Chair drawn by 6 or more horses or beasts of burden', to a halfpenny for pedestrians. Funeral processions were free, which tended to swell the ranks of mourners.

It is interesting to note, in relation to today's concern about global warming and extreme weather events, that the Suir and Waterford experienced a number of exceptionally cold spells in the nineteenth century, during which the river was iced over. In January 1814 there was a period of extremely cold weather accompanied by prodigious falls of snow, and it lasted long enough for ice flows to develop on the river. The ice sank two boats above Mount Congreve, and for a while threatened the new bridge at Waterford.

In the 1860s there was severe flooding on the Suir at Waterford, and at high tides the river waters rose to several feet high on the façades of the buildings facing the Quay.

In December 1878, during a prolonged severe frost, the Suir froze over again. The ice on the river at Carrick was up to six inches thick, and the tug *Father Mathew*, which belonged to the Grubb family of Clonmel, had iron plates fixed to the bows and stern to help create a navigable passage up and down river. Two years later, in January 1881, there was another extremely cold spell of weather that lasted for almost two weeks, after which ice began to build up against Timbertoes at every outgoing tide. The bridge at New Ross over the Barrow was wrecked by the ice, and there were fears that Waterford bridge might be severely damaged, so the *Father Mathew* was rented again by the Bridge Commissioners to break up the accumulation of ice. Their concern is understandable, because some of the 'icebergs' were reported to be up to 3 feet thick and measured 80 feet by 40 feet. Another steam tug, the *Suir*, was employed with the *Father Mathew*, and their work, assisted by a screw-driven steam ship, bearing 600 tons of coal, forcing her way through, soon showed results with much smaller sections of ice being shepherded safely under the bridge.

By the last quarter of the nineteenth century the old timbers of the bridge were in poor condition and needed replacement: Cox's first Irish bridge, across the Foyle at Derry, had to be replaced in 1863. A look at the meticulously kept accounts for Waterford's bridge between the years 1883 and 1892[9] show that it continued to be profitable, making more than £3,500 a year, although maintenance costs averaged £1,500. Gas lighting cost £62, while administration costs came to about £110: the thrifty owners had old timber that had been removed from the bridge sold off each year for about £25.

The toll bridge, however, had become an anachronism by the beginning of the twentieth century, and the idea of a modern city being accessible only on payment of a toll was generally regarded as a ridiculous state of affairs. As a result, a viceregal commission sat in Waterford Courthouse in October 1902 to consider a proposal by the Corporation to erect a new toll-free bridge 200 yards above the existing bridge. The proposal, naturally, was opposed by the toll bridge proprietors, but the commission subsequently reported in favour of the Corporation. Legal challenges ensued that lasted for a few years, but eventually the courts decided that, although the rights held by the toll bridge proprietors were antiquated, they still could not be legally interfered with and the individuals would have to be bought out.

On 31 December 1907 the Corporation bought the toll bridge, lock stock and barrel, for a sum of £63,000, after which the mayor, Alderman Quinlan, entertained 200 citizens to dinner at City Hall in celebration of a great event for all Waterfordians. After the dinner, the mayor and corporation led a great concourse of people up the Quay, and as

9   Author's Waterford archive: *Waterford Bridge Accounts.*

'New bridge' completed in 1913 and later named Redmond Bridge

midnight was greeted by the ringing of church bells, the sounding off of ships' sirens and the discharging of cannon, the gates of the bridge were opened, and the crowds followed the mayor across the bridge free of toll for the first time.

The design for the new bridge attracted more controversy: the vice-regal commission proposed a steel bridge that would be mainly fabricated in England and erected at a cost of £115,000. This was strongly objected to in Waterford, where, after considerable debate, the citizens favoured a ferro-concrete bridge which at £47,000 would cost the ratepayers considerably less, and the work would give a boost to local employment.[10] The ordinary citizenry of Waterford were familiar with ferro-concrete, at the time a relatively novel form of construction, because they had watched or worked on the building just a few years before of Messrs

10 Letter by Edmund Harvey of Suirview, to the *Irish Times*, 4 November 1908.

Hall's 'immense' new corn stores on the north bank of the Suir, which had used the same method. These structures are still there today, and although they do not look particularly impressive, in the early 1900s they must have seemed like a series of gleaming skyscrapers compared to the rest of Waterford.

Waterford Corporation eventually got its way, but a study of the machinations involved in the seemingly simple matter of an Irish local authority building a bridge across an Irish river brings home how demeaning, inefficient and unsatisfactory it must have been to be ruled from Westminster. To achieve what was needed for a modern city, the Corporation had first to plead with the Viceroy, the queen's representative in Ireland, then become deeply immersed in legal wranglings involving the Viceroy's powers and rights, the rights and wrongs of laws passed three hundred years before by a foreign king, with the Master of the Rolls arguing with the Attorney General, a dozen King's Counsels at battle, and prolonged legal wrangles that would make any modern tribunal lawyer's mouth water.

Work finally began on the new ferro-concrete bridge in 1910, and it was completed and opened in 1913 by John Redmond MP, the Nationalist politician, and served well for over sixty years. As Timbertoes before it, there are many stories about the 'new bridge', which was later named Redmond Bridge. One in particular captured my imagination. At the height of summer in 1937, local papers reported that Patrick O'Mahony, a fourteen-year-old schoolboy, had climbed to the top of one of the bridge towers and dived 60 feet into the river. He had told a companion who had dived twenty feet from the parapet that his dive was too easy, and had been bet sixpence that he wouldn't dive from the top. Having got a taste for this showmanship, O'Mahony went down to the Halls flourmills to attempt to climb to the top, 120 feet above the water, for a dive, but the Garda Síochána prevented him from doing so. He was in the news again, however, the following week when he 'thrilled hundreds of spectators' by diving into the river again, swimming out to rescue a pigeon which had fallen into the water, and swimming back with the bird in his mouth, retriever fashion!

The river, with its glistening mudbanks, tar-black mooring hulks and ships seemingly constantly on the move, belching smoke and steam, and frightening the seagulls with their deep horns, and the long Quay lined with shops, was a central part of my Waterford childhood. The SS *Great Western*, a mixed passenger and cargo ship that plied between Waterford and Fishguard, provided those who needed it a direct passage abroad, and she brought scarce visitors to the city. I well recall the blast of its klaxon, and the drama of the great ship turning in the river in strong tides, smoke billowing from her funnel, the noise of the engine roaring, and the explosion of turbulence at her stern. With the SS *Rockabill*, which plied between Waterford and Liverpool twice a week, the *Great Western* provided a lifeline to Waterford trade throughout World War II. During that war they braved the U-boat-infested waters of the Irish Sea, bringing a taste of war exotica to the neutral city in the form of bulbous barrage balloons, designed to deter bombers from getting too close.

Besides the passenger and cargo vessels that regularly came and went from Waterford, another ancient small black ship was ever present, moving up and down river with smoke pumping out of its tall funnel, a craft called the *Portlairge*, built in Scotland in the early years of the twentieth century. It was the harbour dredger, commonly known as the 'Mud Boat', constantly working with clanking of chains and rattling of great steel buckets, scooping mud into its hold, just barely keeping pace with the constant build-up of solids washed down from the good lands of Tipperary, west Waterford and Kilkenny and deposited along the margins of the river. When it was retired in 1984, it was bought by a Scottish firm which clearly appreciated its heritage value, but while it was being towed to Scotland, it was driven back by bad weather, and washed up at Saltmills, County Wexford, where it remains today, battered but unbowed.

As a child I watched the activities of the *Portlairge* and other shipping in the river from the front windows of my grandfather's apartment, which overlooked the quays and the busiest berths along the south bank near Reginald's Tower. The apartment was over his motorcar showrooms, which he opened in 1916. In 1923, he installed, on the pavement outside, what was possibly one of Ireland's earliest electrically operated petrol pumps. It was just one of a number of motoring

WATERFORD FERRY

firsts for Waterford: the first motor garage in Ireland is thought to have been in nearby Catherine Street, founded by Captain W. F. Peare, and it was there that the first car to be registered in Waterford was bought, by Sir William Goff.

Postcard depicting the ferry boat near Reginald's Tower

In the late 1920s my mother daily took the ferry boat across the river to school. Two large 15-feet long, open rowing boats provided the service, plying between Adelphi Quay and a slip near Abbeyside, from which it was only five minutes' walk to Ferrybank Convent School. Every fifteen minutes, apart from breaks, each ferry would set out, one from the north bank, the other from the south, and the journey took about five minutes. There were two oarsman and room for about twenty passengers, and the fare was one old penny, a fraction of today's one cent, but school children had a reduced weekly fare of threepence for ten journeys. My mother told me that the ferry operated in all conditions other than severe gales and thick fog, when the danger was not so much getting lost and ending up at sea, but being run over by one of the many large ships that came up to Waterford at that time. She remembered that it was nothing to travel across on surging tides, strong winds and stormy rain, sleet and snow: it wasn't so bad when you were on your way home, but if you got wet on the way to school, you had to sit in damp clothes all day. The 'senior' ferryman, Larry McCarthy, always wore a nautical hat to signify his rank, and my mother remembered one of the men always rowing with a pipe between his teeth, even on a stormy, rainy crossing. On some occasions when a very strong tide was running, the crew was doubled to four and the trip, a cacophony of slapping water, the grunts of the oarsmen, and the rhythmic creaking of the oars, lasted for about twenty minutes. She never remembered being scared on any of her many ferry journeys, and, in spite of the total lack of safety equipment, there do not seem to have been any casualties.

Waterford was still a loyalist city as the twentieth century began, as is suggested by a newspaper report of the visit on 2 May 1904 of Edward VII, Queen Alexandra and Princess Victoria to the city and the Waterford Agricultural Society's Show.

The assemblage on the stands and in the jumping enclosure was one of the largest and most fashionable ever seen in Waterford. Along the roadway leading to the show the crowds that lined the sidepaths and hedgerows gave Their Majesties a very warm reception...1,500 children, representing the Protestant and Catholic schools of Waterford assembled, waving tiny flags and cheering heartily. Their Majesties were greatly pleased by this demonstration, and bowed graciously and smiled upon the children as they passed.

Within sixteen years, however, Waterford had become emphatically nationalist when Dr Vincent White, a Sinn Féin councillor, was elected mayor in February 1920. He was a flamboyant character and at his inauguration wore, instead of the usual red and black robes, a cape of green white and gold. When the Corporation officials brought the ancient maces of office to him on the mayoral chair, he called out in a stentorious voice, 'Take away those English baubles!' I remember Dr White marching in the St Patrick's Day parades as an alderman of the

The motorcar showrooms of the author's grandfather, near Reginald's Tower in 1923

Corporation in the nineteen fifties, wearing a bunch of shamrock that all but covered his chest.

In March 1922, after the Treaty had been signed and the general election campaign was in full swing, Michael Collins visited Waterford as part of a nationwide tour to speak on behalf of the Treaty. The *Irish Times* reported that Waterford's efforts to frustrate the holding of a Pro-Treaty rally were 'worthy of the Wild West'. Roads into Waterford were trenched, telephone wires cut, the speech platform was burned down, and the band that was to play at the rally had its instruments stolen. The train carrying Collins and his party was stopped for an hour at Ballyhale in County Kilkenny while cut signal wires were repaired. Attempts were made to raise the bridge and prevent the party crossing after their arrival at the station, but the Pro-Treaty reception committee had arranged for vital mechanical parts to be removed from the bridge mechanism so the bridge would not lift. With no speech platform, the visitors had to speak from the back of a lorry, constantly interrupted by shouting, singing and whistling, but at least no shots were fired as they had been in Cork a fortnight before. The *Irish Times* reported that the bulk of the populace, however, was disgusted by the activities of the Anti-Treaty faction.

In July 1922, Waterford became the last city in these islands to come under siege when a force of the National Army arrived on the north bank of the Suir, opposite the city, to attempt to eject the 300-strong Anti-Treaty garrison, which had been in place in Waterford since the British Army had left in March.

Civil strife had been threatening for some time between the Pro- and Anti-Treaty factions, but the war began in earnest when the Pro-Treaty National Army opened fire on Anti-Treaty forces in the Four Courts in Dublin on 28 June 1922, in an attempt to dislodge the Anti-Treaty forces that had garrisoned them. Up until that time, each side had been reluctant to tangle with the other. When hostilities did begin, however, a vicious civil war began that lasted from that summer's day until 24 May 1923, when Eamon de Valera, who had set up an alternative government in October 1922 claiming legitimate authority, proclaimed a definitive ceasefire, telling his supporters that 'military victory must be allowed to rest for the moment with those who have destroyed the republic'.

At the commencement of hostilities, the Anti-Treaty forces put Waterford under martial law, isolating it from the rest of the country by barricading and trenching approach roads, tearing up railway lines, and cutting telephonic and telegraphic wires. Censors were placed in the local newspaper offices, and many thousands of pounds' worth of goods and foodstuffs, and a number of motor lorries and cars were commandeered, by which time the Anti-Treaty garrison had earned the dislike of the citizenry.

The Pro-Treaty National Army force of about 600 troops which came to oust the Anti-Treaty soldiers from Waterford, was under the command of General Prout, an experienced soldier who had fought in France with the American Army. As soon as the strongpoints of the Anti-Treaty forces had been identified at Waterford Jail and the Army and Artillery barracks, they came under heavy fire. The weather was warm and sunny, and on the commencement of shooting, the civilian population of the city made their way to the seaside resort of Tramore by train and, except for night-time sorties back to the city, there they stayed for the duration of the siege.

On the second day of the siege, an eighteen-pounder field gun was set up near Mount Misery and in the hands of an expert gunner, commenced firing with great accuracy on Anti-Treaty positions in the city. Over a twenty-four-hour period 38 shells were fired, hitting the Barracks, the adjacent Artillery Barracks and the Jail. There was a minimum of what the Americans would call collateral damage, and one miraculous escape when a shell entered a house in King's Terrace, passed through the bedclothes on one bed, through a partition into the next room where it cut two beds in half, and then emerged through a back window before exploding. There were, however, two deaths among the civilian population from the hail of sniper fire raining down on the city from the Kilkenny side of the river.

Under this bombardment, the Anti-Treaty forces soon abandoned the two barracks, setting fire to them as they left. After they had fled, neither the fire nor the danger of exploding shells prevented an excited crowd of men, women and children from rushing into the barracks on a looting spree. In addition to much of the material and foodstuffs that had been requisitioned from Waterford businesses, beds and bedding, clothing, kitchen utensils, food and plumbing fittings were taken, and windows and doors were dismantled. The artillery barracks was gutted by fire, and much of the infantry barracks, some of which survives today, was damaged. Motor cars that had been requisitioned, one from my grandfather, were destroyed.

Early on the morning of the third day, the National Army crossed the Suir in rowing boats to the east end of the Quay and began to edge westwards, taking the Adelphi Hotel and Reginald's Tower before being halted by a garrison at the General Post Office. Signals across the river brought the eighteen-pounder to bear on the Post Office, and after six

The Quay, Waterford, watercolour by Michael Fewer, 1973

hits the garrison hastily withdrew. The rest of the Quay was taken by Thursday night, and the following day the city was abandoned to the National Army, thus ending Waterford's brief siege.

A few days later, searches were carried out through the lanes and backstreets of the Ballybricken area for the goods that had been looted from the barracks and the Jail, and £250 worth of property was returned to its rightful owners.

Following Ireland's independence, Waterford as a port, like the rest of the country, seemed to stagnate. The basic cargo and passenger services to Wales and England continued, but there were no new developments through the nineteen twenties and thirties. World War II and the late 1940s, strangely, brought a slight increase in trade, particularly in exports of foodstuffs to Britain, but by the 1950s commerce had quietened down again. A serious dock strike in the 1960s almost shut down the port permanently, but with the development of container

transport, Waterford got a new lease of life when Bell Ferries established its Irish terminal on the north quays.

The establishment, by a group of Waterford businessmen, of Waterford Harbour as a cruise ship destination twenty years ago gave a boost to the port and to tourism in general in the south-east. The idea had been developed by Waterfordian Anthony Brophy, born within yards of the Suir and a life-long enthusiast of Waterford Port. In partnership with a local travel agent, in August 1989 he arranged for the first of what was to be many cruise ship arrivals when the *Royal Viking Sky* sailed up the Suir.

The initial attraction of Waterford as a port-of-call was that it was the home of world-famous Waterford Crystal, where visitors could watch the glass being manufactured and buy it at a preferential rate, but soon it became clear that Waterford was an ideal day touring centre for many of the attractions of the south east. In 1992 the *Crystal Symphony*, a cruise ship of 700 feet, sailed upriver, the longest ship by 300 feet to do so. The QE2 has visited also, but ships of her size have to moor off Dunmore

East in Waterford Harbour and have their passengers ferried ashore. Altogether, Waterford Harbour has welcomed an average of 20 cruise ships and 12,000 passengers a year since 1989.

Cruise liner off Dunmore East

(*Above*) Cormorants on the Quay, Waterford

The planned ambitious development of the north quays of Waterford, essentially the other half of the city centre, was initially delayed by disputes over ownership, and subsequently by the downturn in the economy. When it does proceed, however, it will probably bring about the erection of another bridge, to provide a connection from the Quay to the north shore, taking people and traffic from near Reginald's Tower to Ferrybank, along the route that my mother and so many others once travelled by ferry.

Chapter Eight

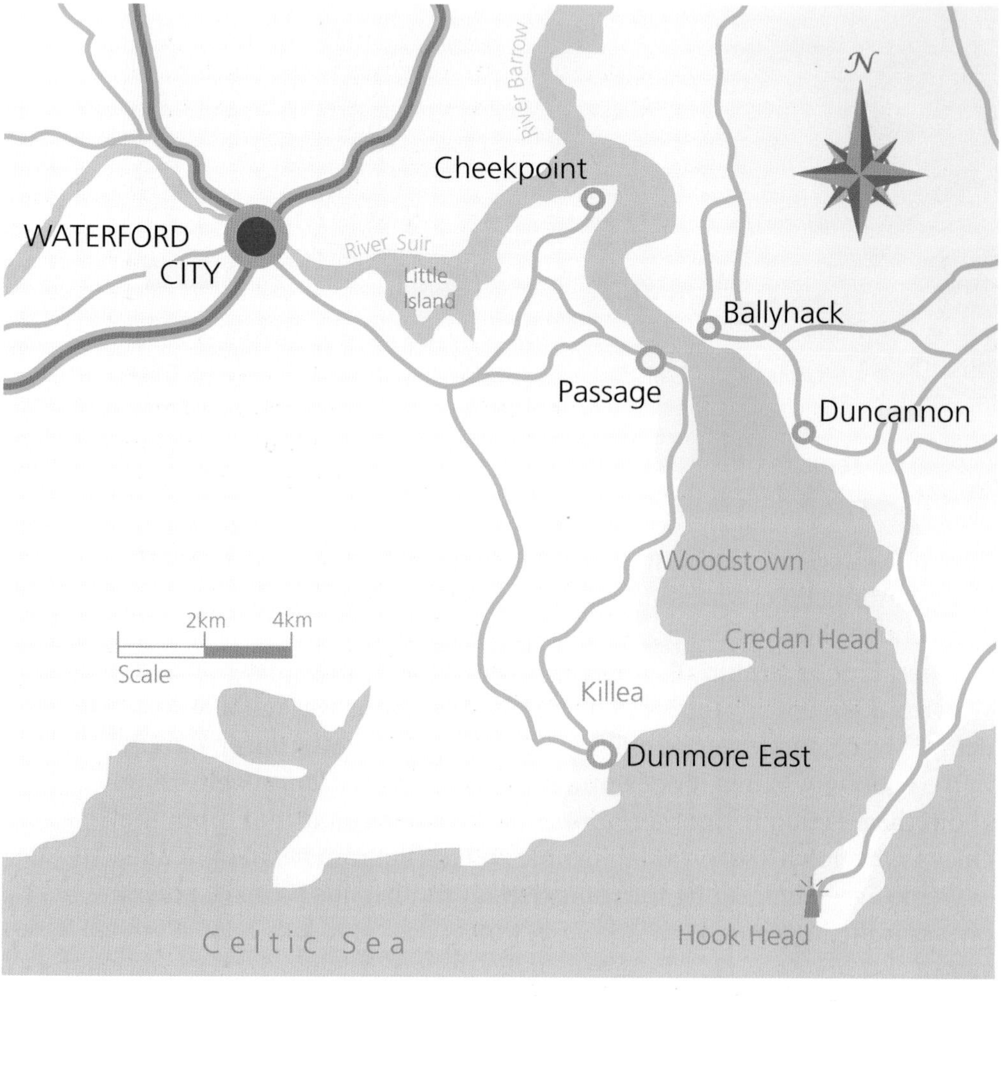

N
River Barrow
Cheekpoint
WATERFORD
CITY
River Suir
Little
Island
Ballyhack
Passage
Duncannon
Woodstown
2km
4km
Scale
Credan Head
Killea
Dunmore East
Celtic Sea
Hook Head

Waterford to the Sea

OWNSTREAM OF THE ROTUND Reginald's Tower, St John's Pill joins the Suir. For many years not much more than a smelly drain lined with viscous mudbanks, since the removal of the gas works a short distance upstream, it has improved greatly. I have always considered what a wonderful amenity the little river could be to the parts of the city through which it flows if it were thoroughly cleaned out of centuries of spoil that fill it, and barraged at its meeting with the Suir, ensuring that it always maintained a good depth. One could expect enough archaeological finds to fill a small museum, and it does not take a lot of imagination to conjure up how the watercourse might look when properly finished, with a board-walk along its length, its banks planted with trees and shrubs, nesting islands for wildfowl established, and footbridges located at appropriate places.

Below St John's Pill is Canada Street, the name of which recalls both the nineteenth-century importation of Canadian timber and the export of young Irish pioneers to populate the province of Upper Canada, an area that is now part of southern Ontario. The Canada Company was allocated a seventh of the province, and a million acres on the shores of Lake Huron, and they sought to offer to emigrants from Europe land at very low cost or in certain cases free of charge if they settled there.[1] The Canada Company wanted emigrants with 'sober, honest and industrious habits', and used ships that had taken lumber to Europe to accommodate emigrants on the return journey, at very low fares. Their efforts bore fruit, and the population of Ontario expanded by 10 percent year on year,

---

1   Daniel Dowling, *Waterford's Streets, Past and Present,* Waterford Corporation, 1998.

increasing between 1825 and 1840 from 157,000 to 432,000.

Downstream from Canada Street ship-building was carried on in the eighteenth and nineteenth centuries. Waterford-built ships, like Waterford seamen, enjoyed a high reputation, and sailing vessels of all sizes were constructed and launched by the ship-building firms that flourished at the time. Ambrose Congreve, whom we met previously upstream at Mount Congreve, established repair docks with a dry dock for dealing with large vessels in Waterford as early as 1737: Dublin port was not able to offer dry dock facilities until around 1794.[2]

By early in the nineteenth century Messrs Pope and Company, local merchants and ship-owners, began to build its own schooners and brigantines for the cross-channel trade. Another firm, Albert White and Company, built some early paddle-steamers. One of theirs, the PS *Kilkenny*, a craft of 1,000 tons with a 280 horsepower engine, was launched in 1837: later, as the *Zenobia*, she was one of the first paddle steamers to voyage around the Cape of Good Hope to India, where she was still in service on the Bengal Station in 1854.[3] In 1856 the largest wooden ship ever built in Ireland, *Merrie England*, 280 feet in length, was launched from White's ship-building yard.

Another Waterford ship of the period was *The Pathfinder*, a fine and fast 131-feet sailing ship that was used on the copper-ore trade between Swansea and the west coast of South America via Cape Horn. The figure-head on the ship's prow, evidence of the skill of Waterford craftsmen at the time, was described as follows:

> Her figure-head represented Fenimore Cooper's Pathfinder, standing full length on top of the stem head. The figure-head carver was careful to be correct in his portrait to the smallest particular. The Pathfinder was clad in fringed leggings of buck-skin, embroidered shirt, coon-skin cap and beaded moccasins, whilst about his middle were slung his powder horn and shot pouch, water bottle and hunting knife. Trailing his rifle from his right hand, he was leaning forward with left knee bent, and gazing ahead with his left hand shading his eyes.

---

2   Colin Rynne, *Industrial Ireland 1750-1930: An Archaeology*, The Collins Press, 2006.
3   Ernest B. Anderson, *Sailing Ships of Ireland*, Morris & Company, 1951.

John Malcolmson, the fourth son of David Malcolmson who founded Portlaw, looked after the family business at Waterford in the 1830s, which depended greatly on shipping. It imported coal from Swansea for the factory at Portlaw, the raw cotton for the factory was imported via Liverpool and the finished products were exported around the world. In order to gain more control over the shipping of these raw materials and their products, the family helped found, in 1835, the Waterford Steam Navigation Company. The Malcolmsons were visionaries and they kept abreast of newly emerging technology: they were convinced that the future lay in steel-hulled, steam-powered vessels, and after they had two steel-hulled steamers built for them in Britain, in 1836 they commissioned Albert White's yard to build for them Waterford's first paddle steamer.

By 1843 the Malcolmsons had nineteen ships, and in the same year they built a repair yard called the Neptune Works just below Canada Street; Joseph Malcolmson, another son of David's, managed it. With a workforce of 300 skilled workers, the Neptune Works soon began to build its own iron-hulled ships, and by 1858 it had turned out twelve large steamships, some of them 200 feet or more in length. Perhaps the best known of their ships was the 172-feet iron-hulled screw-driven SS *Neptune*, specially built for the London to St Petersburg service. On her first arrival at the Russian port of Cronstadt after a hazardous crossing, she was boarded by the mayor of St Petersburg to sail up the river Neva into the city. On the way, Czar Nicholas I, in his state barge, formed up on the *Neptune*, and they sailed together into the harbour which was decorated with bunting. She was the first screw-driven iron steamship to sail into St Petersburg and, to commemorate the occasion, the Czar granted the *Neptune* freedom from port dues for life.

One of the biggest ships to be built at the Neptune Works was the 316-feet long *William Penn* of 1,799 tons, which spent her early years on the London-Le Havre-New York route, at one stage carrying 680 passengers across the Atlantic.[4] She must have been an impressive sight towering over the banks of the Suir before her launch in 1865.

Over 100 ships were built at the three Waterford shipyards between

4   Bill Irish, *Shipbuilding in Waterford*, Wordwell, 2001.

Villas and holiday homes along the shore at Dunmore

1820 and 1882 and, but for the decline of the Malcolmson family fortunes and their bankruptcy in the 1870s, it is possible that ship-building would have become a major industry in Waterford during the following fifty years, the greatest era of ship-building.

As the Suir flows out of Waterford city, its south bank is lined with fine villas embowered in trees and facing the river over beautiful terraced gardens. Some of the properties, particularly houses that have been built in recent years, have private docks on the river. Among the more historic of the older houses is Newtown Park, now much altered and converted into apartments. It was here that Field Marshal Lord Roberts of Kandahar lived for a while as a child. The most glorious exploits of his career occurred during his time in India, particularly during the rebellion of 1857, when he won the Victoria Cross, after which he fought in Abyssinia and led an army of 10,000 for the relief of Kandahar during the Second Afghan War in 1878.

Three kilometres east of Waterford the Suir divides to encompass Little Island. It was described in a guide book at the end of the nineteenth century as 'well furnished, umbrageous...throwing up luxuriantly wild herbage and thickly planted trees, by which it adorns so well the spreading waters.' With an area of 300 acres, it is today the largest

island on the Suir: Great Island farther downstream used to be larger, but it is now connected to the Wexford shore. It is possible that aeons ago Little Island was similarly joined to County Kilkenny, for, although broad and straight, the depth of the dividing channel was up until 1816 as little at times as 60 centimetres, and its old name was the Ford Channel. The river to the south of the island, King's Channel, was deep enough for the vessels of the sailing era, but is narrower and meandering, and in those days there had to be ideal wind conditions to achieve a good passage. In 1816 the Ford Channel was dredged and deepened, and from then on it became the primary navigation up to Waterford port.

Little Island's location made it strategically important from early times and the oldest extant structure on the island is a sixteenth-century castle that forms the core of a house built by the FitzGeralds in the nineteenth century. This in turn was further extended and heavily battlemented about 1900 by Gerald Purcell-FitzGerald, great-grand-nephew

Waterford Castle, now a hotel

of Edward FitzGerald, translator of the Rubaiyat of the Persian poet Omar Khayyam. Ownership of the island came into the aristocratic Italian Caracciolo family through the marriage of Mary Augusta FitzGerald to Don Fernandino Antonio Giuseppe Maria d'Ardia Caracciolo in 1938. A descendant of his, Prince Francesco Caracciolo, an admiral in the Neapolitan Navy, was hanged by Lord Nelson from the yardarm of *The Victory*. When Caracciolo family moved to Dublin in the early 1950s, the island was sold, and sold again in 1987, reportedly for a half million pounds, when the castle was converted into a luxury hotel.

Downstream of Little Island is Waterford's new port at Bellvue: in line with an international trend to liberate ports from their historic urban locations, Waterford port was relocated in 1992 as a modern container facility four kilometres downstream at Bellevue, nearer the open sea and with its own rail connection on the Waterford-Rosslare line. It can accommodate ships of up to 40,000 tonnes.

Just downstream of the new port is a place called Glasshouse, a name it has had since 1729 and, although still in common use and marked on

earlier ordnance maps, it is absent from the Ordnance Survey Discovery series of maps. In this way, old names and often history are lost. The name comes from a glass factory that was established here in 1728 which made glass tableware, window glass, and glass for greenhouses. Manufacture seems to have ceased in the 1740s when the Westminster Parliament passed a protectionist act forbidding exports of glassware from Ireland.

The picturesque hamlet of Cheekpoint

Along this stretch of the Suir crumbling stones of ancient piers reach out from under riverside trees, and blackened poles of old fish weirs, which at one time would have trapped in season as many as 200 salmon on each tide, protrude from the river mud in places. After the King's Channel the banks of the river to the left and right rise to form two wooded hills through which the Suir squeezes to meet its sisters, the Barrow and Nore, which have drained most of the rest of the south-east of Ireland before reaching this point. The amalgamated rivers swerve east and west and east again as they flow towards Waterford Harbour and the Atlantic. County Kilkenny is left behind beyond the Barrow, where County Wexford forms the eastern bank.

Ruins of Dunbrody Abbey by George du Noyer, c.1850

The Barrow railway bridge at 2,132 feet long, is said to be the longest in Ireland across water, and carries the railway line that runs between Waterford and Rosslare Harbour. Erected in 1906 by the firm of Sir William Arrol of Glasgow, builders of the Forth Railway Bridge in Scotland, it has thirteen spans and a swivel section to allow access by ships. The new rail line was inaugurated on 23 July 1906, when a special luxury train was laid on by the Fishguard and Rosslare Harbour and Railway Company to take the Lord Lieutenant, captains of industry, skilled surgeons, eminent professors and heads of government departments from the capital to Waterford and then along the new line to Rosslare. The train paused on the Barrow Bridge so that the passengers could enjoy the fine view before travelling on to Rosslare where they were entertained to an elaborate luncheon at the new harbour.

Opposite the confluence of the sister rivers Cheekpoint Hill rises dramatically 129 metres above the river, with Glazing Wood hugging its steep northern and western flanks. Just downstream, the scattered and picturesque hamlet of Cheekpoint snuggles into a wooded shore. A little more than two hundred years ago it was a bustling industrial village and had the potential to become an important town on the Suir. In 1779, the local landowner, Cornelius Bolton, transformed the sleepy fishing hamlet of Cheekpoint into a linen and cotton manufactury, and arranged its establishment as the chief packet station for the south-east. For the next couple of decades the place was a hive of activity, with 22 cottage looms and 30 stocking frames in operation; it seems that one of the main products was cotton stockings, an important feature of the male apparel of the period. The name of the place was changed to Bolton, and until recently there were still three stone-carved Bolton mileposts on the main road out from Waterford.

As an important landowner and having held the posts of Sheriff and Mayor of Waterford, Bolton influenced the decision to transfer the packet station from Passage East, a couple of miles downstream, to his own village in 1785. This was a major coup for Bolton's new 'town': packet sailing ships were the authorised transporters of Royal Mail, official dispatches, goods and passengers between Britain and the south-east of Ireland, and by the early years of the nineteenth century seven vessels performed the task on regular sailings, as weather permitted. Bolton became an important transport hub, attracting visitors, revenues and business: a new coach road was built from the village to Waterford and a pier was constructed to serve the lighters from the packet ship. A packet hotel was built in an imposing position overlooking the river, but it seems that it was never a success. One visitor in 1800 described it as 'a very dirty, dear, bad Inn, only staid there to breakfast, or more properly speaking to dine on bad bread and tea.'

The success of the new town was short-lived, however. By 1813 it had become clear that Bolton was not a suitable location for the packet station, it was relocated downriver at Dunmore East. Cornelius Bolton had incurred considerable debts in his various ventures, and began to get into financial difficulties. He delayed the inevitable by selling off parcels of land, his slate quarries, and his extensive woodlands for timber. But it was too late, and when the final collapse came, he had to dispose of the fine mansion he had built at Faithlegge in the 1780s, together with all his furniture, his pictures and his library. [5]

Bolton reverted to its original name, Cheekpoint, and returned to being a quiet fishing hamlet. There are two pubs there, and in one of

5   Julian Walton, 'The Boltons of County Waterford', *The Irish Genealogist* 1988.

them years ago I can remember convivial drinking and singing going on long past closing time. To help her customers on their way home, the landlady used to bring out a large dish of potatoes and salmon, and as she doled out portions, she proudly announced that the salmon had been poached twice that night.

There are few records of the works or buildings that existed in Cornelius Bolton's time and little evidence of the extent of the development, other than the old hotel high on the hill, which after a long period of neglect has been well refurbished as a fine family home.

Downstream from Cheekpoint on the Wexford side are the picturesque ruins of Dunbrody Abbey. Hervey de Montmorency, Strongbow's uncle, was granted so much land in Ireland after the Norman invasion that he could afford to offer 10,000 acres of land in this area to the monks of Buildwas Abbey in Shropshire, hoping they might build a monastery here and develop the lands and fisheries. The lay brother they sent to assess the site, however, was not welcomed by the natives and had to spend his time living in a hollow oak tree, so he was not impressed. When he reported on the wildness of the place, the sterility of the land and the ferociousness of the 'barbarians', the Buildwas monks declined Montmorency's offer. Subsequently it was the monks of St Mary's Abbey in Dublin who took up the offer, and in 1182 they began to build the Abbey, one of Ireland's finest Cistercian monastic complexes. The abbey and its lands were taken over by the Etchingham family from Suffolk in

The stunning view upriver from Whort Hill

1536, no doubt as part payment to Sir Osbourne Etchingham for his services to Henry VIII as marshal of the army in Ireland. They converted part of the abbey into an Elizabethan manor house, but when they eventually moved to more modern quarters in nearby Dunbrody Castle, the great monastery eventually fell into disrepair.

The stone structure of the abbey remains in good order: until recent years one could climb to the top of the tower, which provided good views up and down the Suir, but today one pays an entrance fee to simply walk about the abbey at ground level.

Below Dunbrody, the Campile tributary enters the river, south of which is a tiny, picturesque cove called Nook, where I once spent a pleasant half-hour watching shelducks feeding along the water's edge. I discovered the place in the 1980s when I was looking for the ruined church of St Catherine, which may have been built on the site of the cell of an early Christian hermit, St Inioque. At that time it was an off-the-beaten-track kind of place with a few tiny disused cottages. One of the boreens I followed had as paving the bedrock, into which the ruts of

R.S.A.I.

cartwheels had been worn, reminding me of those in the stone paving at Pompeii. The old church was heavily overgrown, a tiny place with the remains of a priest's living quarters on an upper storey, reached by a staircase within the thickness of the wall. Visiting the area again in 2008 on my journey along the Suir, I found there were many new bungalows at Nook, and a house had been built so close by the old church that I felt I could not get to it without passing through their garden.

Downstream, hidden in modern forestry at the shore are the remains of Buttermilk Castle, from where the monks of Dunbrody controlled a network of fish weirs in the river.

The Waterford side of the river here is dominated by Whort Hill, after the whortleberries or fraughans that were once common in this area but are now very scarce. It is one of the high points in the Barony of Gaultier, 'the Land of the Foreigner', apparently named after the Vikings and eventually the Normans who settled it. The hill rises in a steep wooded escarpment almost a hundred metres from the waters of the Suir, providing a spectacular viewpoint, a panorama that encompasses a

Passage East

(*Above*) Waterford Harbour between Passage East and Arthurstown

horizon of Brandon Hill in County Kilkenny, the Blackstairs mountains in Carlow, rounded Slieve Coillte and ragged-topped Fort mountain in Wexford, before the land flattens as it stretches southwards towards the Hook peninsula. In the foreground the Suir conjoined with its two sister rivers, flows onwards and sweeps down past Ballyhack on the Wexford bank and Passage East on the Waterford side.

The village of Passage East probably owes its existence to the broad gravel spit on which it stands, projecting into the river from the base of steep-sided cliffs at a narrow point on the river before it broadens to form Waterford Harbour to the south. It was the last place where sailing ships heading upriver could safely pause at anchor awaiting suitable winds and tides to tackle the navigation of narrower waters ahead, and its gravel beach provided a safe landing place.

It is almost certain that it was on this gravel beach that Strongbow, Richard le Clare, landed to march on Danish Waterford in August 1170, and this is also where his king, Henry II, came ashore in October of the following year, after bringing a great fleet up Waterford Harbour carrying an army of 500 knights and 1,000 men-at-arms. The show of force was not just to fill the native Irish with fear and respect, but to emphasise for Strongbow and his fellow adventurers that Henry was taking control of the situation in Ireland, notwithstanding Strongbow's hurried visit to him a short time before in Wales to assure him of his loyalty.

Henry II was used to organising expeditionary forces after his campaigns in France, and the preparations made for his Irish visit were, even in modern terms, impressive. As was common in those times, a king leaned heavily on his friends and supporters, and called in diverse debts to assemble the costly wherewithal to allow an army to travel overseas, well-armed, well-fed and well-clothed. The city of Winchester supplied two thousand ells (about 2,300 metres in length) of burel, a coarse woollen cloth for the soldier's tunics, and food supplies collected included enormous quantities of beans, salt, cheese, bacon, wheat and oats, together with portable mills for milling the flour and portable ovens for baking bread. From the city of Gloucester and county of Gloucestershire came a contribution of 1,000 shovels, 60,000 nails, 2,000 pickaxes, 1,000 spades and iron for 2,000 more, probably for the building of earthworks such as the Norman motte. The cities of Lancaster and Carlisle sent between them five wooden towers in prefabricated form, for erection on the earthen mounds of mottes. Henry had to be dressed appropriately for his first appearance before the Irish. It is recorded that he was supplied with a large amount of scarlet and green cloth, silk, two skins of mountain cat and five otter skins, and ten pairs of boots. His swords were given an overhaul and plated with sterling silver, and the scabbards were decorated with gold.[6]

All this materiel, in addition to his army, was carried in 400 ships, begged and borrowed from English merchants, each of whom could expect to eventually benefit by generous grants of Irish land. This great armada must have been an astonishing sight to the native Irish, whose experience of shipping up until this would have been limited to the small numbers of merchant craft constantly sailing in and out of the harbour.

A few years later Henry's son John, Earl of Morton, whom he had created Lord of Ireland, probably landed here or nearby, accompanied by

6   J. F. Lydon, *The Lordship of Ireland in the Middle Ages*, Gill & Macmillan, 1972.

a large retinue which included a group of his contemporaries and the historian Giraldus Cambrensis. It is said that John feasted so well on Passage salmon that he almost died, but I am sure there was also drink involved!

Probably the greatest gathering of ships the harbour has seen, however, occurred in October 1394, when Richard II entered it with about 500 ships, bearing an army of nearly 7,000 men, its horses, equipment and supplies, in addition to its heavy artillery, the contents of his Tower of London armoury. It was by far the largest army to arrive in Ireland in the Middle Ages, and not less than any English army that fought in France in the Hundred Years War, which indicates the importance that Richard, like Henry II before him, put in his mission to Ireland. It must have been a sight to remember. Their coming ashore, however, was less than magnificent, according to Richard's chronicler, Jan Froissart, who reports that they had to wade up to their waists in ooze to get from the ships to dry land. Richard stayed in Waterford for almost three weeks planning and consolidating his force before setting off north to attempt to chastise the Leinster clans, particularly Art Mac Murrough Kavanagh.

Passage East was also the embarkation point for number of important departures. Perkin Warbeck, the Yorkist pretender to the throne of Henry VII, left Ireland from here after his failure to take the city of Waterford in 1497. Captured in England, he and John Water, Mayor of Cork, who was travelling with him, were hanged for treason in 1499, finally bringing to an end the War of the Roses.

In the wake of the battle of the Boyne in 1690, James II was particularly concerned to avoid capture when he might have to spend the rest of his life in the Tower of London. In case his armies might be defeated by William's forces, he had made contingency plans to escape to France. There was no point boarding a ship at Dublin, since there was every chance it would be intercepted before it got south to the open Atlantic. So, some time before the fatal battle, he sent Sir Philip Trant to Waterford to arrange transport by a vessel from a southern port. When James arrived in Waterford a couple of days after the battle, a French trader was anchored at Duncannon awaiting him. He spent his last night in Ireland in Ballynakill House overlooking the Suir, and was escorted the following day to Passage, and rowed out to the French ship. It took him to Kinsale, where he was picked up by a French warship detached from the fleet moored off the Devon coast at the time, and conveyed to France.

The broad waters between Passage East and Duncannon on the Wexford side were used for assembling convoys of ships during the French wars of the late eighteenth century. The Tall Ships Race provided a recent reminder of what the harbour must have looked like in those days of sail. In July 2005 ninety sailing ships, manned by 3,000 sailors and including 23 of the largest tall ships in the world, sailed up the harbour to Waterford to take part in the biggest free open-air festival that Ireland has ever seen. The international organisers were so impressed by the welcome given and the atmosphere in the city for the three days the ships were docked that they have included the city as a stage in their 2011 race.

To fully appreciate the harbour at Passage before it broadens towards the open sea, you have to climb the old stairs by the road at the back of the village. They take you up to the clifftop on which the former chapel of St Anne stands, high above the rooftops. It has been in private ownership for some years now, transformed into a residence with a marvellous view. An oratory dedicated to St Anne existed here as early as the thirteenth century, but the present building dates from about 1730, at which time it was the main chapel serving the barony of Gaultier.

Queen Victoria mentions this chapel in her journal of her first visit to Ireland in August 1849. The Royal Yacht anchored 'between two little villages, one on either side, each with its little chapel, picturesquely situated on the top of the rock or hill'. She wrote that Passage was 'famous for salmon: we had an excellent specimen for our dinner'. Albert went upriver in their pinnace with their young sons but, feeling 'giddy and tired', the monarch preferred remaining quietly on board, sketching. She was quite a good watercolourist, and I wonder where the sketches she made are to be found today. The chapel she mentioned on the Wexford side, above Ballyhack, was named the Temple of St James on Frances Jobson's chart of Waterford Harbour dated 1591, and is today an ivy-covered ruin surrounded by long grass and tombstones.

Passage East is mainly known today for its car ferry, which plies between the County Waterford village and the hamlet of Ballyhack on the

R.S.A.I.

Wexford side. Until the early 1980s there was a traditional ferry here, a motorised half-decker boat about 20 feet long: it accommodated about a dozen passengers and you could bring your bike if there was room. When a Waterford man had the vision to establish a car ferry to replace the open ferry boat, local people were amazed at the idea, and wondered how he could ever recoup his considerable investment. Within months, however, the service was booming, and it was a major factor in opening up the Hook peninsula to tourism and business. Tourism in the south-east in general, and the Hook area in particular, was greatly improved, as was business communication between Waterford and Wexford.

Before the establishment of the car ferry, the triangle of land that makes up the Hook peninsula was a coastal cul-de-sac, remote from the rest of the hinterland, where old ways were retained long after the modern world had come to the rest of the mainland. Our annual family outings from Waterford to Hook lighthouse in the pre-car-ferry days were like a trip back in time. Clusters of men still gathered at crossroads

Ballyhack at low tide

(*Above*) Ballyhack Castle from the pier, a pencil sketch by du Noyer c.1860

[255]

The remains of the
Templars' preceptory at
Crook

on Sundays after mass, wearing navy suits with waistcoats, and played pitch and toss with pennies. Tiny roadside shops where we would stop for ice-creams, had on their shelves glass globes for paraffin lamps, jars of concentrated sheep-dip, packets of Murphy's Pure Rice Starch, and jars of boiled sweets. Along the road one would see country people sitting on makeshift seats in the hedge outside their cottages watching the world go by, and at harvest-time one could watch the traditional *meithil*, neighbours working together in the fields to bring in the crop.

The ferry port on the Wexford side is the village of Ballyhack, overlooked by a fine towerhouse, said to have been built by the Templars, although to me it looks later in date and is probably an establishment of another religious order, Knights of St John, also called the Hospitallers. In common with Dunbrody, it came into the ownership of the Etchinghams in the sixteenth century. Evidence that they used Ballyhack for continental trade is indicated by the large amount of pottery from France, Portugal, Spain and the Low Countries that was excavated from one of the

garderobes or cupboards in the castle. The castle has survived centuries of depredations and a threat to demolish it in 1649, when it was thought that it might be taken by Cromwell's forces and disrupt communications up and down the river. The Model Army did take the castle, and caused a little damage, but some fine carved stone survived, and on one of the upper floors there is a perfect little oratory complete with an altar flanked by two corbels for holding candles. The stone to build the castle came from a quarry on the tall hill of sandstone at the back of the village, from which, until the end of the nineteenth century, millstones were also cut and exported by river. An account of 1684 reports how the heavy millstones were transported to the Quay: they 'with noe small skill nor less danger are rowled downe a very high precipice to the aforesaid Key, and soe carried by water as occation requires'.

Duncannon Fort and Credan Head

Below Ballyhack is the hamlet of Arthurstown, a nineteenth-century estate village attached to Dunbrody Park, a rambling mansion of the same date built by the Chichester family. The Chichesters also built a substantial 300 feet-long harbour to deal with the considerable exports from the area of poultry, fish, pigs butter, eggs and honey, and imports of coal and slate from Wales, but within years it became silted up and therefore redundant.

A kilometre south of Passage at Crook are the ruins of another Knights Templar establishment, founded in 1172, on a grant of land made to them by Henry II, as part of his penance for his involvement in the murder of Thomas Becket. When in 1312 the order was abolished by Pope Clement V, Crook passed into the hands of the Knights of St John. They built a tall castle on the site, some vestiges of the ruins of which can still be seen. It was probably occupied down to the mid-seventeenth century at least,[7] when the Down Survey refers to it as 'a fair castle in repair' but it was a ruin by the mid-nineteenth century. Other than the stump of the castle, the ivy-clothed gable of an old church and an overgrown holy well, there is little left above ground today of the Hospitallers', or indeed the Templars' presence in Crook.

Opposite Crook on the Wexford shore the holiday and fishing village of Duncannon has grown up around a large Elizabethan fort. It was originally built to defend Waterford Harbour against invasion by the Spaniards and to protect shipping and the local fishing fleet from pirates. The harbour and the seas off the coast were rich fishing grounds at the time: as many as 450 fishing boast were based in Dunmore, Passage, Cheekpoint, Duncannon and Ballyhack at the end of the sixteenth century, harvesting an abundance of cod, gurnard and whiting, lobster, crab, prawns, shrimp and oysters.

Built on the site of an Iron Age fortification on a high rocky promontory jutting into Waterford Harbour, Duncannon fort was protected from the land side by a 30 feet deep dry moat, and it constituted a formidable barrier to ships trying to enter the river. Its strategic location ensured that it played an important part in the military history of the south-east, particularly during the wars of the seventeenth century, when it came under siege three times. Having seen James II slip quietly out of Waterford Harbour in the wake of the battle of the Boyne, the fort surrendered to his son-in-law, William of Orange, when he arrived a few days later to embark for England. After the end of the Napoleonic Wars there was

7   Julian Walton, 'Aspects of Passage East', *Decies* 10.

only a caretaker garrison, and Queen Victoria, who was used to receiving thunderous gun salutes as she sailed by military or naval establishments, commented in her diary during her visit to Waterford Harbour in 1849 that Duncannon 'had not saluted for fifty years'.

Today the fort is run as a tourist attraction by a local co-operative and has been used for military re-enactments in full period dress. The little maritime museum there is worth a visit, and local artists are encouraged to exibit their work and to avail of the studios provided. An internet café occupies one of the old barrack buildings. I always find it difficult to make a connection with a place and its past if there are crowds around, and on my most recent visit to Duncannon fort the internet café, the school tours, and the hustle and bustle of the place failed to inspire me. After a while I slipped away to investigate the open area between the fort and the little harbour. The sun was bright, and outside the fort it was quiet, with only the sound of a gentle wind wafting from the open sea to the south. I squeezed through an old gateway into what, at first sight, I thought was a meadow of long grass undulating in the breeze, but then I saw that there was a scatter of tombstones reaching their tops above the grass and wildflowers. I waded through the grass to read the inscriptions on the stones, and in the quiet, under a blue sky, with the waters of Waterford Harbour in sight, I felt a sense of the past. I expected to find soldiers' graves, and indeed I did find the last resting place of Gunner Little of the Royal Artillary, who died in June 1860 aged 23, but one forgets that the soldiers manning Irish forts such as these were English, and lived in the forts, often, if they were officers, with their wives and children. So I also found the stone of Susanna Todd, wife of John Todd, Bombardier Commander of the 3rd Battalion of the Royal Artillery, who died in February 1830, aged 37 years, and a stone poignantly inscribed to a child who died aged four years, 11 months and 27 days, erected by the rank and file of her father's detachment, and the lines:

> *In life she was beloved,*
> *And in death much lamented.*

How many such sad graves are spread across the world where the British Empire reigned?

Downstream and opposite Duncannon on the Waterford side is Woodstown beach, spanning a mile between a rocky promontory at the northern end and a beech-wooded headland at the other, and often carpeted with acres of gleaming white cockleshells. There was probably once an inlet connecting the sea to a broad tidal lagoon behind the beach, but changes in sea level after the last Ice Age strung a line of low sand dunes across the inlet cutting off the lagoon from the sea, and, apart from a stream flowing through the beach to enter the sea, all that is left of the lagoon is a reed bed of considerable extent, a wonderful, happily inaccessible, wildlife wilderness. This tidal history has left Woodstown with its fine beach, a place of summer pleasure for count-less Waterford families, and a feeding ground for wildfowl in winter-time. Then the sand flats are home to a glorious host of piping, squealing, trilling, gabbling wildfowl and waders, which include a contingent of Brent geese taking summer holidays from their homes in Greenland. A most welcome addition to the usual range of birds one can see at Woodstown all year round now is the egret, whose numbers, after an absence of fifty years, are on the increase.

At one part of the beach the sand is frequently stripped away, revealing the scattered remains of tree roots and branches, relics of an age gone by when the sea level was lower, possibly during the last Ice Age. The low boulder clay cliff at the back of the beach displays a layer of sand full of seashells six metres above the beach level, another relic of a time long past when the melting ice of the glaciers led to sea levels that were higher than they are today, dramatic physical evidence of a former period of global warming. This sand layer at the top of the boulder clay cliffs has been used since time immemorial by a colony of tiny sand martins that turn up each year for their summer holidays after a long flight from Africa. Here they mate and rear their young before their autumnal return south.

Woodstown has changed little in centuries, and must be one of very few places in Ireland that the Celtic Tiger has missed. One might have expected housing schemes, chip shops and maybe even amusement arcades to have sprung up along its mile-long beach, but just one house, a holiday home for city children and a small caravan park have been developed over the past thirty years. The only significant change has been the establishment of extensive

(*Left*) Colourful shells on Woodstown beach

The quiet unspoiled Woodstown beach

Bluebells in the beach wood on Knockaveelish Head

oyster farms far out on the sands, exposed at low tide as a series of dark seaweed-draped frames. An increasing amount of the detritus of this industry, including rubber straps and vinyl net sacks, is beginning to mar the beach, and one wonders if the local authorities make sure the oyster farmers clean up regularly. I fear they do not.

Among the gleaming cockles that give the beach much of its character are to be found an increasing number of new, exotic shells, the remains of Japanese oysters that have escaped from the artificial beds: I sometimes wonder if this imported species has anything to do with the disappearance from the beach of razor shells, those long narrow shells which my childhood friends and I used as palisades around our sand castles, and there seems to have been a considerable reduction in tiny roseate and pink tellin shells. No place, however, stays the same for long. On my exploration of the coast of Waterford in the early 1990s[8] I met a man who recalled the beach being frequently covered in the 1920s with giant jellyfish, to such an extent that the place would stink of them for weeks. He also remembered how shoals of horse mackerel were often left stranded on the beach when the tide went out. The jellyfish do occasionally still turn up in small numbers, but horse mackerel, similar to the common mackerel we know except for great spines down its back, hasn't been seen for years on the south coast. In the 1920s when these phenomena were occurring, no one trumpeted that their appearance were signs of great climate change.

The stretch of water and the Wexford and Waterford coastlines from Cheekpoint to the open sea are wonderfully scenic and a priceless resource: enjoyed but taken for granted by many, the area came close to being utterly transformed on two occasions in the last couple of centuries.

In the late eighteenth century the people of the Swiss city state of Geneva, for long a spiritual centre of Protestantism, revolted against the aristocrats of the place and took power in a bloodless coup. In short order, France, Berne and Sardinia, which had interests in Geneva, allied to intervene on behalf of the aristocrats, and laid siege to the city. After some negotiations, the Genevans decided to abandon their city and emigrate, and seek asylum in a country where they would be

(*Right*) Knockaveelish Hill south of Woodstown beach

---

8   Michael Fewer, *By Cliff and Shore*, 1992.

appreciated. There were plenty of options available: their craftsmanship in silver and gold and in particular their knowledge of watchmaking, an extraordinarily important and valuable craft at the time, were widely sought after, and there were offers from the Grand Duke of Tuscany, the Palatine Elector, the Landgrave of Hesse-Homburg and George III. The Genevans were particularly attracted to settling in Ireland, a country where the recent establishment of a domestic parliament had encouraged an enthusiastic atmosphere of liberalism, and where there would be no problems of competition from the English watchmaking community. The advantages to the Protestant establishment in Ireland of having a community of enlightened Protestants bringing their skills and financial resources to a relatively poor and strongly Catholic area of the south-east were clear, and Charles Tottenham Loftus, Lord Ely, who owned land on both sides of the harbour, offered them a site at Crook. In his letter to them he stated: 'I wish to benefit the most enlightened people in the universe, the first Protestant colony on earth. When I am called to leave this earth, I shall repose with the serenity worthy of a man who knows that in giving happiness to you, he has reared a monument more durable than marble and shaped by the most able artist.'

The area agreed for the new settlement was a parcel of 11,000 acres near Passage East, and it was decided that a new town would be built on higher ground south of the village. A grant of £50,000 was made for the construction of the town and the transportation of about 1,000 Genevans with all their effects from Europe. The local Catholic priest, Father Hearne, enthusiastically supported the establishment of the new town and ensured that there were no objections from his flock.

In July 1783 an advance party of Genevans arrived in Waterford city to oversee planning and arrangements. James Gandon, the foremost architect working in Ireland at the time, was commissioned to plan New Geneva, as it was to be called, and he laid out a grid iron plan with a subtly curved Bath-like terrace that terminated in a church at each end. The town was to have a university like the Academy of Science in Geneva, employing 44 professors and assistants, to which it was hoped to attract students from all over Europe. In the first phase, fifty houses were to be built, along with a bakery, an inn, a cotton factory and a laundry. Plans were made for a water supply, and it seems that a large new harbour was to be built within the 1,000 acres of tidal land that was to be reclaimed below the boulder clay cliffs at Crook. In parallel with all these arrangements, the government saw to it that the Gold Standard, which had stood since 1729, was altered to suit the Genevans, and three new assay marks were devised for the new assay office planned for New Geneva. Meanwhile, Waterford society was enjoying the presence of the Genevan advance party, and the opportunity to socialise with these refined and accomplished Europeans, which included M. Claviere, an entrepreneur and businessman who later became the Finance Minister of France, and a master watchmaker by the name of Challons, who had travelled throughout Europe for many years extending his knowledge and skills.

Building work on the new town began in late 1783, and the foundation stone was laid in July 1784, but within weeks of that date, with over £30,000 already spent, the project came to a sudden halt and New Geneva was never completed.

Considerable doubts about the settlement had arisen on both sides. First, there was a change of Lord Lieutenant in Ireland, the supportive and sober Lord Temple being replaced by the high-living Duke of Rutland, who had little sympathy for the virtuous Genevans. It had also become clear to the Irish aristocracy that the Genevans, while Protestants, were in political terms far too liberal. With the rural areas of the south-east beset by the activities of the Whiteboys, agrarian protesters, it was not difficult for the advance party of Genevans based in Waterford to be aware of the reality of Irish politics. M. Claviere wrote to a compatriot in Neuchâtel: 'we must not overlook the need to conciliate the poor, who cultivate the soil that is offered to us. The greed and harshness of the great landowners have made the tenants violent and irritable. That is the reason for the disorders of which you have heard. They are in revolt against treachery and abominable outrage. If we behave well we shall gain their confidence'.[9] Word of these sentiments spread, and were not appreciated by the establishment.

Back at Neuchâtel, where the refugees had settled temporarily, they were becoming comfortable and were settling in, and the idea of a further journey to the far-off, cold and primitive western isle of Ireland

---

9   Hubert Butler, *Escape from the Anthill*, Lilliput, 1985.

was losing its appeal. The burgers of Waterford, while charmed by the Genevans, can hardly have been pleased about the idea of a new town and port, outside of their control, on the banks of Waterford Harbour. All these concerns combined to deal a death-blow to the project, which, if it had proceeded, would without doubt have changed the face of east Waterford, and indeed of the city itself.

—◦◦◦—

Nearly two hundred years later another project was being considered that would have had even greater impact on Waterford Harbour. In the early 1970s the geographic location of the port of Waterford in relation to Britain and the Continent suggested, with the advent of the European Economic Community, that it had the potential to expand greatly and provide serious competition for Dublin and Cork. Waterford, after all, had once been the second city in Ireland because of its port, and there was a strong possiblity that it could become such again. A number of problems, however, stood in the way of the comprehensive development that might allow Waterford to exploit its true potential. The port's location in Waterford city centre restricted expansion; transport in and out of the city was difficult and two large sandbanks in the river, one at Cheekpoint and the other at Duncannon, prevented large ships passing up and down stream on an around-the-clock basis.

In 1974 Waterford Harbour Board considered a radical plan to counteract these problems, which involved relocating the port down-stream.[10] The proposal was to reclaim the shallow sandflats between Passage East and Credan Head on the Waterford side, and Duncannon and Hall Point on the Wexford side, creating nine square miles of new land, narrowing down the natural harbour to less than a mile in width and creating a vast new port area with nearly nine linear miles of quayside. Technically, the project was perfectly practical: the Dutch had been doing such reclamation work very successfully for centuries. The project was estimated to cost one billion pounds, the provision of which out of the public purse might be possible, it was thought, particularly if a large oil strike was made in the Celtic Sea. Employment potential in the

---

10 *Development: Waterford Port,* 1972. Author's archive.

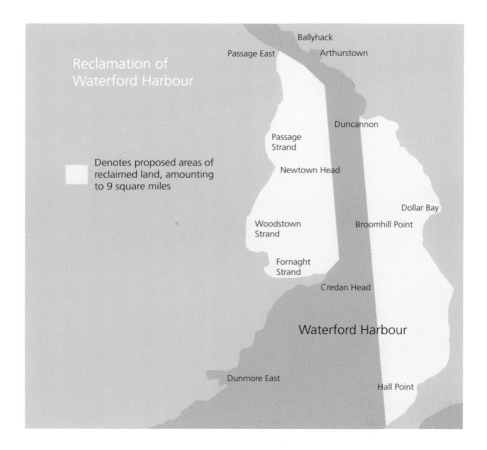

new port area and in industries associated with the port was estimated at 100,000 to 200,000, which suggests a population growth of about one million. At this remove, with the miracle of the Celtic Tiger behind us, none of these figures sounds over-ambitious. In the Ireland of 1974 such visionary ideas, however, while interesting, must have seemed like science fiction and received little more than a cursory examination from the Harbour Board and the politicians. After a limited discussion, the plan was shelved, and the people of east Waterford and south Wexford still have the glorious amenities of the beaches and coastline of Waterford Harbour to enjoy.

Subsequently, a new, more modest, port was established at Bellevue. Located on a site with more than enough potential for expansion, with

Credan Head | adjacent rail and road access and deep water mooring, the new container and bulk port has proved very successful. At the time of writing, however, I understand the question of a 'Superport' in the south-east is being discussed again in relation to the natural development of the east coast of Ireland.

———

Between the point at Passage and rounded Credan Head, a great whale-back of a headland that projects from the Waterford shore deep into the harbour, the navigable channel is quite narrow, bounded on the west by an extensive stretch of mudflats which at full tide would have been invis-

ible to newcomers to the harbour, and on the east by rocky cliffs. In the days of sail, travel by sea had considerable dangers, particularly close to the shore. There have been many reports over the centuries of shipwrecks within Waterford Harbour, and it is likely that the seabed is littered with the remains of ships and cargoes. Larger merchant ships always needed to take a pilot on board when arriving at the mouth of the harbour and when leaving Waterford port to sail downstream to the sea – usually a local man who knew the vagaries of the tide, shifting sand bars and the navigable channel, to guide them safely through.

At the end of Credan Head, cut into the cliffs, is a staircase that harks back to those days. I remember as a boy being brought out along the dramatic headland to fish for bass, or salmon bass as we knew them, and it was on the old red sandstone Forty Steps that we stood and cast our lines into the rising tide. We were told that the steps were made by smugglers of old to land their illicit cargoes of tobacco and brandy, a story that as a boy I found fascinating, and later found not to be far removed from the truth. In the days of sail, pilots operated independently and in competition with one another. The first to be able to board a ship as she entered the harbour usually got the job, so there must have been a lot of watching for sail and many a race rowed across the waves. The Forty Steps, nearly a mile out into the harbour, were, it is said, carved by an enterprising pilot to ensure that he got to vessels first.

There seems to be little doubt, however, that smugglers did on occasion use these steps to land contraband. A series of bohereens can be traced leading from Credan Head inland: the old name of one section of this route is Bothar na mBan Gorm, or the Road of the Black Women, and it has been suggested that the name arose from sightings at night of lines of African slave bearers carrying kegs of contraband brandy or bales of tobacco, and the fact that they were wearing garments like dresses suggested that they were women.

Smuggling was a particularly popular and almost respectable seafaring occupation throughout the eighteenth century, and probably went out of fashion only when the Royal Navy increased its presence around Ireland's coasts during the French wars of the period. There was a strong force of Royal Navy and Revenue warships stationed in Waterford in the early 1790s: the Revenue Cruiser *Rutland* was assisted in dealing with smugglers by the Royal Navy frigates the *Porcupine* and the *Squirrel*, substantial warships which must have been an impressive sight to see beating up Waterford Harbour. A frigate, the next class down from the ship-of-the-line or battleship, had two decks and carried anything from 20 to 50 guns. A well-handled frigate could turn and manoeuvre with the speed of a yacht, and could out-sail and capture any merchant ship. At that time, the navy also had a sloop, the *Swallow*, and two fast cutters on station at Waterford. A sloop was a small but fast cruising warship: cutters were up to 130 tons displacement, with a crew of 40 and about 16 guns.

The most lucrative cargoes for smugglers included rum, brandy and tobacco, and they did not give up their cargoes without a fight. The

Waterford Herald reported in the summer of 1791 that a smuggling cutter called the *Morgan Rattler* had been captured by the *Swallow* off the coast after an exchange of cannon fire, during which five of the *Swallow's* crew were killed. It was not thought necessary to report what casualties the smugglers suffered. On other occasions smugglers were captured complete with their valuable contraband. Another column in the *Waterford Herald* in 1791 states:

> Thursday morning was brought up to Custom House Quay, a smuggling sloop, clinch built, called *The Two Brothers of Fowey*, John Lee Master, laden with 297 ankews of rum, brandy, Geneva, and 37 bales of tobacco, captured off Tramore by the *Rutland* Revenue Cruizer, Captain Wilby, after a chase of twelve hours.

With the permission of Mr Baldwin, the owner of the land, I recently sought out the Forty Steps again, following the line of the Bothar na mBan Gorm out over Credan Head. At the highest point, the full extent of Waterford Harbour can be seen, stretching from the village of Dunmore East and the wooded hills of Gaultier around to a northern horizon that included Mount Leinster, Brandon Hill, Kennedy Park and Forth Mountain, while to the east the long peninsula of Hook, beyond which one of the Saltee islands was visible, shelved into the gleaming Atlantic. From this elevation I could see that the waters of the harbour were divided into two distinct parallel streams stretching northwards, a brown one of fresh water carrying rich nutrients on the Wexford side, and a blue-green stream of the salty Atlantic water on the Waterford side. Since the tides surge inland and retreat twice a day, this meeting of the waters must move with them.

At the north-eastern tip of Credan an overgrown path leads steeply down to the cliff edge, where I was delighted to find again, after fifty years, the Forty Steps. Much eroded today, and with one section apparently dislodged by heavy seas, I counted eighteen steps down as far as the dropping tide, and it looks as if this last concrete vestige of the sailing ship era in Waterford Harbour will last for another century.

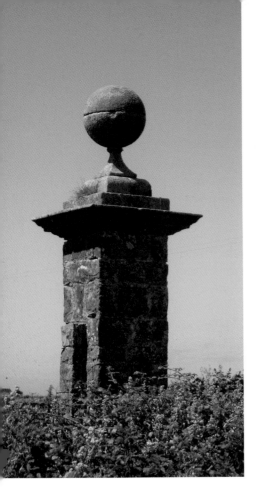

Old gate pillar at Loftus Hall

(*Right*) Templetown Church and cemetery

Opposite Credan Head on the Wexford side, a battlemented tower at Templetown marks the site of yet another Knights Templar establishment, this one founded in 1183. On the low-lying coast farther south, the three-storey, nine-bay pile of Loftus Hall stands out starkly in its treeless, walled demesne. The Hall was erected by George Herbert Loftus, 6th Marquess of Ely in 1871, on the site of an eighteenth-century house that was in turn built on the site of a fourteenth-century castle of the Redmonds. The house and lands came into the ownership of the Benedictine order in 1917, followed by the Rossminian nuns, who came in 1935, and stayed for nearly fifty years. In the 1980s the house, which has 22 bedrooms, was bought by locally born Michael Devereaux and was run for a while as a hotel.

Loftus Hall is said to be haunted. The story told is one that is common

Counsellors Strand at Dunmore East

to many locations in Ireland – of a card game late at night, a stranger turning up and joining in, a card dropped to the floor, and the stranger seen to have cloven hooves. This may just be cover story, but it seems that there was a real problem with possession or evil spirits at the house in the 1760s. It seems that the Catholic Parish Priest of the time, a Canon Broaders, was called in by the Protestant Tottenhams and performed an elaborate exorcism. It is said that his tombstone in Horetown cemetery had the epitaph 'Here lies the body of Thomas Broaders, who did good and prayed for all and banished the Devil from Loftus Hall'. Somehow the curse lived on in the 1871 house, however, and it is said that the nuns kept one of the rooms locked for all the years they were there. At the time of writing, which is also a time of plummeting property prices, the house and 63 acres of land are to be auctioned:

the guide price of 1.6 million euro reflects not only the economic climate, but the building work that will be required to reinstate the house.

Almost directly due west of Loftus Hall on the Waterford side is the pretty village of Dunmore East, the built footprint of which has quadrupled in the last fifteen years. Great numbers of holiday homes and homes of commuters have spread out west and north from the Victorian centre, which is blessed with a rich collection of nineteenth-century seaside villas and cottage ornés of wealthy Waterford merchants. The name Dunmore or *Dún Mór* translates as Great Fort, and there was until the 1960s the remains of a large Iron Age promontory fort above the harbour. It was damaged first during the original construction of the harbour in 1824, and what remained was swept away in the 1960s by the Office of Public Works when the harbour was being extended and improved. In the medieval period, it seems that the Normans built a stone-built fortification overlooking Dunmore's two beaches which would have been safe landing places: only a much-eroded old red sandstone flanker tower survives.

For hundreds of years little happened in this sleepy fishing village until in the 1820s it was decided that Dunmore would become the packet station for Waterford owing to the difficulties and delays caused by trying to get the packet ships farther upriver. A large harbour was designed by the Scottish surveyor and engineer Alexander Nimmo to create a haven, and a direct road was constructed to Waterford. Nimmo had designed many harbours around the coast of Ireland, but at Dunmore he got the opportunity to include a lighthouse, and the building, a great classical Doric column in granite, still graces the much-altered harbour.

The southernmost point of the county of Wexford is Hook Head, a promontory of fossil-rich limestone formed aeons ago when this particular piece of the earth's plate was the bottom of a shallow sea near where the Falkland Islands are today. Such is the dramatic presence of the great and ancient rotund lighthouse, at Hook, however, that most visitors will not notice the myriad fossilised plants, shells and organisms that thrived in warm waters seventy million years ago and which cover the pavements of rock.

Hook Tower is one of the oldest lighthouses still in operation in Europe, albeit these days, like all Ireland's lighthouses, it is operated automatically. It was established by the great feudal knight William Marshall, Earl of Pembroke, in the early thirteenth century, to ensure safe access to and from his newly established town of New Ross, some 45 kilometres upstream on the Barrow. The spectacular 36-metre high structure built then may have been inspired by the Pharos lighthouse in Alexandria which Marshall had seen when he served as a young man on the crusades.[11] The gleaming, lime-washed tower would have been a startling landmark in daylight, and the beacon fire tended by monks on its top was visible for many miles out to sea. The place is a tourist attraction today, both for the historic tower, which is open to the public, and for the experience of the powerful might of the Atlantic, which even in calm weather surges in great waves over and around the black limestone prow of the headland.

Where does the Suir end and the Atlantic begin? Where do the fresh waters of the Suir and its sisters finally dilute themselves in the Celtic

---

11 Billy Colfer, *The Hook Peninsula*, Cork University Press, 2004.

Sea and give themselves up to the great ocean? Because of the movement of tides, the interface, if there is one, is moved twice daily up and downriver by the tides, and further blurred by a myriad sea currents. A symbolic end to my journey down the Suir, therefore, begun in a boggy spring on grassy Borrisnoe in far-off Tipperary, might be between the two great portals of Waterford Harbour, Hook Head on the east side and the Old Red Sandstone bluffs of Dunmore East on the west. There is an appropriate symmetry in the fact that a line between these points, continued inland for a kilometre, passes through a hill where there is a ruined medieval church with the same name as the first medieval church site met along the Suir, Killea.

Hook Tower, one of the oldest working lighthouses in Europe

(*Above*) Ruined medieval chuch at Killea

Select Bibliography

Anderson, Ernest B., *Sailing Ships of Ireland*, Morris & Company, 1951

Anderson, Paris, *Nooks and Corners of the County Kilkenny*, 1914

Annals of Lough Cé at Trinity College, Dublin

Bianconi M. O'C. & S. J. Watson, *Bianconi, King of the Irish Roads*, Allen Figgis, 1962

Brady, C. & R. Gillespie, eds., *Natives and Newcomers*, Irish Academic Press, 1986

Broderick, Eugene, *Devotions at Holy Wells*, Decies 54

Burke Houlihan, Elaine ed., *Tipperary: A Treasure Chest*, Relay 1995

Butler, David J., *South Tipperary 1570-1841, Religion, Land and Rivalry*, Four Courts Press, 2006

Butler, Hubert, *Escape from the Anthill*, Lilliput, 1985

Byrne, Niall J. [ed.] *Liber Antiquissimus Civitatis Waterfordiae*, Irish Manuscripts Commission, 2007

Carlyle, Thomas, *Oliver Cromwell's Letters and Speeches: with elucidations*, Chapman & Hall, 1924

Coady, Michael, *One Another*, The Gallery Press, 2006

—— *All Souls*, The Gallery Press, 2001

—— *Two for a Woman, Three for a Man*, The Gallery Press, 1980

Colfer, Billy, *The Hook Peninsula*, Cork University Press, 2004

Covey, Thomas, *A Scheme for Building a Bridge over the River Suire at the City of Waterford*, 1770

Cuddihy, Thomas, *Boats, Cots, Punts and Wherries*, Coracle, 2004

Doran, Linda, *Thesis Paper: The Suir Valley: A Study of Medieval Settlement in the Suir River Valley*, 2004

Dowling, Daniel, *Waterford's Streets, Past and Present*, Waterford Corporation, 1998.

Fewer, Michael, *By Cliff and Shore*, Anna Livia, 1993

—— *Irish Waterside Walks*, Gill & Macmillan, 1997

Fewer, T. N., *Waterford People*, Ballylough, 1998

Flood, J. and P., *Kilcash: A History 1190-1801*, Geography Publications, 1999

Flynn, Paul, *The Book of the Galtees and the Golden Vein*, Hodges Figgis & Co., 1926

Fraser, Antonia, *Cromwell, Our Chief of Men*, Weidenfeld and Nicolson, 1973

Fullam, Brendan, *The Throw-In: The GAA and the Men Who Made it*, Wolfhound, 2004

Galloway, Peter, *The Cathedrals of Ireland*, Institute of Irish Studies, 1992

Gardiner, Samuel Rawson, *Oliver Cromwell*, Longmans, Green & Co., 1901

Green, Alice Stopford, *The Making of Ireland and its Undoing*, Macmillan, 1913

Griffith, Arthur, ed., *Meagher of the Sword*, M. H. Gill & Son 1917

Gwynn, A. & R. N. Haddock, *Medieval Religious Houses, Ireland*, Irish Academic Press, 1988

Harbison, Peter, ed., *The Shell Guide*, Gill & Macmillan, 1989

—— *The High Crosses of Ireland*, Rudolf Habelt, 1992

Hogan, John, *Kilkenny*, P. M. Egan, 1884

Hore, Philip Herbert, *History of the town and county of Wexford*, Elliot Stock, 1901

Hunt, Tom, *Portlaw, County Waterford, 1825- 1876*, Four Courts Press, 2000

Hurley, M. & O. Scully, *Late Viking Age and Medieval Waterford: excavations 1986-1992*, Waterford Corporation

Irish, Bill, *Shipbuilding in Waterford*, Wordwell, 2001

Kickham, Charles, *Knocknagow*, James Duffy, 1918

Laffan, Kathleen, *The History of Kilmacow*, private, 2005

Lincoln, Siobhan, *Along St Declan's Way*, private

Lydon, J. F., *The Lordship of Ireland in the Middle Ages*, Gill & Macmillan, 1972

Monk, M. and J. Sheehan, eds., *Early Medieval Munster, Archaeology, History and Society*, Cork University Press, 1998

Moss, R., C. O'Clabaigh & S. Ryan, eds., *Art and Devotion in Late Medieval Ireland*, Four Courts Press, 2006

Mulvihill, Mary, *Ingenious Ireland*, Town House, 2002

Murphy, Donal A., *The Two Tipperarys*, Relay, 1994

O'Connor, Frank, *Irish Miles*, Macmillan, 1947

O'Connor, Nuala, *Bring It All Back Home*, BBC Books, 1991

Ó Corrbuí, Máirtín *Tipperary*, Brandon, 1991

O'Donovan, John, ed., *Annals of the Kingdom of Ireland*, Castlebourke, 1998

O'Kelly, Owen, *The Place Names of the County of Kilkenny*, The Kilkenny Archaeogical Society, 1985

O'Leary, Patrick, *Half Hours with the old boatmen*, 1895

O'Neill, Eoghan, *The Golden Vale of Ivowen*, Geography Publications, nd

Power, Patrick *Waterford and Lismore: A compendious History of the United Diocese*, Cork University Press, 1937

The Place-Names of Decies, Cork University Press, 1952

Power, Patrick C., *Carrick-on-Suir Town and District, 1800-2000*, Carrick Books, 2003

Queen Victoria, *Leaves from the Journal of Our Life in the Highlands*, 1868

Radner, Joan, ed., *Fragmentary Annals of Ireland*, Dublin Institute for Advanced Studies, 1978

Rynne, Colin, *Industrial Ireland 1750-1930: An Archaeology*, The Collins Press, 2006

Smith, Charles, *The Ancient and Present State of the County and City of Waterford*, 1746

Somerville-Large, Peter, *The Irish Country House*, Sinclair Stevenson, 1995

Stokes, G.T, *Ireland and the Anglo-Norman Church*, Hodder & Stoughton, 1889

Titmarsh, M.A., (W.M. Thackeray) *The Irish Sketchbook*, 1843

Walsh, Paul P., *A History of Templemore and its Environs*, Private, 2006

Walsh, Jim, ed., *Sliabh Rua – a History of its People and Places*, Slieverue Parish Pastoral Committee, 2001

Walsh, John Edward, *Sketches of Ireland Sixty Years Ago*, McGlashan, 1857

White, James, *My Clonmel Scrap Book*, Dundalgan Press, nd

Young, Arthur, *A Tour in Ireland*, Cambridge University Press, 1925

JOURNALS:

The Irish Sword

Cork Historical and Archaeological Society Journal

Waterford and South East Ireland Archaeological Society Journal

Decies: The Journal of the Waterford Archaeological and Historical Society

The Irish Genealogist

Index

Abbeyside, Waterford, 229
Aherlow (Aherloe), 85
  Glen (Vale) of, 83, 86, 100
  river, 83, 86
Aidan of Ferns, Saint, 152
Albert, Prince Consort, 254
Alexandra, Queen, 230
America, United States of, 77,
  166, 191–93, 219
An Mainistir Mhuire, see Lady's
  Abbey
Annals of the Kingdom of Ireland,
  203
Anner, river, 52
Anti-Treaty forces, 161–62,
  184, 232–34
Aongus, King, 107
Araid Cliach, clan, 209
Arbuthnot, Eleanor, 30
Ardcloyne, 182
Ardfinnan, 103–9
  Castle, 104
Ardmayle, 72
Ardmore, 106
Ardnacrusha, 218
Armagh, County, 131, 141
Arrol, Sir William, bridge
  builder, 246
Arthurstown, 257
Athassel, 77
Attaeemore, 202
Aughall Bridge, 41, 43
Augustinian Order, 79, 86
Augustinian nunnery, 113
Axtell, Colonel,, 182

Bagwell, Colonel John, 118
Bagwell, William, 118
Bagwell family, 119
Baldwin, Mr, Waterford
  landowner, 271

Balleen Castle, 200
Ballinahinch Castle, 74
Ballingarry, 53, 158
Ballybrada House, 98
Ballybrada Quaker burial
  ground, 99
Ballybricken, 234
Ballydine, 151, 152
Ballygorey, 194, 196
Ballyhack, 251, 254, 256–58
Ballyhale, 231
Ballynakill House, 253
Ballyragget Castle, 200
Ballyslatteen, 83
Ballylooby, 99
Bansha Castle, 82
Barbados, 218
Barnane, Castle, 30, 31
Barnane School, 30
Barrow railway bridge, 246
Barrow, river, 11, 41, 156, 197,
  209, 245, 275
Becket, Thomas, 258
Bell Ferries, 235
Bellvue, port, 244, 267
Benduff (mountain), 13
Benedictine Order, 272
Bernard of Clairveaux, Saint,
  119
Beresford, Sir Marcus, 141
Beresford Poers, see le Poers
Bessborough Estate, 170, 184
Bianconi, Charles, 70, 72
Bilberry Rock, 205
Bindon, Francis, 184
Black and Tans, 37, 59
Blackfeet, see Cummins family
  group
Blackrock, County Dublin, 53
Blackstairs mountains, 24, 251
Blackwater, river, 125, 201

Blaise Hamlet, 96
Blessington, Earl of, 133–34
Blessington, Lady, 133–35
Blueshirts, the, 163
Boharnarooda, 14
Bohernamona, 52
Bolton, County Waterford, see
  Cheekpoint
Bolton, Cornelius, 246–48
Borrisnoe Mountain, 13–15,
  24, 277
Boru, Brian, 63
Bothar na mBan Gorm, 270,
  271
Bourke, William, 149
Boyne, Battle of, 184, 253, 258
Bradshaw, William, 57
Brandon Hill, 24, 251, 271
Brann's Fort, 199
Breack, Teig, 211
Breen, Dan, 161
Bremor, County Dublin, 178
Bridge Castle, Thurles, 52, 60
Bristol, 169
Britain, Roman, 20
British Army, 37, 59
British Empire, 34
British Parliament, 218
Brittas, estate, 51–52
Broaders, Canon Thomas, 273
Bronze Age, 24, 196
Brookes Hanley (Company),
  20
Brophy, Anthony, 235
Buildwas Abbey, 248
bullaun stone, 27
Bulmers cider, 130, 141
Burges, 99–100
Burke, Patrick, 99
  'the Barrister Burke', 99
Burke, Peter and Liz, 13–14, 28

Burnt House, The, 19–20
Butler, Christopher,
    Archbishop of Cashel, 149
Butler, Edmund Mac Richard,
    157, 182–83
Butler, Ellen, wife of Thomas,
    1st Baron of Cahir, 129
Butler, Lady Iveagh, 148, 149
Butler, James, 3rd Earl of
    Ormond, 199
Butler, James, 12th Earl and 1st
    Duke of Ormond, 56, 69,
    128, 149
Butler, James, 2nd Duke of
    Ormond, 149
Butler, James, 9th Baron Cahir,
    91
Butler, James, nephew of Piers,
    91
Butler, Sir James, son of 6th
    Earl, 200
Butler, John, 6th Earl of
    Ormond, 182–83
Butler, Margaret,
    granddaughter of Richard,
    96
Butler, Piers, 8th Earl of
    Ormond, 91, 199–201
Butler, Richard, 91, *see also*
    Cahir, Baron
Butler, Thomas, 1st Baron of
    Cahir, 129
Butler, Thomas, (Black
    Thomas) 10th Earl of
    Ormond, 64, 171–73
Butler, Thomas, Colonel, of
    Kilcash, 149
Butler, General Sir William, 82
Butler, John, Mayor of
    Waterford, 212
Butler army, 183
Butler family, 32, 74, 86–96,
    113, 149
Buttermilk Castle, 248, 250
Byron, Lord, 134, 158

cabbage-patch revolt, the, 158
Cabragh, 63
Cahir, 86–93, 95–101, 131, 133

Cahir, Baron, 95–96
Cahir Abbey, 86
Cahir Bridge, 88
Cahir Castle, 88–90
Cahir Cavalry Barracks, 95
Cahir Community Council, 96
Cahir House and Hotel, 92–93
Cahir to Clonmel, 94–135
Cambrensis, Giraldus, 86, 253
Campile, river. 249
Camus Bridge, 73
Canada, 82, 239
Canada Company, The, 239
Canada Street, County
    Waterford, 239–41
Cantrell and Cochrane, 141
Cappoquin, 125, 130
Caracciolo, Italian family, 244
Carden family, 22, 29–33, 51
    John Rutter ('Woodcock')
        Carden, 30
    Sir John, 31
Carden's Wild Demesne, ballad,
    149
Carew, Sir George, 66, 213
Carlisle, city, 252
Carlow, County, 24
Carmelite Order, 108
Carrick Boat Club, 167
Carrick Bridge, 157
Carrick Castle, 171–73
Carrick on Suir, 41, 123, 125,
    130, 131, 155–75,
Carrick on Suir to Waterford,
    176–205
Carrickbeg, 162, 170
Carrickmagriffin, *see* Carrick
    on Suir
Carroll, Teig, 211
Carron, County Clare, 58
Cashel, 41, 52, 74, 106, 107
Cashel, Rock of, 13
Castlelake, house, 73
Castleleiny, 41–43
Cathair Dun Iascaigh, *see* Cahir
Cathedral Church of the
    Assumption, Thurles, 54–
    55
Catholic Church, the, 68

Cavan, County, 19
Ceitinn, Seathrun, see Keating,
    Geoffrey
Celtic Sea, 11, 266
Challons, Swiss watchmaker,
    265
Charles II, 152
Charteris, family, 96
Cheekpoint, 246–48, 258, 266
Cheekpoint Hill, 246
Cheshire, Leonard, 69
Cheshire Homes, 69
Childers, Erskine, 162
China, 191
Chichester family, 257–58
Church of Ireland, 68
Churchill, Winston, 69
Churchtown, County
    Tipperary, 152
Cinaed, King of Deise, 113
Cistercian Monks,
    Holy Cross Abbey, 63, 68
    Roscrea, 31
Cistercian Abbey De Surio,
    118–20
Civil War, the, 144, 157
Clais na nAlbanach, see Dyke
    of the Foreigner
Clancy Brothers, the, 166–67
Clancy, Liam, 167
Clancy, Mary, 166
Clancy, Paddy, 166
Clancy, Tom, 166
Clare, County, 24
Claviere, M. Finance Minister
    of France
Clement V, Pope, 258
Clodiagh, river, 69, 191–93
Clonakenny, 28, 41
Clonamuckoge, 51
Cloncully Castle, 111
Clonmel, 30, 44, 122–35, 160–
    61, 191, 220
Clonmel to Carrick on Suir,
    136–175
Clonmore, 189
Cluain na Meala, *see* Clonmel
Coady, Michael, 155–58, 160,
    167

Coillte, 97
Collins, Michael, 231
Comeraghs, 13, 15, 24, 111, 123, 137, 196
Comgan, Abbot of Inislounaght, 119
Congreve, Ambrose, 195, 196, 240
Congreve, John, 195
Conn of the Hundred Battles, King, 13
Coolfinn Marshes, 194
Coolmore Stud, 70
Coolnamuck, 151
Coracle Press, 114
Corcomroe Abbey, 119
Cork, city, 76, 160, 232
Cork, County, 77, 152
Cornwall, 161
Cottagehill Wood, 96–98
Country Life, 207
Covey, Thomas, 222
Cox, Samuel, 223, 225
Craig, Maurice, 50
Credan Head, 266, 267, 269–72
Croke, Archbishop Thomas William, 54, 58–59
Croke Park, 59
Cromwell, Oliver, 90, 106, 126–27, 184, 213
Cromwell's Well, 81
Cromwellian New Model Army, 148, 222, 257
Cronin, Dick, 114
Crook, County Waterford, 258, 264, 265
Cruiskeen racing skiff, the, 130
Cuddihy, Thomas, 188–89
Cummins, family group, Tipperary, 26
Cunningham, John, 57
Curraduff, Killea, 31
Curraghmore House, 141, 185–86
Cusack, Michael, 58
Cutts, Simon, 114–15

Darrigal, 164

Darrigal Marshes, 194
Darrigs, family group, Tipperary, 26
Davin family, 130, 154–55
Davin, Maurice, 58, 154
Davin, Pat, 154–55
Davitt, Michael, 58, 59
de Burgo, Richard, 123
de Burgo, William, 79, 145, 146
de Camville, Geoffrey, 86
de Glanville, Ranulf, 180
de la Rochell, Fitz Norman, 191

de La Tocnaye, the Chevalier, 207
de Lacy, Walter, 72
de Montmorency, Hervey, 248
de Poher, Robert, 141
de Valera, Eamon, 161–63, 232
Declan, Saint, 107, 113
deiseal, 121
della Porta, Giacomo, 55
Demsey clan, 111
Denmark, 141, 221
Denny, Henry, *see* Henry Denny
Derry, *see* Londonderry
Desii, tribe, 121
Desmond, James Fitzgerald 6th Earl of, 182–83
Desmond, Gerald Fitzgerald 15th Earl of, 172, 173
Eleanor, wife of, 172
Desmond army, 183
Devanney, Marie Tynan, 15
Devereaux, Michael, 272
Devil's Bit Mountain, 12–14, 20–21, 24–27, 29–31, 41, 47
Dillon Bridge, 160, 161
Dillon, John Blake, 157
Disert Nairbe, cemetery, 152
Donoughmore, 8th Earl of, 116
Donoughmore, Baron, *see* Hely Hutchinson, Richard
Donoughmore, family 115–16
Dool, Herman, 195
Doornane, 196
Dowley, Daphne, 180–81
Dowley, Leslie, 164, 165

Dowley, Louis, 181
Drish, river, 61
Driver, Thomas and Rosemary, 191
Drogheda, 163
Drohan, Patrick, 167–70
Drom and Templemore, established church parish, 27
Dublin, city, 39, 89, 133, 211, 222
Dublin, County, 209
Dublin Port, 240
du Noyer, George, 80, 134, 210–11
Dun Bhrain, *see* Brann's Fort
Dunbrody Abbey, 248–49, 256
Dunbrody Castle, 249, 256–57
Dunbrody Park, 257
Duncannon, 216, 253, 254, 258–59, 266
Dundry Hill, Bristol, 79
Dungarvan, 124
Dunmore East, 235, 247. 258, 271, 274–77
Dunkitt, 201–2
Dyke of the Foreigner, Ardcloyne, 182

Edward VI, *see* Simnel, Lambert
Edward VII, 230
Edward J Dowley and Co., 164
Education and Science, Department of, 140
Elizabeth, Viscountess of Thurles, 56
Elizabeth I, 64, 172, 213
Elizabethan wars, 89
England, 182, 209, 211
English, Denis, 118
English Island, 104
Eoghanacht, 83
Eohgan Mhor, chief of, 83
Eoghanachta, 83, 85, 107, 209
Essex, Earl of, 89, 90
Etchingham, Sir Osbourne, 249
Etchingham family, 248–49, 256

Fachtna, Saint, 179
Fairbairn, William, 88
Faithlegge House, 247
Father Mathew, steam tug, 164, 224, 227
Fedamore, 86
Fenians, the, 53, 54
Fennel, John, 91
Fennel, Mary, 131
Fennel, family, 91–92, 96, 99
|Fergus, river, 146
Ferrybank, 208, 229, 237
Fethard, County Tipperary, 148
Fermoy Abbey, 119
Fewer, Michael, 234
Fewer, Teresa, 13, 116, 118
Fiddown, 188
Fionan Lobhar, Saint, 104
First Fruits, Irish Board of, 101, 119
Fishguard and Rosslare Harbour and Railway Company, 246
fitzGriffyn, Raymond, 157
FitzGerald, Edward, translator, 244
Fitzgerald, Gearoid Mór, the Great Earl of Kildare, 200
Fitzgerald, Margaret, wife of Piers Butler, 199–201
FitzGerald, Mary Augusta, 244
FitzGeralds, the, 243
Flanders, 211
Florence, 134
Foras Feasa ar Eirinn, 86, 100
Fort Mountain, Nth County Wexford, 251
Fort Railway Bridge, 246
Forth Mountain, Wexford, 271
Forty Steps, cliff staircase, 269–71
Foyle, river, 153, 225
France, 209, 216, 218, 253, 262
Franciscan Friary, Clonmel, 129, 146
Franciscan Third Order, 108
Free State, the, 161, 218
From the Source of the Suir to Templemore, 10–39

Gaelic Athletic Association (GAA), 34, 58–59, 155
Gaelic League, the, 82
Galtee (Galty) Mountains, 24, 47, 73, 85, 113
Galway, County, 24, 30, 213
Gandon, James, 264
Garda Training College, 39
Gardiner, Charles John, *see* Blessington, Earl of
Garret's Mill, 20
Garret's Mill Bridge, 20
Garryroe, 100
Gaultier, barony of, 250, 254, 271
Geneva, 262–64, *see also* New Geneva
Genoa, 134
Georgian Society, the, 96
George IV, 92, 218
Germany, 193
Gibbet Hill, 205
Girouard, Mark, 207
Glasshouse, County Waterford, 244–45
Glazing Wood, 246
Glen, County Tipperary, 154
Glen Castle, 154
Glen Poer, 152
Gloucester, city and shire, 252
Goff, Sir William, 229
Goggins, Brian, 165
Goings, family, Cahir, 92
Golden, village, 73, 76, 77
Golden Castle, 74
Golden Vale, the, 77, 163
Gough family, 120
Gowran Castle, 200
Grace, Tom, 166
Grand Canal, 41
Grange Cross, 98
Grange Moore, 98
Grannagh Castle, 196, 199–201
Grant, Captain Jer, 44
Grant, Mary, 44
Great Island, 242
Great Western, SS, 228
Green Man, the, 108

Gregory I, Pope, 120
Gregory XV, Pope, 67
Grubbs, family, Cahir, 92, 224
Grubb, J. Ernest, 164
Guinness, Waterford, 207
Gurteen le Poer, 141

Half River, The, Ardfinnan, 104
Hall, R& H, corn store
Hall Point, County Wexford, 266
Hampshire, 133
Harrington, Padraig, 118
Harty, Archbishop, 39
Haughey, Charles, 39
Hausmann, city planner, 191
Hayes, Lizzie, 58
Heads and Commoners of Clonmel, 108
Healy, Archbishop, 106
Hearne, Father, Waterford priest
Heavey, caretaker, 96, *see also* Swiss Cottage
hedge schools, 42
Helnwein, Gottfried, 142
Hely Hutchinson, John, 116
Hely Hutchinson, Richard, 115
Henry II, 74, 107, 141, 251–53, 258
Henry VII, 171, 213
Henry VIII, 64, 249
Henry Denny, 220–21
Herbert, Dorothea, 92, 216
Higgins, Reverend Paul, 27–28
holloways, 109–11
Holy Cross Abbey, 30, 63–69
Home Rule, 82
Hook Head, 216, 251, 255, 271, 275, 277
Horetown cemetery, 273
Horn, Erica Van, 114–15
House of Lords, British, 141
House of Lords, Irish, 218
Hudson Bay Company, Canadian, 218
Hundred Years War, the, 253
Hurley, Shay, 131, 133

Hyland, Edmund Keating, 92

India, 70, 191
Inioque, Saint, 249
Inis Leamhnachta, 119
Inishlounaght, 119
  holy well of, *see* St Patrick's
  Well
IRA, 2nd Tipperary Brigade, 37
Ireland, 11, 154, 253, 254
  and Westminster rule, 125,
  192
  and the Great Famine, 158
  and English intrigues, 182
Ireton, General, 213
Irish American Foundation, 96
Irish Georgian Society, 70
Irish Free State Hospitals'
  Sweepstake, 218
Irish Miles (1947), 131
Irish Times, 231, 232
Irish Volunteers, 36
Iron Age, 88
Isabella, Queen of England,
  64, 69

Jacob Brothers (Jacobs), 221–
  22
Jacobites, 153
James II, 128, 152–53, 253, 258
Jeffereys (Jefferyes), Mrs of
  Blarney Castle, 91
Jeffereys, Emily, 91
Jenkins, Captain Thomas, 133,
  134
Jersey, 218
Jobson, Frances, 254
John, son of Henry II, 252–53
  King of England, 69, 104
  Prince, 179, 180
Jones's Wood, 197

Kandahar, Lord Robert of, 242
Keating, Geoffrey, 85, 86, 99–
  102
Keeper Hill, 24
Keepsake for a living, journal, 134
Kennedy Centre, New York,
  219

Kennedy, Jacqueline, 93, 219
Kennedy, Jim and MB, 28–29
Kennedy Park, New Ross, 271
Kickham, Charles Joseph, 52–
  54
Kickham House, 52
Kilcash, song, 148–149
Kilcash Castle, 148–150
Kildalton, *see* Piltown
Kildare, County, 209
Kildroughtan, 155
Kilduff Mountain, 13
Killahara, 48
Killaly, John, 41
Killawardy, 13, 29
Killea, parish, County
  Tipperary, 27
Killea, church, County
  Waterford, 27, 277
Killough, 20
Kilkenny, city, 39
Kilkenny, County, 178, 181,
  195, 201, 208, 219, 243
Kilkenny, PS, 240
Kilkenny Castle, 200
Kilkenny Grammar School,
  200
Kilmacow, 201
Kilmanahan Estate, 116
Kilsheelan, 143–47
Kiltilane, townsland, 31
Kilwatermoy, 106
King, Giles, 215
King's Channel, 243, 245
Kingsbridge Station, 53
Kinsale, 254
Kirke, General, 153–54
Knights of St John
  (Hospitallers), 256
Knights Templar, the, 72, 258,
  272
Knockademsey, 111
Knockanaffrin ridge, 139
Knockanagh, 195
Knockgraffon, 83, 99, 100
Knocklofty bridge, 117
Knocklofty House and
  demesne, 115–18

Knockmealdowns
  (mountains), 13, 24, 85, 98,
  106, 113
Knocknageragh Bridge, 29, 41
Knocknagow, novel, 53
Knocknagow and Knocknagow II,
  steam tugs, 164, 165

Lachtnafrankee, 123
Lacken, 109–10
Lady's Abbey (Ladysabbey),
  107–8
Laffan, Elinor, 86
Land Commission, 96
Lancashire, 193
Lancaster, 252
Landscape, 151
Langley family, 51
  Major Henry, 51
Laois, County, 24
Larcom, Thomas, 203
le Clare, Richard, 251
le Poer, Catherine, Countess of
  Tyrone, 186
le Poer, Edmund James, 141
  see also Power family
le Poer Beresford, John Hubert
  de, 185
le Poer, James Count de, 141
le Poers, Beresford, 141, 185
le Poers, Norman, 186
Leahy, Archbishop Patrick, 54,
  55
Leahy, Commandant, 37–39
Leahy, Fiona, 143
Lebanon, the, 57
Lecky, W.E.H., 42
Leinster, 178, 209
Leitrim, County, 19
Lemass, Sean, 141
Licketstown, 196
Lidwell, brothers Arthur,
  George and Robert, 35
Life of St Malachy, 119
Life of St Patrick, 106–7
Limerick, city, 88, 213
Limerick, County, 77, 79
Lindville, 151
Lingaun, river, 178

Lismore, 106
Little Island, 242
Liverpool, 192, 217, 228, 241
Llangollen, 184,
Loch Dacheach, *see* Port Lairge
Loftus, Charles Tottenham, 264
Loftus, George Herbert, 272
Loftus Hall, 272–74
London, 134, 172, 241
London, Tower of, 253
Londonderry, 153
Long, English family, 70
Long Hill, 139
Long Reach, river Suir, 196, 197
Longfield House, 70
Lords, House of, 185
Lough Derg, 24, 41
Loughmoe, 43, 44, 48, 51
Loughnane, William, 56
Loughtally, 122
Luffany, 194–95
Lugnaquilla, festival of, 15
Lughnasa, 24, 25
Lynn, Dr Kathleen, 162

McCarthy, J.J., 54
McCarthy, Larry, 230
McCormack, Widow, 158
McCormack brothers, the, 48–50
McGrath, Joe, 218–19
McKinley, Richard, 35
Mac Murchú, Diarmuid, 74
Mac Murrough Kavanagh, Art, 253
McQuaid, Archbishop John Charles, 57
Mac Richard Butler, Edmund, *see under* Butler, Edmund
Madeira, 218
Magee, Brownie, 166
Magner, William, 141
Maher, Gilbert, 44
Makem, Tommy, 167
Malcolmson, David, 130–31, 241
Malcolmson, John, 241

Malcolmson, Joseph, 241
Malcolmson family, 98, 191–93, 220, 242
Manson, Marilyn, 142
Marie Antoinette, 95
Marshall, William, 82, 275
Marlfield House, County Tipperary, 117–20, 122
Marlfield House, Gorey, 117
Markievicz, Countess, 162
Mary B. Mitchell, sailing ship, 163
Mathew family, 76
    Francis, 76
    George, 76
    Father Theobald, 76–77
May, Algernon, 191
Mayfield House, 191, 193
Maynooth, 76
Mayo, County, 19
Meagher, Liam, 42, 43
Meagher, Thomas Francis, 130, 157, 158–60
Meath, County, 209
Megalithic tombs, 196
Merck, George W., 152
Merck, Sharp & Dohme, 152
Merriman, Brian, 42
Merrie England, ship, 240
Mesolithic peoples, 11, 196
Milford Haven, 216
Millar, Richard, 165
Mó-Dhomnóg, Saint, 178
Mogue, Saint, *see* Aidan of Ferns
Molough Abbey, 112
Mooncoin, 195
Moonveen, 195
Moore, Arthur, 139–40
Morgan Rattler, cutter ship, 271
Morrison, Sir Richard, 130
Morrison, William Vitruvius, 29, 51
Morton, Earl of, see John, King of England
Mortlestown, 100
Mount Congreve, 195–96, 224
Mount Leinster, 15, 24, 271
Mount Misery, 205, 233

Mulleen, river, 74
Mullinabro district, 197
Mullinahone, 52–54
Mullinavat, 148
Munster, 66, 178, 209
Munster Express, 197
Munster Fusiliers, 36–37

Na Srona, Seamus, 154
Naples, 134
Napoleonic Wars, 258
Nash, John, 92, 96, 101
Nation, The, 52
National (Free State) Army, 38–39, 162, 232–34
National Garda Training Depot, 39
Neddans House, 111
Newfoundland, 217–19
Nenagh, 48
Nenagh Gaol, 30, 48
Neolithic peoples, 11, 196
Neptune, SS, 241
Neptune Works, shipyard, 241
Neuchâtel, 265
New Bridge, County Tipperary, 81
New Geneva, County Waterford, 264–66
New Ross, 130, 163, 224, 275
New York, 166, 218
Newcastle, 111
Newport, Simon, 222
Newtown Park, Waterford, 242
Nicholstown Castle, 100
Nimmo, Alexander, 275
Nire, river, 111
Nook, 249
Nore, river, 11, 156, 197, 245
Normans, the, 44, 88, 209, 248, 250, 274

Oblate Fathers, 184
O'Brien, Catherine, 128
O'Brien, Domhnal Mór, 63, 74, 118, 179, 180
O'Brien, Donough, 86, 100
O'Brien, Margaret, 69
O'Brien, Muirchertacht, 63

O'Brien, Murrough, 90
O'Brien, William Smith, *see* Smith O'Brien, William
O'Connell, Daniel, 70
O'Connor, Frank, 131, 133
O'Donnell, Hugh, 66
O'Donovan, John, 202–3
O'Donovan, William, 202–3
O'Donovan Letters, 203
Ó Dubhtaigh, Eoghan, 100
O'Duffy, General Eoin, 162–63
O'Fyne, Donogho, 211
O'Dwyer, Rev. Dr. Michael, 60
Office of Public Works, 96
O'Fogartys, clan, 68
O'Malley, Tony, 155
O'Meara, Andy, 14, 19
Onslow, Richard, 159–61
O'Neill, Owen Roe, 213
O'Neill, Hugh, 64
O'Neill, Hugh Dubh, 126–27
Ordnance, Survey of Ireland, 203
Ormond Castle, 157, 173, 177
Ormond, Dukes/Earls of, *see* Butler family
O'Riordan, Michael, 54
O'Rourke, Tiernan, 85
Osbourne family, 140
Ossory, 209
Ó Suilleabháin, Amhlaoibh, 148
Ó Suilleabháin, Eoghan Rua, 42
O'Sullivan, clan, *see* Eoghanachta
O'Sullivan Beare, Donal Cam, 85
Otway and Watt, 98
Outragh, 100
Owen, Robert, 192

Paris, 134, 191
Parnell, Charles Stewart, 58, 59
Pascal II, Pope, 63
Passage East, 247, 250–55, 258, 264–67
Pathfinder, The, sailing ship, 240

Patrick, Saint, 97, 106, 107, 121
Paul V, Pope, 122
Peare, Captain W. F., 229
Penal Laws, 42
Penane Bridge, 43
Pennsylvania, 218
Penrose, George and William, 217
Pentonville Prison, 53
Perrot, Sir John, 172
Pharos lighthouse, Alexandria, 275
Philip of Worcester, 83, 85
Picts, 182
Pil, river, 184
Piltown, 160, 170, 179, 184, 185, 188
Poer(s), *see* le Poers
Pompeii, 250
Ponsonby, Myles Brabazon, 185
Ponsonby, Sir John, 184
    Elizabeth, wife of, 184
Ponsonby Packet, mail boat, 216
Ponsonby, Sarah, 184
Porcupine, frigate, 270
Port Lairge (Waterford), 209,
Portlairge, ship, 228
Portlaw, 131, 191–94, 220, 241
Portlaw Spinning Company, 193
Portnahully, 196
Portnascully, 194
Portugal, 211, 218
Pope and Company, 240
Poulakerry Castle, 147–48
Power, Canon, 152, 195
Power, Jim, 167
Power, Lady Catherine, 141
Power, Margaret, *see* Lady Blessington
Power, Rev. P., 106
Power, Patrick, 193
Powere, Joan, 113
Powers family, 140, 141
Powerstown, Manor of, 140
Presentation Brothers, 22, 25
Presentation Sisters, Thurles, 33

Prout, General, 234
Purcell, family, 44–47
Purcell, Philip, 64
Purcell-FitzGerald, Gerald, 243
Purser, Sarah, 128
Purtoga, 164

Quakers, the, 91, 98
QE2, 235
Quinlan, Alderman, Mayor of Waterford, 225

Rahan, 82
Rathronan House, 30
Raven's Rock, 139
Red Bridge, railway, the, 203
Redmond Bridge, *see* Waterford Bridge
Redmond, John, 227
Reformation, the, 64
Reginald the Dane, 209
Reginald's Tower, 209, 214, 228, 233, 237, 238
Request, poem, 82–83
Rian Bó Phádraig, 106–8
Richard II, 253
Richard IV, *see* Warbeck, Perkin
Richard Coeur-de-Lion, 63, 69
Richie, Jean, 166
Richmond Barracks, Templemore, 33, 35–39
    and prisoners-of-War, 35–36
Ring, Lieutenant Colonel James, 34
Ring, Robert, 34
Riverquarter, 189
Roadstone, 165
Roberts, Samuel, 141
Robinson, Seamus, 162
Robinson, Sir William, 128
Roche, George, 201
Roche, Colonel James, *see* the Swimmer Roche
Roche, Suzanna, 154
Roche family, 152
Rock of Bearnan, *see* Devil's Bit
Rock of Cashel, *see* Cashel, Rock of

Rock Sunday, 20–21
Rock Tower, Devil's Bit, 22
Rockabill, SS, 228
Rockett's Castle, 191
Rockett's Tree, 191
Rocksand, steam-boat, 163
Rogerstown Castle, 183
Rome, 27, 55, 120, 191
Rome (Catholic Church), 120
Rosminian Order, 140, 272
Rossestown Bridge, 51
Rosslare Harbour, 246
Royal Hospital, Kilmainham, 128
Royal Irish Constabulary, 158
Royal Navy, 270
Royal Ulster Constabulary, 59
Royal Viking Sky, cruise ship, 235
Rutland, cruiser, 270
Rutland, Duke of, 265
Ryder, Lady Sue, 69
Rynne, Etienne, 181

Sadler, Adjutant General, 148
St Anne's chapel, 254
St Canice's Cathedral, 201
St Catherine's Church, Wexford, 240
St Edmund, Priory of, see Athassel
St George's Channel, 216
St James, Temple of, 254
St John's Pil, river, 209, 239
St Joseph's School, County Tipperary, 139–40
St Mary's Abbey, Dublin, 248
St Mary's Church of Ireland, Clonmel. 127,
St Mary's Church of Ireland, Thurles, 55–57
St Michaels Franciscan friary, 170
St Molleran's Church, 170
St Patrick's Church, Marlfield, 118
St Patrick's Cow, see Rian Bó Phádraig

St Patrick of the Abbey of the Suir, Church of, 122
St Patrick's Seat, 121
St Patrick's Stone, 98
St Patrick's Well, 120–22
St Pauls, church, Cahir, 92, 101
St Petersburg, 241
Sally Kavanagh, novel, 53
Sallypark, 207
Saltee Islands, 271
Scandinavians, see Vikings
Scilly Isles, 196
Scotland, 182
Seeger, Pete, 114, 166
Shannon, river, 41
Shannon Estuary, 41
Shee, Mary, 163
Sheehy, Father Nicholas, 128
Sheridan's Motor Garage, 231
Showerings, 141
Sidney, Sir Henry, 213
Siemens, 218
Silean, Saint, see Kiltilane
Simnel, Lambert, 212
Sinn Fein, 218
Skehanagh Bridge, 20
Skye, Isle of, 30
Slieve Aildiuin, see Devil's Bit
Slieve Aill Deamhan, see Devil's Bit
Slieve Bloom Mountains, 15, 44
Slieve Coillte, 251
Slieve na Mban see Slievenamon Mountain
Slievenamon Mountain, 15, 52, 139, 148
Slievenanard, 83
Smith, Charles, writer, 215
Smith O'Brien, William, 130, 157, 158
South Irish Horse, 95
Soviet Union, 163
Spain, 163, 209, 211
Spenser, Edmund, 86, 205
Squirrel, frigate, 270
Stalley, Roger, 68
Statistical Survey of the County of Kilkenny, 180

Strongbow, Earl of Pembroke, 74, 251, 252
Struell, 121
Sue Ryder Home, 69
Foundation, 69
Suir, proposed canal, 41–42
Suir Castle, 80
Suir Island, 130, 131, 133, 134
Suir Lodge, 151
Suir, river, 11, 155–56, 275–77
building and construction works, 164, 188, 197, 201, 205, 207–9, 245
climate and weather, effects on, 224–25, 242
fishing on, 109, 146, 168–69, 177
flora and fauna, 74, 137–38, 144, 169–70, 182, 184, 187, 194, 261–62
poaching, 146–47
river trade, 123–25, 164–65, 188, 192–94
source, 11
Suir Steam Navigation Company, 164
Suir, steam tug, 225
Suirdale, Viscount, see Hely Hutchinson, John
Suirville, 82
Swallow, sloop, 270, 271
Swansea, 163, 241
Swift, Jonathan, 76, 184
Swimmer Roche, the, 152–54
Swiss Cottage (Cahir), 95–97

Tar, river, 100, 106
Teampull Mór, see Templemore
Temple, Lord, 265
Templemore, 28, 29, 31–39, 41
Abbey, 29, 31, 37, 51
Castle, 29
Church of Ireland, 34
Priory, 29+C75
Templemore to Thurles, 40–61
Templeton, 272
Tenants Rights League, 53
Terry, Sonny, 166

Thackeray, William Makepeace, 73
The Book of Beauty, 134
The Great Lone Land (1872), 82
The Fair of the Glen, song, 152
The Princess Charlotte, steamship, 220
The Repealer, novel, 134
The Suir at Waterford City, 206–237
Thomas Bridge, County Tipperary, 139, 140
Thomastown Castle, 76, 77
Thonoge, river, 99
Three Sisters, rivers, 11–12, *see also* Barrow; Nore
Thurles, 33, 52–61
Thurles Sarsfields Club, 59
Thurles to Cahir, 62–93
Tibroughney Castle, 178–84
Ticincor Castle, 140–41
Timbertoes, *see* Waterford Bridge
Times, The, 30
Tinsley, William, 92
Tipperary, County, 12, 24, 44, 70, 103, 123, 178, 181, 208, 219
  and cricket, 33–34
  children of, 140
  and the Suir, 11
  and tombstones, 145
Tipperary County Council, 155
Tipperary Heritage Way, 73, 79, 81
Tipperary Militia, 118
Tober Fachtna holy well, 179
Todd, John and Susanna, 259
Total Abstinence, Society for, 77
Tower Hill, 185
Tramore, 196
Trant, family, 34
Trant, Sir Philip, 253
Treaty, the, 231–32

Treese, Dita Von, 142
Trinity College, 27
Tubbrid, 100–3
Tullaghmelan, 115
Tullaghorton, 100
Turkstown, 164, 188
Tynan cottage, 16, 19, *see also* Devanney, Marie Tynan

United States, *see* America

Van Diemen's land, 158, 177
Vedrafjordr (Waterford), 209
Victoria, Princess, 230
Victoria, Queen, 254, 259
Vikings, 88, 130, 197–98, 208–9
Virginia, USA, 218

Wales, 163, 182, 209, 252, 258
Walsh, John Edward, 42–43
Walsh Mountains, 181, 183
Walsh, Peter, 170
War of Independence, 37, 60
War of the Roses, 182, 253
Warbeck, Perkin, 212, 253
Warwick Castle, 51
Washpin Bridge, 41
Water, John, 253
Waterford, city, 88, 123–25, 165, 179, 182, 199, 200, 205–37, 251, 253
  glass factory, 217–19
  and the Malcolmsons, 131, 191–94, 197
  and river trade, 165
Waterford, Marquess of, *see* le Poer Beresford
Waterford Bridge, 207, 222–27
Waterford Castle, 243–44
Waterford coastline, 13, 262, 267
Waterford County, 24, 98, 106, 116, 141, 178, 181, 193, 255
  and the Genevans

Waterford Crystal, 218–19, 235
Waterford Harbour, 27, 177, 196, 216, 235, 237, 245, 258, 266–71, 277
  and smuggling, 270–71
Waterford Herald, 216, 271
Waterford Port, 207, 235, 266–67, 269
Waterford Regattas, 189
Waterford Steam Navigation Company, 241
Waterford to the Sea, 238–277
Westminster, 125, 192, 227, 245
Wexford, County, 201, 219, 228, 245, 255, 256, 262
When Irish Eyes are Smiling, 167
White, Albert, and Company, 240, 241
White, Dr Vincent, 230
Whitefeet, *see* Darrigs family group
Whort Hill, 250
Wicklow, hills, 24
William III, *see* William of Orange
William Henry, *see* George IV
William of Orange, 153, 184, 222, 253, 258
William Penn, ship, 241
Willington, family, 31
  Major Richard, 34
Winchester, city, 252
Woodstown Beach, 261–62
Woodstown House, 219
Woodstown Viking settlement, 180, 197, 198, 209

Youghal, 125
Young, Arthur, 140, 215, 219
Young Ireland movement, 53, 157
  insurrection, 130, 157–58

Zenobia, *see* Kilkenny, PS